# The Political Economy ot
# Special-Purpose Government

# American Governance and Public Policy

A SERIES EDITED BY

## Barry Rabe and John Tierney

This series examines a broad range of public policy issues and their relationship to all levels of government in the United States. The editors welcome serious scholarly studies and seek to publish books that appeal to both academic and professional audiences. The series showcases studies that illuminate the successes, as well as the problems, of policy formulation and implementation.

# The Political Economy of Special-Purpose Government

Kathryn A. Foster

GEORGETOWN UNIVERSITY PRESS / WASHINGTON, D.C.

Georgetown University Press, Washington, D.C. 20007
© 1997 by Georgetown University Press. All rights reserved.

10  9  8  7  6  5  4  3  2                              1997

**Library of Congress Cataloging-in-Publication Data**

Foster, Kathryn Ann
    The political economy of special-purpose government / Kathryn A.
Foster.
        p.    cm. — (American governance and public policy)
    Includes bibliographical references and index.
    1. Special districts—United States.  2. Municipal powers and
services beyond corporate limits—United States.  I. Title.
II. Series.
JS426.F67   1997
352.19′0973—DC21
ISBN 0-87840-638-7 (cloth)                              96-46603

# Contents

# List of Tables

# Preface

At one time or another, most of us face a choice between an institution with a specialized focus and one with a more general perspective. Perhaps you once deliberated whether to pursue your love of painting at the state university, which offered a major in art, or at a dedicated art institute, which offered *only* a major in art. Or perhaps you decided to seek treatment for a ringing in your ears and had to choose between calling a general practitioner or an otolaryngologist. Maybe, more simply, you want fish for dinner tonight and have the option of shopping at either the fish counter of your local supermarket or the specialty fish store nearby. In these and other instances of institutional choice, your decision depends, of course, on personal circumstances and the specifics of the case. Nonetheless, most of us have an intuitive sense that one or the other of the specialized or generalized alternatives holds the edge in terms of cost, service quality, range of offerings, expertise of the personnel, or long-term value.

This book is about society's analogous choice between which kind of government, special-purpose or general-purpose, to rely on for service delivery. The impetus for the study is an observation: for several decades, society, especially metropolitan society in the United States, has favored the specialized over the generalized option. Although relatively rare as recently as the 1950s, special-purpose governments are today the most common and fastest growing government type in the nation, far outnumbering and outpacing traditional general-purpose alternatives like counties, municipalities, and townships. The central questions of the book are why this trend toward specialized governance is occurring and whether and how it makes a difference.

Some people may regard these questions as trivial. Does it really matter, they might ask, whether the provider of, say, water service is a single-purpose water district or a municipal water department, provided that decent water comes out when you turn on the tap? I believe, and seek to demonstrate in this book, that the institutional choice to rely on special-purpose entities does matter, for a variety of economic, political, and social reasons. I further believe that understanding the causes and consequences of specialization in the public sector helps us better understand unresolved issues of institutional choice and specialization in personal and public affairs.

In an earlier incarnation, this book was a dissertation completed at the Woodrow Wilson School of Public and International Affairs at Princeton University. From the vantage point of several years and an eight-hour drive, the gifts of my graduate training and trainers are more evident than ever. I thank again the members of my dissertation committee, Michael N. Danielson, Thomas Romer, and Julian Wolpert, for their encouragement and smarts, both of which improved the process and product. I am especially grateful to Mike Danielson, chair of my committee, for his learned insights, spirited and thorough critiques, and ongoing interest. Although this book is several iterations away from the original product, there undoubtedly remain a few ideas or expressive phrases that owe their distinction to Mike.

The wisdom of my own institutional choice to accept a job at the University at Buffalo has been affirmed repeatedly by the collegial and talented group of students, staff, and faculty I have found there. I thank especially my colleagues in the Department of Planning and the School of Architecture and Planning for many kinds of support, from reading early chapters to creating the intellectual and congenial environment within which education can flourish. I was fortunate in the final stages of manuscript preparation to have able graduate assistance from Kristen E. Sosnicki, who checked references and kept me on track in other matters, and Tara L. Hoyt, who spent precious end-of-semester hours preparing tables and figures that required more sophisticated treatment than my meager computer graphics skills could handle.

Material and moral assistance for this project came from numerous sources. The Woodrow Wilson School at Princeton University provided generous fellowships and research support. I acknowledge in particular the Center for Domestic and Comparative Policy Studies and the Princeton Society of Wilson Fellows, both of which provided funding and stimulating discussions on this project and grander themes in the social sciences. I thank also the Association for Public Policy Analysis and Management for the considerable intellectual boost it provided by awarding my dissertation the 1994 APPAM Ph.D. Dissertation Award. The Center for Regional Economic Issues at Case Western University kindly made room for me in the summer of 1995 when I needed a quiet place and a word processor to transform a dissertation into a manuscript. The subsequent transformation of manuscript to book I owe to the support, good advice, and professional care that I and my manuscript received from the accomplished staff at Georgetown University Press, notably director John Samples and production manager Patricia Rayner.

Once again and as usual, my family and friends met the needs of both head and heart. They sensed brilliantly when I needed applause, encouragement, solitude, diversions, advice, cash, reassurance, and celebrations. For all these, but even more so for providing perspective and a firm foundation, I thank my parents, siblings and their families, and grandmothers recently gone but still with us in many ways. There are also numerous friends to thank but it is no contest to single out Paul Gottlieb who knows more than anyone else what this took.

In retrospect, the topic of this book is a curious one for an ardent generalist. Although I do not believe this predilection biases my analysis, in the interest of full disclosure readers should know that hanging above my desk for years has been the following credo, which I believe we would all do well to live by:

A human being should be able to heal a wound, plan an expedition, order from a French menu, climb a mountain face, enjoy a ballet, balance accounts, roll a kayak, embolden a friend, tell a joke, laugh at a joke, laugh at oneself, cooperate, act alone, sing a children's song, solve equations, throw a dog a stick, pitch manure, program a computer, cook a tasty meal, love heartily, fight efficiently, die gallantly. Specialization is for insects.[1]

## NOTE

**1.** The original version of this credo, which varies somewhat from the version above my desk, is from Robert A. Heinlein, *Time Enough for Love: The Lives of Lazarus Long* (New York: G. P. Putnam's Sons, 1973), pp. 265–66. Heinlein's version reads: "A human being should be able to change a diaper, plan an invasion, butcher a hog, conn a ship, design a building, write a sonnet, balance accounts, build a wall, set a bone, comfort the dying, take orders, give orders, cooperate, act alone, solve equations, analyze a new problem, pitch manure, program a computer, cook a tasty meal, fight efficiently, die gallantly. Specialization is for insects." I confess to a preference for the doctored version— the genesis of whose alterations I do not know—primarily because I am used to it.

# 1

# Special Delivery

Concerned about the cumulative effect of postwar urban development on water quality in Puget Sound and Lake Washington, Seattle-area voters in 1958 approved formation of a two-county district to collect and treat sewage throughout the region. Fourteen years later, voters extended the powers of the district, known as Metro, to encompass regional transit services. In recent years, reformers have lobbied for further expansions of Metro's scope and powers to include regional land use planning and transportation, and for direct election of Metro governing board members.[1]

*     *     *

In 1965, the forward-looking developer of an exurban tract of land near Houston Intercontinental Airport formed the 320-acre Harris County Water Conservation and Improvement District #91. The district, which provided water, sewer, and drainage services, was one of what would soon be 400 similar districts serving unincorporated subdivisions in rapidly urbanizing Harris County. By 1974, two years prior to the projected build-out date, the district served an overcapacity customer base of 941 households. Subdivision residents, five of whom sit as the district's governing board, raise revenues for services through property taxes and utility user fees.[2]

*     *     *

In 1991, caught between the competing desires of maintaining high-quality city services, avoiding tax increases, and meeting the pressing need for overdue maintenance of the city's infrastructure, New York City officials proposed formation of two city-sized public authorities, one for solid waste management and one for bridge and tunnel maintenance. Because several dozen public authorities already operated in the city, officials were familiar with the tradeoffs associated with these independent entities. The administrators reasoned that what they might sacrifice in financial and policy control over maintenance and solid waste services would be outweighed by the benefits of off-loading

*Completeness throws of
Scope*

politically tough spending and service decisions and freeing the city to devote revenues and bonding capacity to other immediate needs.[3]

\*                    \*                    \*

For all their differences in size, function, funding, and governing structure, Seattle's Metro, Harris County's Water Conservation and Improvement District #91, and New York City's proposed public authorities have in common their basic character as special-purpose governments. As such, they are illustrations of one of the most fundamental and significant shifts in institutional arrangements over the past half-century: the increased reliance on independent, special-purpose local governments for service delivery. The purpose of this book is to examine the causes, consequences, and implications of this trend toward specialized governance, specifically as it affects U.S. metropolitan regions.

Special-purpose governments, which I also refer to as special districts,[4] are autonomous local governments that provide a single or limited services. Most people are familiar with the larger ones, not only Seattle's Metro perhaps, but also the Metropolitan Water District of Southern California, the Massachusetts Bay Transit Authority, the Chicago Sanitary District, and the Port Authority of New York and New Jersey. Less publicized and far more common are the thousands of special districts providing metropolitan-area residents with specialized provision of health, fire protection, sewer, transit, water, gas and electric utilities, airports, housing, drainage, libraries, parks and recreation, highways, ports, sanitation, and other services.

In the four decades between 1952 and 1992, the number of special-purpose governments in the United States grew by 19,215 units, or 156 percent, while the number of general-purpose governments (counties, municipalities, and townships together) increased far more modestly by 1,917 units, or 5 percent. Though often far from the public eye, special districts are, and have been since the early 1970s, the most common type of local government in the nation. As of 1992, the 31,555 special districts nationwide outnumbered the second most common government type, municipalities, by over 12,000 units.[5]

Although the rise of specialized governance has occurred throughout the nation, it has been most rapid in metropolitan areas. Nowhere is the challenge of meeting service needs more demanding and complex than where large diverse populations live, work, play, move about, and interact in close quarters. Between 1952 and 1992 the number of special districts in the 785 counties comprising U.S. metropolitan areas grew from 4,943 to 13,343, an increase of 8,400 units, or 170 percent (figure 1–1). By contrast, over the same period the number of independent school districts fell 67 percent from around 18,000 to under 6,000, while the number of municipalities and townships together increased 11 percent to slightly over 12,000 units. At the individual metropolitan level, the trend toward specialized governance reveals itself in the 169 percent increase in the mean number of special districts per metropolitan area (from sixteen to forty-three) compared to a modest 9 percent increase in the number of general-purpose governments (from thirty-eight to forty-one).[6]

More significant than the sheer growth in district numbers, however, is the unheralded but notable increase in district influence on metropolitan society. Bus or subway riders in New York, Boston, Chicago, Philadelphia, Denver, Minneapolis–St. Paul, Washington, D.C., Atlanta, San Francisco–Oakland, Houston, and dozens of other metropolitan areas, for example, consume district-provided transit services. Nearly half of the total local government expenditures on public housing nationwide is made by independent housing authorities.[7] The proportion of total local government expenditures and revenues represented by special districts has grown two to three times faster than that of other local government types every decade since 1962.[8] As of 1992 (the latest data available) special districts held over $151 billion in long-term debt, an amount representing 26 percent of total local government debt and surpassed only by municipal governments.[9] If trendwatchers are correct, the importance of special districts will

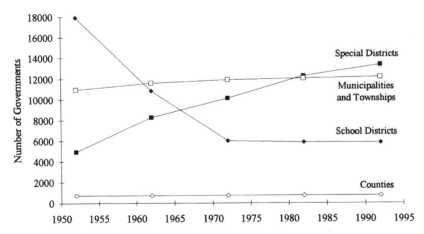

**Figure 1-1** Local Governments in Metropolitan Areas, 1952–1992
(N = 312 metropolitan areas, constant 1987 boundaries)

continue to grow: districts are often the service provider of choice in metropolitan edge cities alleged to be "the crucible of America's urban future."[10]

Perhaps it is no wonder that society turns increasingly to specialized governments for service delivery. Districts enjoy the financial reach, tax-exempt status, and quasi-monopolistic service delivery advantages of public governments, together with the political isolation, management flexibility, and financial discretion of private corporations. Still, despite the growing pervasiveness and apparent advantages of special districts, knowledge of their causes and consequences remains modest. Libraries fill stacks with books on municipalities but offer a relative handful of volumes on special-purpose governments. Collective ignorance of these specialized entities is of increasing concern. In the words of one research team, "special districts may have more profound political and economic implications than many features of sub-state relations, yet they have received little serious attention."[11]

This study seeks to narrow that breach through detailed analysis of the trend toward reliance on special-purpose governments in metropolitan regions. In broadest terms, the study focuses on the relevance and ramifications of a world in which service delivery occurs not by a single government providing many services, but by many governments each providing a single service.

## QUESTIONS OF INSTITUTIONAL CHOICE

I organize the investigation around four principal questions. First, *what is the most useful way to think about special-purpose governments?* Much of the theoretical and empirical work on urban service delivery overlooks or treats vaguely the role of special districts in the metropolitan political economy. For example, most researchers classify and treat special-purpose governments as undifferentiated entities under the rubric "special districts." Yet even a cursory glance at the diversity of units so classified reveals the analytic hazards of such a tidy classification. How should we conceive of a local government type that includes entities as varied as a regionwide, revenue bond–financed sports authority and a subdivision-sized, tax-financed drainage district? How might we reframe traditional conceptualizations of special-purpose governments to better understand their multiple roles and outcomes in the metropolitan political economy?

Second, *what factors explain the rise of special-purpose governance?* There is considerable debate over the answer. Some theorists see specialized governments as an ill-guided attempt to alleviate the burdens of metropolitan political fragmentation. Others suggest that districts are the logical institutional result of efforts by rational, utility-maximizing citizens to satisfy their diverse demands for services. Still others view districts as a politically expedient means for prodevelopment forces to undermine popular will and control the pace, location, and costs of growth. A fourth school of thought contends that special-purpose governments arise from a complex set of economic, political, and cultural forces, which are further conditioned by legal and institutional factors in the metropolis. How useful are these alternative explanations for understanding the appeal of special-purpose governments? And if special districts are so appealing, what accounts for the considerable variation in the degree to which different metropolitan areas rely on these governments for service delivery?

Third, *what are the cost consequences of service provision by special-purpose governments?* Some observers argue that the presence of special districts, by applying a competitive brake to monopolistic tendencies of general-purpose governments, will lead to lower public expenditures for urban services. Other observers suggest that reliance on functionally specialized, independent, politically obscure governments will inevitably lead to higher costs, either by default or design. Do district-reliant metropolitan areas spend more for services than their general-purpose–reliant counterparts? If so, what accounts for this upward spending bias?

Fourth, *what are the policy implications of specialized governance?* In any metropolitan area, funds are allocated to different public functions in accordance with citizen preferences, legal and policy constraints, and local political, economic, and social circumstances. Perhaps, as some contend, reliance on special districts leads to a disproportionately high share of resources allocated to district-provided functions. Maybe, as others more particularly argue, district service provision skews spending in favor of development-oriented functions at the expense of social welfare functions. What are the resource allocation effects of specialized governance? Does specialized governance promote an implicit bias toward certain spending choices?

In investigating these questions, I draw upon a body of thought known as institutional choice theory. Institutional choice theory argues that changes in institutional arrangements occur when interested parties see opportunities to capture profits from "arrangemental adjustments."[12] Arrangemental adjustments are changes in the existing social, legal, or political frameworks that establish society's ground rules for economic interactions in public and private spheres. These adjustments may be as rare as amendments to the U.S. Constitution or as relatively commonplace as the formation of new corporations, the expansion of local government boundaries, or the enactment or modification of laws related to elections, investment, or property rights.

Opportunities to profit from institutional adjustments arise from changes in market conditions, technology, income distribution, or other exogenous factors related to the political-economic environment. To capture profits, interested parties pursue specific institutional changes, such as, for example, a new law to enable provision of both cable TV and telephone services by the same operator. Following an institutional adjustment, the system achieves equilibrium until new changes in markets, technology, or policy inaugurate fresh opportunities to profit through institutional reorganization.

Institutional choice theory offers a useful starting point for examining the trend toward specialized service delivery. Fundamental to understanding the rise of specialized governance is understanding the often-overlooked reality that such growth is the outcome of hundreds of discrete choices to rely on a special-purpose government rather than an alternative public, private, or nonprofit service delivery option.

This way of thinking about special-purpose governments differs from that found in the theoretical and empirical literature on specialized governance. Conventional analyses generally overlook the specificity and importance of choosing a special-purpose government, as opposed to alternative choices, for service delivery. In particular, analysts tend to either overspecify or underspecify the nature of special districts. Proponents of structuralist and metropolitan ecology perspectives, for example, tend to make inferences about the universe of special districts from observation of a single district type or attribute. By contrast, proponents of an institutional reform or public choice perspective automatically consider districts a burden or blessing, respectively, thereby overlooking consequential differences in district types and purposes.

An institutional choice framework recognizes that different geographic and financial subtypes of districts may well respond differently to institutional, economic, political, and legal factors hypothesized to motivate district formation. Likewise, districts of different functions may well generate different fiscal and policy consequences. Conceptualizing "special districts" as a plural, rather than singular, concept permits drawing important geographic, financial, and functional distinctions that influence the causes and consequences of particular district subtypes. Because current theoretical and empirical analyses have failed to make such distinctions, they have led to an incomplete and skewed understanding of specialized governance.

For institutional choice theory to aid in understanding specialized governance, however, several modifications, which I employ in this study, are required. The first is expanding the traditional theory's notion of profits to include the noneconomic objectives of metropolitan interest groups. This modification is particularly important in the realm of public sector service delivery where agencies often use noneconomic criteria to guide institutional choices.[13] The second modification is discarding the implicit presumption that competing interest groups bring equivalent skills, resources, and clout to the process of institutional change. The modified framework explicitly recognizes the existence of political and social constraints that impede some interest groups from engaging in and achieving profits from institutional change. The final modification is expanding the traditional theory's focus on the *causes* of institutional choices to embrace also their *consequences*.

## A PRIMER ON SPECIAL DISTRICTS[14]

Before turning to these investigations, it is important to clarify the nature and functioning of the often-misunderstood entities known as special districts.

### District Types

Students of local government make a traditional and useful, though by no means rigid, distinction between two types of special-purpose governments. The first type, known as *taxing districts* (or, often, "special districts" in a narrower sense than used in this study), comprises local government entities with the power to tax and levy special assessments. For many taxing districts, user charges may and often do supplement other revenues. Nearly all taxing districts have elected governing boards, a structure consistent with the core democratic principle demanding no taxation without representation.

The second type of special-purpose government, known as *public authorities,* comprises government corporations without property-taxing powers. Public authorities raise most revenues through user fees, grants, and private revenue bonds. Authorities tend to provide services that are divisible and chargeable, that is, those for which the benefits of a service can be attributed to specific individuals (for example, tolls for road users), and for which administrative costs are not so high that they outstrip the practical ability to set user fees at a level to recoup costs.[15] Public authorities are also common providers of large-scale, typically costly capital projects that might go wanting under a pay-as-you-go system. As nontaxing entities, public authorities ordinarily operate under appointed rather than elected boards, with most appointments made by officials of the parent government (city, county, or state, for example) that created the district.

Throughout this study, I use the labels "special districts" and "special-purpose governments" interchangeably to signify the universe of taxing districts and public authorities. When the discussion concerns one or the other subtype of special-purpose government, I use its specific label. Special districts and special-purpose governments do not include school districts, which, although functionally specialized and administratively independent, are sufficiently different from districts in purpose, origin, geographic scope, and local financial importance to be excluded from consideration in this analysis.

## Public Versus Private Status

A common source of confusion about special-purpose governments is their public or private status. In legal terms, special districts are public sector institutions, located toward the public end of a public-to-private continuum, as illustrated in figure 1–2. Taxing districts fall into the same category as municipalities, the most public of government corporations. Nontaxing public authorities are one notch closer to private enterprises.

The public character of special-purpose governments reveals itself in districts' range of public powers. Like other public corporations, districts may enter into contracts, adopt joint powers agreements, sue and be sued, employ workers, acquire real property, and raise funds through bonds, user charges, and, sometimes, property taxes. Districts must comply with state laws regulating elections, public health and safety, bonded indebtedness, and financial accounting. Districts also enjoy many public-sector financial powers, including exemption from property or corporate taxes, and the power to offer tax-free proceeds on investment in district revenue bonds.

Despite their legal status as public, however, a hallmark of special-purpose governments is their mix of public and private character, which earns them labels such as quasi-public governments or the businesses of government. Special-purpose governments typically lack fundamental powers authorized to general-purpose governments. Foremost among these are police powers, a broad category that includes the power to regulate behavior and adopt land use controls, such as zoning, subdivision regulations, and building codes. In the relatively rare cases where districts do possess police powers, these powers are limited to regulating specific behavior on district property. A metropolitan parks district, for example, might prohibit consumption of alcohol in its parks. Of note is that many, though not all, districts possess eminent domain powers to take private land for public purpose with just compensation.

Districts' public powers are also limited with respect to determining functions and raising revenues. Unlike general-purpose governments, which generally have broad constitutional and statutory powers to

FIGURE 1-2   Entities Along a Public-Private Continuum

|  | Type | Example(s) |
|---|---|---|
| Public |  |  |
|  | Government corporation, tax-funded | municipality; library district |
|  | Government corporation, user fee-and/or revenue bond-funded | transit authority; Port Authority of New York and New Jersey |
|  | Government-sponsored enterprise | Federal National Mortgage Association |
|  | Government corporation, private vendor-dependent | Medicare program |
|  | Nonprofit, government grant-dependent | Atomic Energy Commission |
|  | Private corporation, government contract-dependent | General Dynamics McDonnell Douglass |
|  | Private corporation, public shares | General Motors; IBM |
|  | Private corporation, owner-managed | flower shop; independent grocery store |
| Private |  |  |

Source:   Adapted and revised from Hal G. Rainey, *Understanding and Managing Public Organizations* (San Francisco: Jossey-Bass, 1991), pp. 27–30, figs. 1.1, 1.2, 1.3, and table 1.1, which were adapted in turn from Robert A. Dahl and Charles E. Lindblom, *Politics, Economics, and Welfare* (New York: Harper and Row, 1953); Gary L. Wamsley and Mayer N. Zald, *The Political Economy of Public Organizations* (Lexington, Mass.: Heath, 1973); Barry Bozeman, *All Organizations Are Public: Bridging Public and Private Organizational Theories* (San Francisco: Jossey-Bass, 1987); and James L. Perry and Hal G. Rainey, "The Public-Private Distinction in Organization Theory: A Critique and Research Strategy," *Academy of Management Review* 13 (1988): 182–201. Used by permission of Jossey-Bass Inc.

determine and modify their mix of functions, special-purpose governments usually require state legislative approval before adding services or changing their functional portfolio. Districts also ordinarily lack several staples of municipal fund-raising. Districts are ineligible for certain federal and state grants, for example, and for numerous state and local subventions, including gas taxes, license fees, and hotel taxes. This restriction has softened in recent years in some states where districts have gained access to taxes and funds traditionally beyond the legal reach of special-purpose governments.[16]

The private character of special-purpose governments stems from administrative and financial powers that districts share with private-sector enterprises. Like private firms, districts are generally exempt from civil service, procurement, and pension fund regulations governing public agencies. Districts also share with private entities broad discretion to establish personnel policies, salary schedules, management techniques, and internal operating procedures. Districts tend to be less unionized than general-purpose governments, although, like private corporations, the level of union involvement varies by location and function.[17] Perhaps most important, districts have relatively few restrictions on revenue raising and are exempt from state constitutional ceilings on municipal property taxing and borrowing. Many special-purpose governments turn a profit and channel extra revenues into projects of interest to their governing board.[18]

## Independence

The attribute that makes special districts so potentially influential in fiscal and political affairs is institutional independence from other local governments.[19] As independent entities, districts have sovereignty over their administrative and financial affairs and enjoy substantial freedom from oversight by their parent government.

Because criteria differ across states, determining a district's independence status can be problematic. To enable comparisons, the U.S. Bureau of the Census establishes and applies uniform criteria to determine an entity's independence. By these criteria, a local government (special district, school district, municipality, township, or county) is independent if it possesses each of three attributes: existence as an organized entity, government character, and substantial autonomy. Existence as an organized entity requires evidence of corporate powers (for example, perpetual succession or the right to make contracts), institutional character (for example, elected officials), and the conduct of activities (for example, raising revenues or holding regular board meetings). Governmental character refers to the presence of elected or appointed officials, financial powers to tax or incur debt, and responsibility for provision of public services. Substantial autonomy entails fiscal and administrative independence. Fiscal independence requires that districts have the power to determine their budgets, levy taxes, set tax rates, determine service charges and fees, and issue debt without review or extensive modification by other governments. Administrative independence requires either a popularly elected governing board distinct from the legislative body of the parent government or an appointed governing board that either performs functions distinct from its parent government or performs similar functions without oversight by the parent government.

The U.S. Bureau of the Census formally defines special districts in reference to the local governments they are not:

> Special district governments are independent, special-purpose governmental units (other than school district governments) that exist as separate entities with substantial administrative and fiscal independence from general-purpose local governments.[20]

## Legal Basis and Creation

The legal basis for a special district is found in the enabling legislation of the state(s) in which the district operates. Most districts form pursuant to general enabling legislation, which sets forth the rules for all districts of a particular type in a state. For example, Florida general law governs the formation and operation of mobile home park recreation districts in the state. States differ in terms of the number of general statutes and the types of districts they permit. A tally of district-enabling laws in California, for example, counted 206 state statutes enabling 55 varieties of special districts providing 30 different service functions.[21]

Other districts form pursuant to special enabling legislation, statutes that pertain to a single special-purpose government. District creators tend to use special legislation when a proposed district will provide a unique combination of services, require special financing arrangements, or encompass geographic territory in two or more states. For example, the Arizona State Legislature used special enabling legislation in 1937 when it formed the Salt River Project Agricultural Improvement and Power District, a unique entity created to control water use and distribution throughout much of the state.

There are three common ways to create special districts. First, one or more state legislatures may create state- or region-level districts through special enabling legislation. The Delaware River and Bay Authority, for example, was established by joint compact between the state legislatures of New Jersey and Delaware. Second, one or more general-purpose governments may create districts by resolution pursuant to the state's general enabling legislation. For example, municipal officials in Novato, California, formed the Novato Sanitary District to provide sanitary services to city residents. Third, one or more citizens may initiate districts by petition, pursuant to state general enabling legislation. A developer in suburban Houston, Texas, for example, initiated formation of Harris County Municipal Utilities District #145 to provide water, sewer, and drainage services to a proposed residential subdivision.

## Governing Boards

Special districts are governed by independent boards whose members are elected or appointed, pursuant to state enabling legislation. Board sizes range from a few to several dozen members. An extreme example, the governing board of the Metropolitan Water District of Southern California, has forty-seven members representing over 130 constituent municipalities and 26 constituent water districts.

Most nontaxing authorities have appointed boards with members selected by the chief executive or legislative body of the parent government. Taxing districts are typically, though not necessarily, governed by boards elected by district residents. The initial governing board for utility districts formed prior to residential development, for example, often comprises members selected by the chief executive officer or legislature of the parent government, sometimes upon recommendation of the developer.[22] In some instances, district property owners, rather than residents, have the authority to elect board members, a stipulation that has generated legal activity in a number of states.[23]

## Functions

The "special" in special-purpose governments refers to districts' specialized functional focus. Over 29,000, or 92 percent, of the 31,555 districts nationwide are classified as single-function districts. Some of these districts possess latent powers to provide other services. A port district, for example, may have legal authority to provide transit, airports, and economic-development services in addition to port functions. The remaining 8 percent of districts are multifunction districts, which most often provide water services in combination with either sewer, fire protection, or natural resource functions.

Although individual districts have narrow functional breadth, in the aggregate districts provide a wide array of functions, as shown in table 1–1. Despite a reputation as providers of infrastructure services, the four most numerous categories of special-purpose governments are natural resources, fire protection, housing and community development, and water. The functional profile of metropolitan-based special-purpose governments differs slightly from the national profile. Based on figures from 1987 (the latest year for which disaggregated data are available at the metropolitan scale), compared with nonmetropolitan areas, metropolitan areas have a higher proportion of fire protection,

TABLE 1-1 Distribution of Special Districts by Function

| | Percentage of Districts | |
|---|---|---|
| Function | Total U.S., 1992 | Metropolitan Areas, 1987 |
| | (N = 31,555) | (N = 12,590) |
| Natural Resources[a] | 19.7 | 13.8 |
| Fire Protection | 16.7 | 18.2 |
| Housing and Community Development | 11.0 | 11.4 |
| Water | 10.5 | 11.4 |
| Sewer | 5.4 | 8.0 |
| Multifunction Water-Sewer | 4.3 | 6.8 |
| Other Multifunction | 3.7 | 4.4 |
| Parks and Recreation | 3.7 | 4.4 |
| Health and Hospitals | 4.2 | 3.6 |
| Libraries | 3.3 | 2.7 |
| Highway | 2.0 | 1.7 |
| Utilities (gas, electricity, transit) | 1.5 | 1.9 |
| Airports | 1.4 | 0.9 |
| Other Transport (ports, parking) | 0.7 | 1.4 |
| Other Single-function[b] | 12.0 | 9.7 |

Sources: U.S. Bureau of the Census, *1992 Census of Governments*, vol. 1, no. 1, pp. 20–21, table 15; and U.S. Bureau of the Census, *1987 Governments File*.
Notes: Totals exceed 100.0 percent due to rounding. Data for metropolitan areas are the latest available.
a. Includes drainage, flood control, soil and water conservation, irrigation, and other.
b. Includes solid-waste management, cemeteries, school buildings, industrial development, and other single-function.

water, sewer, multifunction, parks and recreation, and utilities districts, and a lower proportion of natural resources, health and hospitals, libraries, and airports districts.

## Geographic Scope

The conventional perception that special-purpose governments are primarily regional is not accurate. Fewer than 20 percent of the 26,783 districts that reported geographic data in the *1992 Census of Governments* are countywide or larger, with only 15 percent of these (3 percent overall) comprising two or more counties. Another 10 percent of the total have territory within two or more counties but are not coterminous with other local government areas. Another 20 percent of districts are coterminous with a municipality. The modal district type, representing the remaining 60 percent of districts nationwide, is subcounty in scope and noncoterminous with another local government. The geographic scope of metropolitan-based districts generally mirrors these national patterns and is discussed more fully in chapter 5.

## Revenue Raising

Special-purpose governments rely on a variety of revenue sources, which are set forth in their enabling legislation. Taxing districts draw primarily on property tax levies but may also receive funds from bond issues, grants, user fees, rents, special assessments, and other taxes. Nontaxing authorities have similar funding options, with the exception of property taxes. Nationwide, 63 percent of the approximately 24,000 districts that reported revenue characteristics raised some revenues from property taxes. Over 41 percent relied at least in part on service charges and fees. Special assessments, a staple funding source for dependent districts, are used by around 24 percent of independent districts. Sales, payroll, and other nonproperty taxes are a relatively minor revenue source drawn upon by only 5 percent of districts.

Although not a major revenue source overall, nonproperty taxes provide a means for nominally nontaxing public authorities to acquire a tax base. Some transit authorities, including the Metropolitan Atlanta Rapid Transit Authority, Bay Area Rapid Transit in the San Francisco Bay Area, and Capital Metropolitan Transit Authority in Austin, Texas, enjoy the proceeds of a 1/2 to 1 percent locally added sales tax.[24] Other transportation authorities may raise revenues from gas taxes and a variety of state fees, including auto registrations, license fees, and lotteries.[25] Even hotel taxes have provided an innovative source of district funding. Financing and construction of the Georgia World Congress Center's new domed stadium, for example, relied on hotel taxes earmarked for that project.[26]

Contrary to the folklore of district self-sufficiency, districts are frequent recipients of public support. Over half of all districts receive at least partial funding from grants, shared taxes, rentals, or reimbursements from other governments. Especially important is aid from the federal government, which in 1992 (the latest data available) totaled $7.4 billion and represented approximately 37 percent of all federal aid to local governments. Direct state aid to districts is less significant in absolute and percentage terms than is federal aid. In 1992, districts received 1.8 percent of total state funding to local governments, a total of $3.6 billion.[27]

Although direct state aid is relatively minor, indirect state aid to special-purpose governments can be considerable. Most districts receive their initial funding from the state and may obtain appropriations and subsidies as they gain financial footing.[28] More important, districts are often exempt from state taxes on income and property. State legislatures may also exempt districts from complying with land use and environmental regulations. States have routinely bailed out districts in default or near-default circumstances, as the well-publicized cases of the Washington Public Power and Supply System (WPPSS) and the New Jersey Sports and Exposition Authority attest.[29]

## THE EMERGENCE OF SPECIAL DISTRICTS

The backdrop for examining specialized governance is the evolution of districts' role in U.S. metropolitan regions. Special-purpose governments have played an active role in service delivery for over two centuries.[30] As early as the 1600s, colonial governments chartered private and public corporations to provide goods and services beyond the then-limited responsibilities of local governments. Early public corporations catered to the needs of the commercially oriented municipalities of the era. Most of these pre-1800 districts were created to construct canals, roads, bridges, and harbors that would expedite, and thereby lower the costs of, moving goods and people. These corporations were quasi-public in scope: they were financed by a combination of public revenues and privately raised capital, managed by boards of directors who often sold the corporation's stock back to the government, and endowed with considerable autonomy over service levels and operations.

A review of districts' role in shaping metropolitan political economies reveals multiple and sometimes contrary motivations for functionally specialized governments. The original impetus for special districts was to regionalize service delivery in what by the 1800s were increasingly interdependent, politically decentralized metropolitan areas. The earliest known use of districts as a regionalizing mechanism was the joint creation in 1790 of a Board of Prison Inspectors by the City of Philadelphia and its ten independent neighboring suburbs.[31] Over the next six decades these municipal neighbors collaborated on nine more regionwide districts, including boards of poor relief, health, police, port wardens, and education. Precursors of today's metropolitan districts, the Philadelphia boards levied taxes, formulated their own budgets, and determined levels of service provision without interference from their municipal creators.

Philadelphia's special districts provided a model for other nineteenth-century metropolitan areas facing similar challenges of population decentralization. In the late 1850s and 1860s, for example, the New

York State Legislature approved the formation of metropolitan police, fire, excise, and sanitary districts encompassing New York City, the City of Brooklyn, and the surrounding counties of Kings, Westchester, and Richmond. Between 1869 and 1889, Illinois officials created three parks districts and a sanitary authority in the Chicago Metropolitan Area. In the late 1880s and early 1890s worsening water pollution and a desire to develop a metropolitan park system convinced state lawmakers to heed the recommendations of Boston-area officials to create independent water, sewer, and parks districts to serve that metropolitan area.[32] The ability of districts to readily fulfill regional service demands has remained a prime motivation for district formation at the metropolitan scale.

In the meantime a very different form of specialized government, the special-assessment district, was gaining wide acceptance for its ability to localize, rather than regionalize, service delivery.[33] Special-assessment districts operated according to the equity principle of proportional payment for proportional benefit. Most districts were small in size, wholly contained within municipal boundaries, and responsible for chargeable improvements such as road construction and street lighting. Because assessment levels were based on a quantifiable measure of potential benefits from the improvement—a fee based on the length of frontage abutting a new road, for example—implementation of assessment districts was considered "above politics." Although administration was not always apolitical in practice, assessment districts earned a reputation as fair, incorruptible, and nonpartisan.[34] The legacy of this reputation is the popular view of districts as neutral, technocratic institutions, a status commonly cited by contemporary proponents of special-purpose governments.

Three powerful and familiar forces affecting metropolitan areas between 1870 and 1920 stimulated a second wave of regionwide and small-area districts, and also prompted formation of a new district type, the municipally coterminous special district.

The first force was population decentralization, spurred by the advances in transportation and communication technology of the late nineteenth and early twentieth centuries, and the needs and practices of industrialists and social elites.[35] Deconcentration of people and jobs led to increased demand for urban services beyond city boundaries. Despite efforts by some cities to annex outlying areas or create consolidated regional governments, the extent and pace of decentralization outstripped efforts to politically contain it.[36] In response to the growing geopolitical mismatch between regionwide service needs, existing jurisdiction boundaries, and the location of public facilities, local officials initiated a second round of the now tried-and-tested metropolitan district. Among the regional districts formed in the era were several that served as models well into the twentieth century: Metropolitan (Boston) Transit District, Cleveland Metropolitan Parks District, Baltimore County Metropolitan District, and East Bay (San Francisco-Oakland) Utility District.[37]

A second and corollary force kindling the formation of special-purpose government during this era was the home rule movement and associated pressures for local autonomy and control. Starting in the 1870s and continuing into the early 1900s, rural- and suburban-controlled state legislatures sharply limited the ability of municipalities to annex outlying territory, while simultaneously enacting permissive statutes for municipal incorporation and district formation.[38] In response, many resource-poor but annexation-resistant urban fringe settlements either incorporated of their own accord or retained their status as unincorporated communities adjacent to municipalities. These fledgling communities desired both autonomy and service viability, a wish well met by functionally specialized, relatively easy-to-create special districts. The result was formation of a new breed of districts, one designed to serve small towns or unincorporated settlements. The desire for local autonomy and limited services remains a prime stimulus for formation of districts in unincorporated communities.[39]

The third impetus for districts was the legislative response to the macroeconomic boom-bust cycles of 1870–1900, which prompted formation of a new district type, the municipally coterminous district. Prior to 1870 rapidly growing municipalities borrowed heavily from private bond markets to finance large-scale public improvements. The depression of 1870 caught indebted cities in a fiscally vulnerable position, triggering a wave of local government defaults or near-defaults. To combat future economic failures, state legislatures placed stringent limitations on the ability of municipalities to incur debt. Citizen groups, fearful that local governments would make up the inevitable revenue shortfall through higher property taxes, lobbied successfully for state enactment of municipal tax limitations. As a result, municipalities found themselves in a doubly tight financial vise, constrained on the one hand by debt ceilings and on the other by property tax limitations, with no reduction in urban service demands.[40]

Municipal officials responded by turning to municipally coterminous special districts. The usefulness of these special-purpose governments was reinforced by court rulings holding that districts were exempt from state-imposed constraints on county or municipal revenue raising. To local officials, the special district offered a legal, easy-to-implement means for circumventing municipal debt and tax constraints without wholly sacrificing control over services. Hundreds of municipalities, particularly in states that had stringent restrictions on municipal debt and taxation (notably Illinois and Pennsylvania), capitalized on districts' financial powers to evade state-imposed ceilings on revenue raising.[41] This fiscal impetus remains a significant motivation for formation of municipally coterminous districts.

In the 1920s and 1930s, widespread embrace of the tenets of Progressivism provided a favorable political climate for a fourth type of special-purpose government, the public authority. A major goal of Progressive reform was to wrest control over public sector functions from political bosses whose governing styles and policies were thought to spawn corruption, inefficiency, and social and physical deterioration of urban society.[42] Consistent with that goal was a reform platform emphasizing the values of efficiency, neutral competence, and professionalism in municipal affairs, in short, "good government."[43] Not surprisingly, the independent, nonelected, professionally managed, nontaxing public authority was seen by many as a key to, if not the epitome of, good government.[44] Early successes of the nation's first—and probably still best-known—authority, the Port of New York Authority (today the Port Authority of New York and New Jersey), formed in 1921, allayed the doubts of many authority skeptics.[45] The public-authority model caught on, leading to formation of hundreds of these nontaxing entities over the next several decades.

By the 1930s, then, four different district subtypes—regional, small-area (submunicipal or unincorporated), municipally coterminous, and nontaxing (of any scale)—had gained a foothold in metropolitan affairs. An early enumeration by political scientist William Anderson estimated that in 1931 there were over 1,400 districts providing urban services nationwide. A decade later that total had increased by over 50 percent to around 2,200 districts.[46]

The primary stimulus of this proliferation was federal government intervention in local service delivery. The Great Depression brought failing urban economies and massive job loss, prompting considerable federal effort to create jobs and keep cities afloat. Under President Franklin D. Roosevelt, a foe of big city administrators and staunch advocate of the neutral public authority,[47] the federal government instituted numerous programs that stipulated creation of independent agencies as a condition of receiving federal funding. Hundreds of special-purpose governments, notably soil conservation districts and public housing authorities, formed in response to federal funding enticements.[48] Over the next several decades, federal and state fiscal incentives remained catalysts for a wide range of special-purpose governments in law enforcement, health, planning, air quality control, resource conservation, economic development, airports, transit, and sewers.[49]

A second impetus for the use of nontaxing authorities during the 1930s and 1940s was broad acceptance of revenue bonds as an instrument of local government finance.[50] Under traditional general obligation bond funding, local governments must pledge their "full faith and credit" as security for repayment of debt. By contrast, revenue bond financing permits local governments to borrow funds for public projects by pledging the security of future project revenues from user charges, tolls, and rents. Revenue bond-reliant public authorities thus offered a powerful means for securing private funds for public projects, including dams, bridges, utility stations, port facilities, tunnels, highways, and airports.[51] Although critics at the time forecast grave implications of tying local government fortunes to elusive project earnings,[52] enthusiasm was strong and lasting for non-tax-financed service delivery.

The twenty-five years following World War II brought rapid suburbanization and flux in local government arrangements. Municipal incorporations increased sharply in many areas, accompanied by an acceleration of new special-district formations. The reasons for districts' appeal were similar to the motivations for the specialized governments of the nineteenth and early twentieth centuries. Local officials formed metropolitan transit, airport, port, highway, sewer, library, parks, and zoo districts to meet regional needs in rapidly growing areas. Newly incorporated suburbs turned to districts of various types to craft service bundles specially tailored to local preferences. Central cities confronted growing fiscal, political, and physical pressures by forming municipally coterminous districts to operate development-oriented functions and make controversial decisions about housing, urban renewal, and social services. Many unincorporated urban fringe communities rejected the orthodox service options of incorporation and annexation in favor of new forms of contracting for services from new or existing special-purpose governments.[53]

By 1972 the U.S. Bureau of the Census reported over 8,054 special districts in 264 metropolitan areas.[54] This tally was up from 5,411 districts in 212 metropolitan areas ten years earlier, and 2,600 districts in 168 metropolitan areas in the early 1950s.[55] Special-purpose governments could no longer be considered isolated or occasional phenomena.

Since the early 1970s, the number of metropolitan-based special districts has increased steadily, driven not only by traditional motivations but also by two new reasons for district formation. The first is the de facto control many districts hold over the location, size, and timing of urban facilities. As growth controls, environmental regulations, and service moratoria replaced the postwar mentality of growth for growth's sake, property developers found service satisfaction in the relatively autonomous, easy-to-create, politically isolated, financially powerful, and administratively flexible special district. Of particular appeal were districts' bonding powers, which enabled private developers to secure up-front capital for expensive infrastructure projects.[56] Aided often by cooperative public officials and permissive growth policies, developers initiated hundreds of community or subdivision-sized districts to provide water, sewer, drainage, road, street lights, and other development-oriented services.[57] The most exceptional growth of developer-initiated districts occurred in the early 1970s in booming Houston Metropolitan Area. Developers formed nearly 400 municipal utilities districts, over 130 of them in 1971 alone, to serve new residential developments in the Houston suburbs and exurbs.[58]

The most recent motivation for district formation also stems from districts' financial powers. Over the past two decades the onerous combination of taxpayer revolts, popular antagonism toward government spending, and citizen demands for high-quality public services has placed severe fiscal pressure on state and local governments. One response has been the creation of special-purpose governments to fund and administer capital projects that parent governments desire but cannot afford, financially or politically.[59] Because districts enjoy exemption from many administrative controls and voter referenda, they have the ability and power to expedite costly and/or unpopular development projects. As a consequence, state and local officials have turned increasingly to public authorities to fund, construct, and operate convention centers, sports stadia, industrial parks, and other often-controversial economic-development facilities.[60] In 1992, over 7,000 of the nearly 24,000 special-purpose governments reporting their type of operation indicated as one of their purposes the financing of public facilities through issuance of public debt.[61]

## THE ROAD AHEAD

Modified institutional choice theory, the primer on special districts, and the historical overview of special-purpose governments already equip us to take several giant steps down the path toward understanding the nature, motivations, and implications of specialized governments. The remainder of the study carries us farther along the way.

I begin the investigation in chapters 2 and 3, which together offer a comprehensive critique of the current literature on specialized governance. Chapter 2 reviews the four predominant theoretical perspectives on metropolitan political economies, focusing on how these perspectives view special districts and why no single perspective can adequately account for their emergence and implications. Chapter 3 assesses the small but growing body of empirical research on special-purpose governments and outlines the methodological shortcomings that plague district research.

The theoretical and empirical assessments provide the basis for presentation in chapter 4 of a new conceptual framework for understanding and analyzing special districts. The new framework modifies institutional choice theory to link metropolitan interest groups with their goals for service delivery and, in turn, with the attributes that render special-purpose, rather than general-purpose, governments such popular institutional choices. An important product of the framework is identification of six geographic and financial subtypes of special-purpose governments whose distinct attributes influence the use and significance of districts in metropolitan regions.

The next three chapters apply the new conceptual framework to unresolved questions about the emergence and implications of specialized governments. In chapter 5, I test which of the factors hypothesized by the competing theoretical perspectives best explain the uneven distribution of district subtypes across U.S. metropolitan areas. Chapter 6 examines the fiscal consequences of specialized governance by analyzing the relationship between reliance on districts and per capita service costs in metropolitan areas. Chapter 7 examines the policy implications of district service provision by analyzing the extent to which a metropolitan area's reliance on districts alters the allocation of resources to various local government functions.

The final chapter summarizes the findings and lessons of the study, then discusses their application to three issues of enduring concern to policy makers and scholars: the promise of institutional adaptation, the practice of privatization, and the trend toward specialization in the public and private spheres.

Taken together, these analyses demonstrate at least four major points. First, metropolitan interest groups—residents, local government officials, and developers—turn not to special districts in general, but rather to specific geographic or financial subtypes of districts in particular whose attributes facilitate achieving each group's distinct goals for service delivery. Merely choosing a district does not automatically lead to its formation or operation, of course. As the analysis indicates, the likelihood that a special-purpose government will ultimately provide services depends on a metropolitan area's legal, institutional, and political environment for institutional choices.

Second, of overriding significance in explaining patterns of reliance on special-purpose governments is the legal environment within which institutional choices are made. For a wide range of district subtypes, regardless of economic, political, or social motivations for special-purpose governments, districts are simply more common where laws enable them and municipal powers are restricted, and less common where enabling laws are few and municipal powers more expansive. The significance of legal factors to institutional outcomes is not unexpected, given that laws codify an area's collective preferences. Nonetheless, the findings underscore the significance of the legal framework and the consequent potential for shaping institutional arrangements and policy outcomes through manipulation of legal levers.

Third, district-reliant metropolitan areas spend significantly more per capita for services than do their non-district-reliant counterparts, even after controlling for a variety of metropolitan-area attributes. In some cases this inflationary effect stems from administrative costs associated with a multiplicity of district providers. In other instances higher costs stem from distinctive attributes of districts themselves, such as political and financial isolation. Special districts apparently do not foster the institutional competition hypothesized to keep the lid on local expenditures. To the contrary, a key consequence of the institutional choice to rely on special-purpose, rather than general-purpose, governments for service delivery is significantly higher per capita costs.

Fourth, specialized service delivery alters the allocation of resources and does so in systematic ways. Metropolitan areas that rely on special districts allocate proportionately more resources to district-provided services than do less district-reliant areas. More specifically, the most specialized metropolitan areas—those that rely on special districts to a high degree for a wide range of services—devote significantly fewer resources to social welfare functions and significantly more resources to development and housekeeping functions than do less-specialized metropolitan areas. Special districts are *not* policy-neutral substitutes for general-purpose governments. Institutional choices matter.

## CHAPTER NOTES

**1.** Annmarie Hauck Walsh, *The Public's Business: The Politics and Practices of Government Corporations* (Cambridge: MIT Press, 1978), pp. 192–96; and Richard L. Morrill, "State and Local Government Commissions and Governance of the Metropolis," in *Decentralization, Local Governments and Markets*, ed. Robert J. Bennett (Oxford: Clarendon, 1990), pp. 297–308.

**2.** Virginia Marion Perrenod, *Special Districts, Special Purposes: Fringe Governments and Urban Problems in the Houston Area* (College Station: Texas A&M University Press, 1984); and John Thornton Mitchell, "The Uses of Special Districts in Financing and Facilitating Urban Growth," *Urban Lawyer* 5, no. 2 (1973): 185–227.

**3.** Sarah Bartlett, "New York Seeks Long-Term Approach to Big Projects," *New York Times*, 8 July 1991, sec. B, pp. 1–2; and Annmarie Hauck Walsh,

"Public Authorities and the Shape of Decision Making," in *Urban Politics New York Style*, ed. Jewel Bellush and Dick Netzer (Armonk, N.Y.: M. E. Sharpe, 1990), pp. 188–219.

4. In practice, the entities I call special-purpose governments or special districts go by a variety of labels, including authorities, commissions, boards, and corporations, although not all entities with these labels are sufficiently public or independent to be considered special districts. I follow the conventions of the U.S. Bureau of the Census, discussed in greater detail later in this chapter, and consider as special-purpose governments all entities the bureau categorizes as "special districts." U.S. Bureau of the Census, *1992 Census of Governments*, vol. 1, no. 1, *Government Organization* (Washington, D.C.: U.S. Government Printing Office, 1994), p. vii.

5. U.S. Bureau of the Census, *1992 Census of Governments*, vol. 1, no. 1, p. 3, table 3.

6. Calculated from data in U.S. Bureau of the Census, *Governments in the United States in 1952*, State and Local Government Special Studies, no. 31 (Washington, D.C.: U.S. Government Printing Office, 1953), pp. 22–49, table 11; and U.S. Bureau of the Census, *1992 Census of Governments*, vol. 1, no. 1, pp. 44–83, table 28. Figures are for 312 metropolitan areas with boundaries fixed at 1987 limits.

7. Calculated from data in U.S. Bureau of the Census, *1987 Census of Governments, Directory of Governments File* (1989), hereafter referred to as *1987 Governments File*.

8. U.S. Bureau of the Census, *1982 Census of Governments*, vol. 6, no. 4, *Historical Statistics on Government Finances and Employment* (Washington, D.C.: U.S. Government Printing Office, 1985), pp. 38–39, table 15; and U.S. Bureau of the Census, *1987 Census of Governments*, vol. 4, no. 5, *Compendium of Government Finances* (Washington, D.C.: U.S. Government Printing Office, 1990).

9. U.S. Bureau of the Census, *Government Finances: 1991–92* (Washington, D.C.: U.S. Government Printing Office, 1996), p. 16, table 13.

10. Joel Garreau, *Edge City: Life on the New Frontier* (New York: Doubleday, 1991), p. 8 and, generally, pp. 185–208. Similar trends were noted previously by Richard Louv, *America II* (Los Angeles: Jeremy P. Tarcher, 1983), pp. 108–16; and John Herbers, *The New Heartland* (New York: Times Books, 1986), pp. 171–75.

11. Christopher Hamilton and Donald T. Wells, *Federalism, Power, and Political Economy* (Englewood Cliffs, N.J.: Prentice Hall, 1990), p. 134.

12. The seminal statement of institutional change theory is Lance E. Davis and Douglass C. North, *Institutional Change and American Economic Growth* (Cambridge: Cambridge University Press, 1971). This discussion of the theory draws upon their work, pp. 6–63.

13. Burton A. Weisbrod illustrates this point with the example of a public sector agency that intentionally hires physically or mentally disabled workers, even though their disabilities may decrease productivity for certain tasks. See Burton A. Weisbrod, *The Nonprofit Economy* (Cambridge: Harvard University Press, 1988), pp. 18–25.

14. Unless otherwise noted, data in the primer are from U.S. Bureau of the Census, *1992 Census of Governments*, vol. 1, no. 1.

**15.** William G. Colman, "A Quiet Revolution in Local Government Finance: Policy and Administrative Challenges in Expanding the Role of User Charges in Financing State and Local Government." Paper prepared for the National Academy of Public Administration. (Washington, D.C.: National Academy of Public Administration, 1983).

**16.** See Robert G. Smith, "The Changing Role of Funding in Authority Policy Implementation," in *Public Authorities and Public Policy*, ed. Jerry Mitchell (Westport, Conn.: Greenwood, 1992), pp. 84–95; and Donald T. Wells and Richard Scheff, "Performance Issues for Public Authorities in Georgia," in *Public Authorities and Public Policy*, ed. Jerry Mitchell (Westport, Conn.: Greenwood, 1992), pp. 167–76.

**17.** Joel M. Douglas, "The Influence of Labor Unions on Public Authorities in New York State: Problems and Prospects," in *Public Authorities and Public Policy*, ed. Jerry Mitchell (Westport, Conn.: Greenwood, 1992), pp. 55–56.

**18.** See, for example, William B. Eimicke, "Housing New York: The Creation and Development of the Battery Park City Authority," in *Public Authorities and Public Policy*, ed. Jerry Mitchell (Westport, Conn.: Greenwood, 1992), pp. 119–27; and Deborah Wathen Finn, "Public Authorities and Social Problems: The Port Authority of New York and New Jersey Addresses the Homeless Problem in Its Facilities," in *Public Authorities and Public Policy*, ed. Jerry Mitchell (Westport, Conn.: Greenwood, 1992), pp. 129–36.

**19.** Another class of entities, known as dependent districts, is neither tallied by the U.S. Bureau of the Census nor analyzed in this book. Dependent districts, which include road assessment, sewer, and street-lighting districts, are nonautonomous units established, governed, and operated by a parent government. Dependent districts sometimes number in the hundreds for a single jurisdiction.

**20.** U.S. Bureau of the Census, *1992 Census of Governments*, vol. 1, no. 1, p. vii.

**21.** Alvin D. Sokolow, Priscilla Hanford, Joan Hogan, and Linda Martin, *Choices for the Unincorporated Community: A Guide to Local Government Alternatives in California* (Davis: Institute of Governmental Affairs, University of California at Davis, 1981), p. 81.

**22.** Richard B. Peiser, "The Economics of Municipal Utility Districts for Land Development," *Land Economics* 59, no. 1 (1983): 43–57.

**23.** For a review, see Robert Manson, "*Ball* in Play: The Effect of *Ball v. James* on Special District Voting Scheme Decisions," *Columbia Journal of Law and Social Problems* 21, no. 1 (1987): 87–136; and Tim De Young, "Governing Special Districts: The Conflict Between Voting Rights and Property Privileges," *Arizona State Law Journal* 14 (1982): 419–52.

**24.** Peter Hall, *Great Planning Disasters* (Berkeley: University of California Press, 1980), p. 118; and Wells and Scheff, "Performance Issues for Public Authorities," p. 170.

**25.** R. Smith, "The Changing Role of Funding," p. 84.

**26.** Wells and Scheff, "Performance Issues for Public Authorities," p. 170.

**27.** U.S. Bureau of the Census, *Government Finances: 1991–92*, p. 2, table 2.

**28.** Walsh, *The Public's Business*, pp. 41–42.

**29.** On WPPSS, see James Leigland and Robert Lamb, *WPP$$: Who is to Blame for the WPPSS Disaster?* (Cambridge, Mass.: Ballinger, 1986). On the now publicly subsidized New Jersey Sports and Exposition Authority, see Matthew Purdy, "Troubled Sports Empire Seeks New Fields to Explore," *New York Times,* 24 April 1994, p. 35. For other examples, see Donald Axelrod, *Shadow Government* (New York: John Wiley and Sons, 1992).

**30.** The early history of special districts remains largely unexplored. I rely in this section on several sources that provide an overview, namely National Municipal League, Committee on Metropolitan Government, *The Government of Metropolitan Areas in the United States,* prepared by Paul Studenski with the assistance of the Committee on Metropolitan Government (New York: National Municipal League, 1930), chap. 14 (hereafter Studenski); Walsh, *The Public's Business,* pp. 14–17; and Donald Foster Stetzer, *Special Districts in Cook County: Toward a Geography of Local Government* (Chicago: Department of Geography, University of Chicago, 1975), pp. 12–13.

**31.** Studenski, *The Government of Metropolitan Areas,* pp. 257; and Eli K. Price, *The History of the Consolidation of the City of Philadelphia* (Philadelphia: J. B. Lippincott, 1873), pp. 52–55.

**32.** Discussion of these examples is found in Studenski, *The Government of Metropolitan Areas,* pp. 258–64; Victor Jones, *Metropolitan Government* (Chicago: University of Chicago Press, 1942), pp. 93–94; and Jon C. Teaford, *City and Suburb: The Political Fragmentation of Metropolitan America, 1850–1970* (Baltimore: Johns Hopkins University Press, 1979), p. 79. For more on the New York City case, see David C. Hammack, "Comprehensive Planning before the Comprehensive Plan: A New Look at the Nineteenth Century American City," in *Two Centuries of American City Planning,* ed. Daniel V. Schaffer (Baltimore: Johns Hopkins University Press, 1988), pp. 146, 152–53.

**33.** Robin L. Einhorn, *Property Rules: Political Economy in Chicago, 1833–1872* (Chicago: University of Chicago Press, 1991), pp. 83–103.

**34.** Ibid., pp. 204–24.

**35.** Kenneth T. Jackson, *Crabgrass Frontier: The Suburbanization of the United States* (New York: Oxford University Press, 1985), pp. 87–93, 103–15; and David Gordon, "Capitalist Development and the History of American Cities," in *Marxism and the Metropolis,* ed. William K. Tabb and Larry Sawers (New York: Oxford University Press, 1978), pp. 25–63.

**36.** Kenneth T. Jackson, "Metropolitan Government Versus Suburban Autonomy," in *Cities in American History,* ed. Kenneth T. Jackson and Stanley Schultz (New York: Knopf, 1972), pp. 442–62.

**37.** Studenski, *The Government of Metropolitan Areas,* p. 256.

**38.** Teaford, *City and Suburb,* chap. 2; and Ann R. Markusen, "Class and Urban Social Expenditure: A Marxist Theory of Metropolitan Government," in *Marxism and the Metropolis,* ed. William K. Tabb and Larry Sawers (New York: Oxford University Press, 1978), pp. 100–102.

**39.** Sokolow et al., *Choices for the Unincorporated Community,* pp. 81, 90.

**40.** Jon C. Teaford, *The Unheralded Triumph: City Government in America, 1870–1900* (Baltimore: Johns Hopkins University Press, 1984), pp. 284–88, 293–97.

**41.** See Ann Durkin Keating, *Building Chicago: Suburban Developers and the Creation of a Divided Metropolis* (Columbus: Ohio State University Press, 1988); Ted Flickinger and Peter M. Murphy, "Special Districts," in *Illinois Local Government*, ed. James F. Keane and Gary Koch, pp. 151–81 (Carbondale: Southern Illinois University Press, 1990); and Charles Hoffman, *Municipal Authorities in Pennsylvania* (Harrisburg: Pennsylvania Department of Community Affairs, 1988), p. 2.

**42.** Martin J. Schiesl, *The Politics of Efficiency* (Berkeley: University of California Press, 1977), pp. 46–59, 142–43; and Dennis R. Judd, *The Politics of American Cities*, 3rd ed. (Glenview, Ill.: Scott, Foresman, 1988), pp. 88–95.

**43.** See Charles R. Adrian, *A History of American City Government: The Emergence of the Metropolis, 1920–1945* (Lanham, Md.: University Press of America, 1987), pp. 319–46; and Herbert Kaufman, "Administrative Decentralization and Political Power," *Public Administration Review* 29 (January-February 1969): 3–15.

**44.** Jameson W. Doig, " 'If I See a Murderous Fellow Sharpening a Knife Cleverly. . .' The Wilsonian Dichotomy and the Public Authority Tradition," *Public Administration Review* 43, no. 4 (1983): 295–96; and Jameson W. Doig and Jerry Mitchell, "Expertise, Democracy, and the Public Authority Model: Groping Toward Accommodation," in *Public Authorities and Public Policy*, ed. Jerry Mitchell (Westport, Conn.: Greenwood, 1992), pp. 17–30.

**45.** Doig, " 'A Murderous Fellow,' " p. 295; and, generally, Jameson W. Doig, "Expertise, Politics, and Technological Change: The Search for Mission at the Port of New York Authority," *Journal of the American Planning Association* 59, no. 1 (1993): 31–44.

**46.** For the earlier figure, William Anderson, *The Units of Government in the United States: An Enumeration and Analysis* (Chicago: Public Administration Service, 1936), p. 24. For the later figure, William Anderson, *The Units of Government in the United States: An Enumeration and Analysis*, rev. ed. (Chicago: Public Administration Service, 1942).

**47.** Mark I. Gelfand, *A Nation of Cities: The Federal Government and Urban America, 1933–1965* (New York: Oxford University Press, 1975), pp. 24–26.

**48.** John C. Bollens, *Special District Governments in the United States*, 2nd ed. (Berkeley: University of California Press, 1961), pp. 12–13.

**49.** Harold Seidman, *Politics, Position and Power: The Dynamics of Federal Organization*, 2nd ed. (New York: Oxford University Press, 1970), pp. 170–71; Robert M. Stein, "Federally Supported Substate Regional Governments: The Maintenance of Governmental Structure," *Urban Interest* 2 (Spring 1980): pp. 74–81; and Barbara Pate Glacel, *Regional Transit Authorities* (New York: Praeger, 1983), pp. 1–15.

**50.** Robert Lamb and Stephen P. Rappaport, *Municipal Bonds* (New York: McGraw Hill, 1980), pp. 14–16.

**51.** Lamb and Rappaport, *Municipal Bonds*, pp. 345–50; and, generally, Walsh, *The Public's Business*, chap. 3.

**52.** See, for example, Horace A. Davis, "Borrowing Machines," *National Municipal Review* 24, no. 6 (1935): 328–34; and Joseph E. McLean, "Use and Abuse of Authorities," *National Municipal Review* 42, no. 9 (1953): 438–44.

**53.** John C. Bollens and Henry J. Schmandt, *The Metropolis: Its People, Politics and Economic Life*, 2nd ed. (New York: Harper and Row, 1970), chap. 7 and pp. 313–24; and Gary J. Miller, *Cities by Contract: The Politics of Municipal Incorporation* (Cambridge: MIT Press, 1981).

**54.** U.S. Bureau of the Census, *1972 Census of Governments*, vol. 1, no. 1, *Government Organization* (Washington, D.C.: U.S. Government Printing Office, 1973).

**55.** U.S. Bureau of the Census, *1962 Census of Governments*, vol. 1, no. 1, *Government Organization* (Washington, D.C.: U.S. Government Printing Office, 1963); and U.S. Bureau of the Census, *Local Government in Metropolitan Areas*, State and Local Government Special Studies, no. 36 (Washington, D.C.: U.S. Government Printing Office, 1954), p. 2.

**56.** Mitchell, "The Uses of Special Districts,"; Douglas R. Porter, Ben C. Lin, and Richard B. Peiser, *Special Districts: A Useful Technique for Financing Infrastructure* (Washington, D.C.: Urban Land Institute, 1987); and Gerald E. Mullen, "The Use of Special Assessment Districts and Independent Special Districts as Aids in Financing Private Land Development," *California Law Review* 53, no. 1 (1965): 364–85.

**57.** Porter, Lin, and Peiser, *Special Districts*, pp. 18–34.

**58.** Mitchell, "The Uses of Special Districts," pp. 193–96; Perrenod, *Special Districts, Special Purposes*, pp. 14–17; and William P. Barrett, "Clear as Mud," *Forbes*, 15 June 1987, 96–98.

**59.** Jerry Mitchell, "Policy Functions and Issues for Public Authorities," in *Public Authorities and Public Policy*, ed. Jerry Mitchell (Westport, Conn.: Greenwood, 1992), pp. 3–4, 10–11.

**60.** See Heywood T. Sanders, "Building the Convention City: Politics, Finance, and Public Investment in Urban America," *Journal of Urban Affairs* 14, no. 2 (1992): 135–59; and Annmarie Hauck Walsh and James Leigland, "The Only Planning Game in Town," *Empire State Report* 9, no. 5 (1983): 6–12. On district involvement in industrial development bond projects, see Lamb and Rappaport, *Municipal Bonds*, pp. 221–35.

**61.** U.S. Bureau of the Census, *1992 Census of Governments*, vol. 1, no. 1, p. 25, table 18; see also Jerry Mitchell, "The Policy Activities of Public Authorities," *Policy Studies Journal* 18, no. 4 (1990): pp. 928–42.

# 2

# Theoretical Perspectives

To appreciate the recent rise and implications of specialized governance requires understanding how social scientists and public officials have conceived of the organization and functioning of metropolitan political economies. The literature offers four predominant perspectives—institutional reform, public choice, metropolitan ecology, and structuralist—each of which uses a fundamentally different lens to view and interpret metropolitan political arrangements. Although none of these perspectives trains its sights solely on special-purpose governments, each postulates directly or indirectly about their role, desirability, and implications in metropolitan regions.

How useful are these four perspectives for understanding special-purpose governance? The critical assessment in this chapter highlights the ideological rifts that have long characterized the debate over metropolitan political structure in general and specialized governments in particular. The divergence of views is disclosed in the contradictory labels assigned to special-purpose governments: fragmentary and integrative, efficient and inefficient, apolitical and partisan, competitive and cooperative, growth-inducing and growth-hindering, equitable and inequitable, politically responsive and antidemocratic. In some instances two or more perspectives do reach similar conclusions about district causes or consequences. Such agreement is often coincidental, however, and derives from radically different assumptions and ways of interpreting social phenomena. What stands out is the persistence and contentiousness of an unresolved issue in social science and policy, the implications of institutional arrangements in metropolitan society.

## INSTITUTIONAL REFORM PERSPECTIVE

From the Progressive Era of the 1890s–1920s, through a wave of postwar metropolitan reform proposals in the 1950s and 1960s, and until well into the post-urban crisis 1970s, the dominant view of metropolitan political economies was held by proponents of institutional reform. The institutional-reform view takes a normative approach to metropolitan political organization, de-emphasizing explanation and prediction about institutional arrangements in favor of contentions about how institutions *ought* to be arranged to achieve the efficiency and equity goals that are the hallmark of reform.

The ideals of institutional-reform thought were crystallized in the writings of late nineteenth- and early twentieth-century Progressive Era political scientists and public administrators who sought to modernize government to meet the service needs of rapidly growing and decentralizing metropolitan populations.[1] The means to this end and the primary stated goal of early reformers was efficiency in government, conceived during that time as the promotion of economic growth.[2] A secondary reform goal was the equitable distribution of resources throughout the metropolitan region. To reformers, achieving parity in public service levels and eliminating fiscal disparities between areas of need and resources were essential for the healthy functioning of the metropolis.

The twin desires for efficiency and regional equity persisted in postwar reform thought. Many reform tracts of the late 1940s through the early 1960s supported proposals for political reorganization in rapidly suburbanizing U.S. metropolitan areas.[3] The subsequent generation of institutional-reform literature in the 1970s likewise retained the focus on efficiency and equity goals, but also reflected a greater concern for government accessibility and citizen responsiveness than did earlier reform literature.[4] The most recent incarnation of reform literature revisits its original economic growth-driven premises about the hazards of political fragmentation and the merits of metropolitanization.[5]

Underlying the institutional-reform perspective are two normative assumptions. The first is that the appropriate unit of analysis for studying metropolitan political economies is the metropolitan community itself. To reformers, a metropolitan area constitutes an interdependent economic, social, and political community. Individual jurisdictions are viewed as artificial divisions of the larger, logical whole. The second normative assumption is that the welfare of the metropolitan community takes precedence over the welfare of individuals or individual communities within the metropolis. Accordingly, reformers argue that existing arrangements of local governments as well as any reforms proposed to alter these arrangements should be judged by how they affect regionwide, rather than individual, community welfare.

From these assumptions flow four major tenets of reform that link local government arrangements within a metropolitan area to levels of economic growth, efficiency, equity, and government responsiveness. The first tenet is that metropolitan political fragmentation results in chaotic and inefficient service provision. A regional economy divided into small, autonomous units each acting in its own interest will lack coordination and neglect regionwide concerns. By this logic, inefficiency stems from two sources: the inability of small units to realize economies of scale in production, and the distorted decisions associated with spillover effects in a politically fragmented region.[6]

Second, reformers contend, overlapping units of government lead to wasteful duplication of service. Reform proponents associate service duplication with administrative inefficiency, which they argue results in higher public outlays unrelated to service quality.

Third, reformers argue that local government multiplicity and overlap lead to citizen confusion, voter apathy, and higher costs due to "structural illusion." According to this argument, complex jurisdictional arrangements are associated with higher information and transaction costs, which prevent citizens from effectively articulating their demands for services and acting as the budgetary watchdogs of local government. Structural illusion is the notion that uninformed or misinformed citizens free governments to inflate taxes and expenditures, a condition considered more likely in complex rather than integrated government structures.[7]

Fourth, reformers assume that politically fragmented systems perpetuate fiscal disparities and inequities caused by an intrametropolitan mismatch between service needs and tax resources. To reformers, parity across jurisdictions in levels of public goods and taxes is desirable. The failure to remedy disparities is seen as both morally wrong and dangerous in that it leads to conflict and unrest.

The bête noir of institutional reformers is thus the proliferation of autonomous jurisdictions that "thwart the wholesome development of the enlarged community," and are "administratively inefficient, financially inequitable, poorly organized, and unnecessarily expensive."[8] Accordingly, reformers see the integration of government at the metropolitan level as a logical and necessary antidote to the ills of political decentralization. Placing control over service delivery and governance in the hands of a centralized unit, reformers argue, would boost efficiency and equity by internalizing externalities, realizing economies of scale, lowering transaction and information costs, and distributing more equitably the costs and benefits of service delivery.

## Reform View of Special Districts

Not surprisingly, whether one dips into the writings of Progressive Era reformers, second-wave reformers of the 1950s and 1960s, or contemporary reform proponents, special-purpose governments get largely critical reviews. There are some tempering factors. For example, the reform literature occasionally acknowledges the appeal of special districts for meeting diverse service demands and capturing production economies of scale.[9] Still, most reformers suffer districts grudgingly, emphasizing the widely held reform position that, in the words of one proponent,

> [b]ecause special districts are too numerous, and because they are only palliatives offering no long-range solution [to metropolitan problems], they weaken general local governments and lessen the possibility of attaining a governmental system that is both responsive and responsible.[10]

Institutional reform's condemnation of districts derives from its conviction that a single metropolitan, multipurpose government provides the optimal institutional arrangement for cost-effective service delivery. Special districts thus offend reformers on two counts. First, districts fragment the metropolis geopolitically, adding to what reformers see as the burdens of metropolitan fragmentation. Second, districts fragment the metropolis functionally, adding to service coordination problems and associated administrative inefficiencies. Providing additional affront is districts' low political visibility, which reformers allege exacerbates the ills of geopolitical and functional fragmentation, further hampering effective service delivery.

By these yardsticks, submetropolitan special-purpose governments, such as those found in unincorporated urban fringe settlements, fall particularly short of reform ideals. As low-visibility contributors to geopolitical and functional fragmentation, these "ad hoc" governments, as submetropolitan districts have been pejoratively labeled since the Progressive Era, ipso facto hinder the realization of reform goals.[11]

The specific charges levied at submetropolitan districts are similar to those directed by reformers at small local governments of any type. Small-scale districts are seen as inefficient for failing to realize economies of scale and exacerbating spillover effects. Reform sympathizers point to the problems faced by small-sized districts in providing capital-intensive services such as water and sewer, which are generally agreed to reach efficient levels at large scales.[12] By overlaying additional boundaries on the metropolis, special districts also increase the likelihood of spillover effects, which reformers argue result in distorted and inefficient levels of public goods provision.[13]

Somewhat paradoxically, reformist censure of special-purpose governments extends also to metropolitanwide districts, which because of their scale conceivably overcome the alleged problems of geopolitical fragmentation, spillover effects, and economies of scale. Nonetheless, although reformers occasionally cite metropolitanwide districts as logical stepping-stones to metropolitan unity, they conclude that the economic and policy consequences of functional fragmentation and low political visibility render even metropolitanwide districts a poor cousin to multipurpose metropolitan government.[14]

The institutional-reform literature is characteristically pessimistic about districts' fiscal and policy consequences. With respect to costs, reformers contend that special-purpose governments, whether sub-metropolitan or metropolitanwide, will require higher total public outlays for services than will general-purpose governments.[15] In particular, the reform view criticizes districts for duplicating the services of general-purpose governments, which leads to unnecessary overhead expenses, divisive political controversies, and legal battles costly to the public fisc.[16] Reformers also contend that special-purpose service provision sacrifices the economic benefits of personnel sharing, legal and financial services, and centralized purchasing that are available to general-purpose governments. Moreover, the common practice of including district tax levies on county property tax bills provides districts with lower fiscal visibility than would exist if each district were required to send a separate bill to taxpayers. To reformers, districts can exploit their relative obscurity to levy higher taxes than would be politically possible under an integrated local-government system.[17]

The reform literature more fundamentally cites functional specialization as the source of higher government costs. District officials and board members need not consider alternative service priorities, argue reformers, and so, wearing spending blinders, channel their energies and district financial resources into the single function for which the district is responsible. The district's governing body "is apt to become an official lobby for the activity it oversees."[18] Unlike most municipal departments, moreover, districts typically enjoy a dedicated revenue stream for operations, thereby avoiding the need to share revenues for more pressing government needs. In addition, contend reformers, the low level of coordination associated with functional specialization hampers regional planning, which in turn engenders high social costs of disorderly development.[19]

Functional specialization is an even greater threat to cost containment when combined with the limited political visibility of specialized governments. Low visibility leaves districts susceptible to control by functionally oriented special interest groups, whose intense service preferences encourage higher public outlays. Intensifying the upward pressure on spending is districts' greater potential for structural illusion as consumers are forced to learn about, hunt down, and interact with myriad specialized and limited-access agencies.[20]

With respect to policy effects, reformers emphasize the dangers of decentralizing the locus of public decision making into independent, single-purpose agencies. An underlying premise of reform is that multipurpose governments are uniquely suited to find solutions to communitywide problems of resource allocation and that these solutions "may be of higher value" than those "attained by an aggregation of the choices made by single-functioned organizations."[21] By precluding healthy public debates over the relative merits of competing public resource allocations, districts allegedly thwart articulation of citizen demands and seriously compromise efforts at regional coordination. Functionally fragmented governance, in the words of one observer, "can only dissipate the ability of a region's citizenry to allocate its public resources in a manner consistent with manifest regional preferences."[22] Moreover, "guild autonomy" gives districts virtual control over major policy realms.[23] "And when you stop to think of it," summarized one commentator,

> an independent agency in charge of a basic service that can fix its own rates, determine its own policies for supplying service and making extensions, and formulate and approve its own long-range plans, holds an almost dictatorial control over how, and where, and how much a community is to develop residentially, commercially, and industrially.[24]

## Critique of the Reform View

*But that is not the only option*

Critics often charge that the institutional reform perspective is irrelevant because its proposals for metropolitan government have been repeatedly rejected by voters.[25] Such criticism too hastily dismisses what the reform perspective offers to an understanding of metropolitan political economies, however. The recent resurgence of interest in regionalism, whether through metropolitanwide districts or other forms of local government cooperation, attests to the widespread belief in the need for metropolitan-level coordination of services and governance. Given social and economic interdependence and scarce resources, attending to the public interest requires institutional arrangements that permit regionwide prioritization and coordination across functions. Analysts of all ideological cloth argue that certain services, notably criminal investigation, sewage treatment, and transit, are logically and cost-effectively produced at a regional scale. To the extent functional fragmentation boosts the influence of special-interest groups, moreover, achieving a representative allocation of resources warrants a public forum capable of brokering special-interest demands across the region.

Nonetheless, in four ways the institutional reform perspective fails to accurately represent and account for special-purpose governments. First, reformers tend to underspecify special districts, treating them as

*In some sense these are parts of the argument for special purpose*

a monolithic local government class. Regardless of district size, function, or means of financing, reform proponents assume a priori that
each additional district automatically hinders metropolitan service delivery. By conceiving of special-purpose governments as an undifferentiated class, reformers overlook that particular subtypes of districts—
say a metropolitanwide, multipurpose agency such as Portland's
Metro—may have beneficial outcomes for the region.[26]

 The second difficulty is the reform perspective's failure to come
to grips with the reality of diverse service preferences. The reform
literature largely dismisses the possibility that small government units
can meet the service needs and preferences of residents and that special-
purpose governments might do so also. Because different communities
typically do have different preferences for the quantity and quality of
urban services, such as parks, libraries, and health centers, the finely
tailored offerings of special-purpose governments may improve, rather
than impair, service delivery where preferences are diverse.

The third difficulty with the reform perspective is its presumption,
rather than demonstration, of the ill-effects of politically fragmented
metropolitan organizations in general and special districts in particular.
Reformers leave untested their claims about the links between government multiplicity, special-purpose government service delivery, and
economic or policy consequences. Rather, the perspective presupposes
negative outcomes of small or specialized governments and prescribes
a uniform metropolitan government cure. This is dubious medicine
indeed: in the limited instances where propositions about centralized
arrangements have been tested the results are far from a testament to the
superiority of metropolitan government.[27] Throughout the twentieth
century politically fragmented metropolitan areas suffered few of the
service delivery disasters predicted by reformers, despite the fact that
nearly all metropolitan areas became more complex over time. Much
of the increase in complexity was due to proliferation of special-purpose
governments, which occurred despite the opprobrium of institutional
reformers. The reform literature is devoid of evidence that such proliferation has hindered metropolitan areas from achieving service delivery goals.

 The final difficulty with the reform approach is methodological.
Institutional reformers generalize excessively when they denote
"metropolitanwide" as the ideal scale for efficient service delivery.
With respect to spillover effects, reformers' logic has merit: for certain
services a metropolitan jurisdiction may internalize regionwide spillover effects, thereby increasing efficiency. With respect to other elements of efficiency such as economies of scale, however, reform logic
is flawed. "Metropolitan" encompasses a wide range of scales. By

Bureau of the Census definitions, as of 1992 metropolitan referred to an area as small as 56,735 population (Enid [Okla.] Metropolitan Area) or 46 square miles (Jersey City [N. J.] Metropolitan Area) and as large as 8,854,093 population (New York [N. Y.] Metropolitan Area) or over 27,000 square miles (Riverside-San Bernardino [Calif.] Metropolitan Area). It is impossible to assume inherent efficiency at these varying scales merely because they are designated metropolitan.

## PUBLIC CHOICE PERSPECTIVE

The public choice perspective provides a radically different view from that of institutional reform on metropolitan political economies and special-purpose governance. Rooted in the late 1800s and developed by economists and political scientists largely since the late 1940s, public choice applies economic principles and techniques to political concerns, such as voting behavior, bureaucracies, resource allocation, and processes of collective action.[28] Of central importance is faith in the ability of competitive market mechanisms to ensure efficient service delivery.

The public choice perspective is deductive, basing its predictions and explanations about metropolitan political economies on assumptions about individual and group behavior. A basic postulate of public choice theory is that individuals and groups make rational decisions to maximize their welfare when choosing between alternative courses of action. Individuals are presumed to have diverse preferences for the levels and quantities of goods and services provided in metropolitan areas. From a public choice perspective the most desirable system of metropolitan organization is the one that maximizes the choices available to individual residents to maximize their chances for matching individual preferences to services received.

The central contribution of public choice theory to the analysis of metropolitan political economies is application of the notions of private-market competition and consumer sovereignty to the problem of how to efficiently produce and provide public goods. Public goods are items such as police protection, clean air, city judges, and festivals in the public park, for which there is no cost for an additional consumer to enjoy the benefits of these goods, and for which it is difficult or impossible to exclude an individual from enjoying the good once provided.[29] Classic examples of public goods are national defense and lighthouse beacons. Because of the difficulty identifying and charging each individual user who benefits from such goods, utility-maximizing consumers have no incentive to reveal their true willingness to pay for these goods. Instead, they have an incentive to "free ride" on the generosity of the provider, enjoying the good's benefits without shouldering a portion of its costs. As a consequence, the invisible hand of the market fails to operate. Private producers either do not produce the good at all or produce it in inefficiently small amounts. To achieve efficiency in public goods provision, conventional economic wisdom long held that society must rely on nonmarket—that is, political—mechanisms, such as voting and taxing, to induce consumers to reveal their preferences for public goods and thus compel the sharing of their costs across all citizens.[30]

The now familiar public choice insight set forth by Charles M. Tiebout in 1956 challenged the conventional wisdom that there existed no market for public goods and that political mechanisms were necessary for achieving efficiency in public goods provision.[31] Tiebout argued that market mechanisms could solve the public goods problem in metropolitan areas provided there existed a polycentric political structure. Just as a multiplicity of private firms competing for customers would foster the efficient production of private goods, he contended, so would a multiplicity of public agencies competing for residents foster the efficient provision of public goods. Achieving efficiency required merely a choice among different municipal offerings of services and taxes, and unencumbered mobility to relocate to jurisdictions whose services and tax bundle most closely met residents' service needs.[32] Residents could then "vote with their feet," thereby simulating the interjurisdictional competitition necessary to induce efficient production of public goods.

Public choice logic thus led to a conclusion directly opposite that reached by institutional reformers. Although acceptance was neither immediate nor without criticism, Tiebout's justification for polycentric political systems inspired a large body of theoretical and empirical research on the efficiency of politically fragmented metropolitan arrangements.[33]

One extension with important implications for the public choice approach to specialized governance was the notion that the *provision* and *production* of a public good are distinct and can be accomplished by different entities.[34] *Provision* refers to the collective community choice of whether to offer a good or service and, if so, to determine the appropriate quantity, quality, form of financing, and method of production. *Production* refers to the technical process of manufacturing the good or service. Efficient production levels vary by function: mass transit services, for example, capture economies of scale at relatively high population thresholds, while primary education realizes economies at smaller scales.[35] Public choice theorists underscore that the unit that provides a good need not be the one that actually produces it. As a result, small governments need not forego or pay top dollar for services affordably produced only at large scales. Instead, they may use flexible arrangements—contracting, intergovernmental agreements, or overlying special districts, for example—to achieve production economies of scale and retain economic viability.

Although public choice proponents agree on the benefits of government multiplicity, they divide over its implications for total government costs. Some hypothesize a positive relationship between political fragmentation and public outlays. They reason that "preference-sorted" citizens will be more willing to support relatively high municipal spending (and taxes) because expenditures will presumably be made in accordance with citizens' relatively uniform preferences.[36] Proponents of this view shine favorable light on evidence that more decentralized political structures are positively associated with spending on goods and services.[37] By contrast, public choice theorists who see government as a "budget-maximizing Leviathan" view polycentric systems as an antidote to bureaucratic overspending. They argue that interjurisdictional competition for residents coupled with taxpayer mobility will constrain bureaucratic tendencies for inflating budgets, thus holding down total public outlays for goods and services.[38]

Of fundamental importance, however, is that regardless of whether polycentricity results in higher or lower public outlays, public choice scholars view government multiplicity with none of the alarm expressed by institutional reformers. Government formation represents a rational response to meeting diverse preferences for public goods. A multiplicity of jurisdictions is a necessary condition for ensuring responsiveness to service preferences and engendering the healthy interjurisdictional competition that facilitates efficient production and provision.

## Public Choice View of Special Districts

The principles of the public choice paradigm, like those of the institutional-reform perspective, induce an automatic reaction to special-purpose governments. But whereas the tenets of institutional reform lead to a reflexive *rejection* of special districts, the principles of public choice theory prompt a reflexive *acceptance* of districts as contributors to efficiency-enhancing intergovernmental competition.

The public choice argument in favor of special districts relies on the distinction between production and provision of public goods. In cases where the optimal scale of production differs from the desired scale of provision, public choice scholars see the geographically flexible, functionally specialized district as a logical mode for efficiency.[39]

In this light, districts of all scales, from submunicipal to metropolitanwide, have appeal. Small-sized districts can more finely differentiate the available choice among service bundles, thereby enhancing

*But does this facilitate free rider cost shifting?*

competition, better matching citizen preferences, and promoting efficiency. One proponent went so far as to conclude that, "in areas where
citizens have diverse sets of preferences for public goods and services,
districts are more efficient producers than general-purpose units of
government."[40] The value of small-scale districts is even greater, argue
public choice proponents, where communities desire a narrow range
of services, such as fire protection and sewers only.[41] Forming a special-
purpose government rather than a full-service municipality to meet
limited community needs can lower the marginal costs of operating a
new government unit.

Large-scale districts are likewise appealing because they enable the
efficient production of goods whose technological and cost properties
imply economies of scale or strong spillover effects.[42] By providing
the expensive regional services that are beyond the means of many
individual jurisdictions, large districts make viable a multiplicity of
small government units, the sine qua non of the competitive intergovernmental system advocated by public choice proponents.

*note*

Since the early 1980s, coincident with a swing of the ideological
pendulum toward greater reliance on market mechanisms in public
service delivery, the public choice view of special-purpose governments
has gained sanction in official federal policies on metropolitan organization. These policies are set forth by the U.S. Advisory Commission
on Intergovernmental Relations (ACIR), a federal agency created by
Congress in 1953 to study and recommend improvements to the federal
system of government.[43] Until the mid-1980s ACIR embraced the tenets
of the institutional reform perspective, opposing special-district proliferation as detrimental to efficient and equitable metropolitan service
delivery.[44] ACIR has since embraced public choice theory as the appropriate theoretical framework for analyzing metropolitan political economies. Accordingly, ACIR currently takes a benevolent view of districts
as evidenced by its recent policy statement:

> The Commission finds that special-purpose governments may be a useful
> and efficient form of organization for local citizens. The option of organiz-
> ing a special-purpose government complements the organization of gen-
> eral-purpose local governments. The Commission finds no *a priori* reason
> to reduce the number of special-purpose governments or to restrict their
> growth arbitrarily.[45]

This approach to metropolitan service delivery, known as the local
public economy view, also contends that districts are useful for addressing issues of distributional equity. Rather than enlarge general-purpose
governments to enable redistribution of resources through an expanded

tax base, as the conventional orthodoxy on equity recommends, the public economy view urges the formation of overlying special districts that can accomplish redistribution without jeopardizing jurisdictional autonomy.[46] The only circumstance under which public choice proponents denounce districts is when their purpose is to circumvent citizen-inspired, state-imposed restrictions on municipal borrowing or taxation, which choice adherents argue distorts the efficient operation of the market.[47]

## Critique of the Public Choice View

The public choice perspective offers several important insights for understanding the functioning of special districts in metropolitan political economies. First, it acknowledges that utility-maximizing citizens have a rational basis for forming special-purpose governments when alternative local government options cannot meet consumer service demands. Second, it provides economic justification for the efficiency-enhancing properties of districts of all sizes, from neighborhood-level to metropolitanwide. Third, it separates efficiency arguments from equity arguments, an appropriate distinction for analytic purposes.

The perspective fails to provide a convincing analysis of special districts in metropolitan political economies, however, due to questionable assumptions about district attributes. First, public choice theory assumes that the existence of special-purpose governments is necessarily evidence of more efficient service delivery. The logic is that rational, welfare-maximizing individuals would form districts only if there were "gains to trade." As the historical evidence in chapter 1 chronicles, however, there are myriad noneconomic motivations for district use. It is simply not the case that new special-purpose governments originate solely from economic incentives.

A second problem stems from the public choice assumption that because special-purpose governments are motivated by economic considerations, district boundaries therefore encompass an economically optimal amount of territory and/or population. If this logic is correct, water district boundaries should approximate watersheds, drainage district boundaries should encompass a drainage basin, transit district boundaries should circumscribe a population density threshold, and so forth. Yet a cursory examination of nearly any metropolitan area reveals district boundaries quite different from an economically based standard. The majority of districts are either coterminous with municipalities or counties, or they approximate informal political divisions such as neighborhoods or unincorporated communities. In either case, boundaries are based on political, rather than economic or natural resource, considerations. The public choice view thus neglects the numerous exogenous factors, such as political demands, local intergovernmental relations, the strength and contentiousness of competing interest groups, local leadership networks, and historical practices and events, that determine district boundaries.

A third difficulty with the public choice view is its inability to account for the wide variation across metropolitan areas in the numbers and patterns of special-purpose governments. Assuming there exist diverse preferences within every metropolitan area, public choice theory would hold that every metropolitan area have a large variety of special- (and general-) purpose governments to accommodate the range of service demands. Reality does not sustain this prediction, however. Some metropolitan areas have very few special- (and general-) purpose governments while others have many. Public choice theory would imply that residents of politically integrated metropolitan areas are thus less rational or concerned with cost-effective service delivery than their counterparts in politically fragmented metropolitan areas. A more likely explanation is that the process of government formation and activity is far more complex than the public choice perspective allows.

Fourth, and perhaps most serious, public choice theory assumes that special-purpose governments are competitive producers and providers of public goods and, therefore, that districts are an institutional means for efficient service delivery. Whether special-purpose governments actually compete with other production units is by no means certain, however. The functional and geographic mix of special districts in most metropolitan areas show considerable variety and, hence, relatively little competition across districts. Airport authorities, for example, do not compete with fire districts, nor do either of these types compete with library districts or housing authorities, for example. Indeed, a well-established sociological and economic principle is that specialization is an effective way to *avoid* competition, either by creating new markets or carving out a special niche in an existing one.[48] Moreover, regionwide districts, such as metropolitan transit or sewer authorities, typically enjoy spatial monopolies over their service within an area. As a result, service decentralization through special-purpose governments is as likely to create cost-inducing functional monopolies as it is to create cost-depressing competitive economies.

The potential for competition remains questionable even when multiple districts in a metropolitan area do provide the same service. Except perhaps for the highly preference-oriented service of education,[49] it is unlikely that consumers will move to express dissatisfaction over a single troublesome service.[50] Moving costs are high. Unless consumers are dissatisfied with a wide range of services at their current location, discontent with a single function, say recreation, will not likely induce a move. Despite the public choice perspective's recent focus on voice alternatives to exit as a means for expressing dissatisfaction with service delivery,[51] public choice proponents gloss over the reality that most districts have low political visibility, many have no elected officials, and even more may not operate periodic or open public meetings.

As a consequence, the efficiency-enhancing competitive mechanisms of the market for public goods are largely inoperative in the case of special districts. With exit and voice options attenuated, the demand-articulation option most readily available to citizens is loyalty, that is, the passive choice to resign oneself to less than desirable conditions in the hopes they will somehow improve. This environment provides district boards and officials with ample exploitable margin, the cushion of financial burden consumers will bear relative to service dissatisfaction before actually exiting to another jurisdiction. Far from automatically enhancing efficiency, as public choice proponents argue, districts may instead capitalize on their political isolation and monopolistic status to financially exploit a relatively captive consumer base.

## METROPOLITAN ECOLOGY PERSPECTIVE

The third approach to special-purpose governance is the metropolitan ecology perspective, a view grounded in the human ecology theories of the 1920s and applied most directly to metropolitan political structure since the 1950s. Encompassing a range of social science disciplines, including political science, sociology, geography, public administration, and planning, the metropolitan ecology perspective applies inductive methods, a liberal outlook, realist framework, and institutional focus to analysis of metropolitan political economies.

The underlying premises of metropolitan ecologic thought derive from work on human ecology and urban sociospatial structure conducted by sociologists and geographers at the University of Chicago in the 1920s.[52] Based on evidence that patterns of delinquency and vice in Chicago were concentrated in neighborhoods with high immigration and rapid residential turnover, human ecologists postulated that geographic mobility was linked to social behavior. By ecologic reasoning, different social groups compete to control a spatial niche within the metropolis. Over time other social groups may invade the niche to compete with the incumbent dominant social group for control of the territory, often leading to succession and dominance of the area by a new social group. Ecologists observed that places undergoing invasion and succession experienced instability and social disorganization, manifested in high rates of crime, juvenile delinquency, and unemployment.

The ultimate shakeout of spatial interactions, ecologists argued, was an optimal patterning of human settlement by social groups, "putting every individual and every race into the particular niche where it will meet the least competition and contribute most to the life of the community."[53]

Starting in the 1950s proponents of a metropolitan ecology perspective adapted the premises of human ecology for use in studying issues of metropolitan political structure. The perspective borrowed the notions of interest group competition, socioeconomic differentiation and the disorder of spatial transition, but rejected human ecology's premise that resulting sociospatial patterns were optimal. Instead, metropolitan ecologists argued that the struggle between competing interest groups for control of territory and scarce metropolitan resources was inherently political and contentious, resulting in a hierarchy of winners and losers.[54]

Within this framework, the metropolitan ecology perspective emphasizes four major points about metropolitan political structure that distinguishes the view from the institutional reform and public choice perspectives. The first is the ecologic objection to reformers' prescription of metropolitan government as an appropriate elixir for social and political ills.[55] Reform proposals favoring universalism over pluralism cut against the American cultural and political grain, ecologists argued.[56] There was little reason to believe that metropolitan residents would or should sacrifice the benefits of small-scale democracy for large bureaucracies and unproven gains in service efficiency.[57] To ecologists, institutional reformers were overly idealistic if they thought citizens would willingly replace local autonomy with regional government, especially when the latter meant assuming the responsibility and costs of regionwide redistribution. Ecologists noted that in the relatively few instances where radical metropolitan reforms had occurred, they had been highly contested, and, in the case of Indianapolis's Unigov, effected only by state fiat.[58] Ecologists further noted that the most popular metropolitan reforms were Lakewood Plan arrangements that captured regional economies of scale while leaving intact the underlying autonomous jurisdictions.[59]

Metropolitan ecology's second major point, also critical of the reform perspective, is that institutional change in the metropolis most appropriately occurs through accommodation, adaptation, and adjustment, rather than through the radical government reorganizations advocated by reformers.[60] To justify their point, ecologists presumed two political realities consistent with human ecological principles. First, any existing institutional arrangement benefits the dominant status quo. Second, governmental reorganization by definition alters these institutional arrangements, which threatens the status quo and brings the conflicts and disorder associated with succession.[61] Radical reorganizations, argued ecologists, were excessively disruptive invasions that unduly jeopardized metropolitan political stability. "It must be remembered," warned one commentator,

> that the existing metropolitan areas are going concerns—going systems— as systems we can expect them to react vigorously to attempts to seriously alter them. If the existing system of local government could be easily changed it would be intolerably unstable. If no powerful interests were vested in the status quo, the existing order would have so little allegiance it could scarcely run, much less endure.[62]

In place of radical change, ecologists advocated "muddling through," that is, responding to shifts in demographics, technology, politics, and economic structure with incremental adjustment in policies, intergovernmental relations, and government structure.[63]

The third major point of the metropolitan ecology perspective takes aim at the public choice premise that decentralized political structures represent optimal institutional outcomes in an interdependent metropolis. Citing evidence that political fragmentation is associated with intrametropolitan segmentation on the basis of race, income, ethnicity, and other attributes, ecologists asserted that political fragmentation itself was an institutional means for engendering socioeconomic disparities and fiscal inequities.[64] To be sure, acknowledged ecologists, there existed ample evidence that people seek to live in nonalien and nonthreatening surroundings among persons like themselves.[65] Yet to assume people would freely choose to remain in blighted, high-tax, service-poor environments to be among their own kind challenged reason, if not ethics. The more likely explanations for intrametropolitan segmentation, contended ecologists, were local fiscal practices and societal barriers. Heavy local government reliance on property tax revenues rendered undesirable any potential newcomers who sought more in services than they would likely return in taxes. Undesirables thus included a wide array of groups, from renters and families with children to the elderly, infirm, or poor.[66] De jure and de facto discrimination on the basis of race, religion, ethnicity, and lifestyle, not choice, ecologists argued, prevented people from moving to their preferred locations.[67] Discrimination was expressed in legal and institutional practices such as exclusionary zoning, redlining, and restrictive covenants that further inhibited freedom of residential choice.

Metropolitan political ecology's final theme is the importance of legal and institutional factors in shaping (and being shaped by) local government arrangements in the metropolis. Changes in political arrangements, argue ecologists, are not spontaneous but rather the outcome of deliberate legal and institutional processes established by state and federal governments.[68] These rules for local government, codified in constitutions and statutes, set the limits on institutional choices like annexation, incorporation, special-district formation, and local government revenue raising.[69] Although metropolitan ecologists disagree over the state government's motivations for legislative action on local government organization,[70] they concur about the significance of legal factors in shaping metropolitan structure.

## Ecologic View of Special Districts

Premises of the ecologic framework, namely belief in the importance of local autonomy and small-scale governance, the advantages of accommodation and adjustment, and the ills of intrametropolitan segmentation, induce an ambivalent view of special-purpose governments. On the one hand, ecologists view districts in a relatively positive light because they represent nonradical adaptations to local governmental arrangements and preserve, rather than jeopardize, local autonomy. On the other hand, ecologists criticize districts because they contribute to service inequities by fragmenting the metropolis functionally and often geographically.

Ecologists' positive view of special-purpose governments rests in part on their geographic, functional, and financial flexibility in meeting a wide variety of service delivery needs without jeopardizing the viability of individual government units. Regionwide or joint municipal districts receive praise as institutional innovations that protect local autonomy and save small localities from service diseconomies.[71] Municipally coterminous districts garner high marks from ecologists as politically palatable means for countering fiscal stress, circumventing state-imposed debt and tax limitations, and avoiding politically risky tax increases. Ecologists likewise praise special-purpose governments for their effective response to constituent service needs, from the financing and construction of impressive bridges, tunnels, and highways to the provision of local fire protection and parks.[72]

Metropolitan ecologists temper their enthusiasm for districts, however, with the recognition that society pays hard currency in political accountability and functional coordination for the benefits of district expediency and convenience. As staunch supporters of participatory democracy, ecologists deplore the loss of democratic control and question the "frequently cozy" relations that may occur between a district and its clientele in a politically insulated environment.[73] "However impressive the physical accomplishments of [special districts]," noted one observer,

> the conclusion is inescapable that their operations remove from popularly-constituted governments activities and decisions fundamental to the growth and well-being of the region, or at the very most, subject them to only an indirect type of informal pressure-politics control.[74]

The ecology perspective recognizes many of the political, economic, and service-related motivations for district formation cited by other perspectives. Unique to the ecology perspective, however, is a focus on legal and institutional factors that facilitate or constrain district creation.[75] These factors include the permissiveness of special-district-enabling legislation, statutes governing municipal territorial expansion and revenue raising, and regulations on the scope of contracting, inter-governmental relations, and state-mandated services. The metropolitan ecology literature also notes the importance to district formation of federal policies that tie grant funding to existence of a special district grantee.[76]

Ambivalence about special-purpose governments is also reflected in the perspective's tentative predictions about district fiscal implications. Ecologists hypothesize that district service delivery will result in higher total public outlays, although this outcome is not necessarily considered inappropriate. Indeed, ecologists acknowledge that districts' greatest asset may be their access to and extensive powers to secure private capital for needed public projects.[77] Ecologists also view districts as suitable and acceptable solutions to service problems caused by severe state-imposed constraints on municipal taxing and borrowing. At the same time, however, proponents of the ecology view recognize that districts' low political visibility, functional spending blinders, and administrative independence are ideal conditions for special interest groups to successfully exert upward pressure on district spending.[78] Such attributes may facilitate more nefarious spending practices, listed by one authority analyst as "sloppy investment practices, patronage, conflicts of interest, expense account frauds, purchasing kickbacks, excessive dependence on high-priced consultants, lax internal cost controls, and inflated executive salaries."[79]

The metropolitan ecology literature is less ambivalent with respect to district policy consequences, however. To ecologists, functional specialization, low political visibility, and administrative independence inevitably alter the resource allocations that would occur in a general-purpose environment.[80] In particular, ecologists contend that resource allocations will be skewed in favor of district-provided functions because political insulation impedes citizens' ability to obstruct or delay district projects.[81] Moreover, administrative and financial independence eliminates the need for districts to compete against other public priorities for a share of scarce public resources, thus opening the way for proportionally greater investment in district functions than might otherwise occur.[82] Ecologists also allege that district allegiance to private financial markets induces a bias in favor of capital-intensive, revenue-producing investments at the expense of operations and maintenance tasks.[83]

Given these concerns about district consequences, ecologists tend to qualify their advice on district formation. One observer concluded that "carefully considered and structured" metropolitan districts were desirable, but the more prevalent local-level districts should be discouraged.[84] Another observer highlighted the benefits of public authorities' broad administrative discretion and entrepreneurship, but concluded that because of coordination, citizen participation, and policy bias problems, "we might largely call a halt to new authorities" while "reviewing those already spawned."[85] Another acknowledged that while the financial, political, and management incentives for districts are compelling, residents should continue to expect "a mixture of accomplishments and failures."[86] Consistent with their legal sensitivity, ecologists often suggest legal and regulatory levers to combat perceived shortcomings of special-purpose governments.[87]

### Critique of the Metropolitan Ecology View

Like the reform and public choice views, the metropolitan ecology perspective makes several important contributions to understanding specialized governance. First, ecologists explicitly recognize the many actors and factors that play a part in district causes and consequences. The arena for institutional choice is a complex and dynamic one—no single citizens' group, developer, or public agency, nor single political, economic, cultural, or legal factor determines the arrangement of institutions. Second, the perspective's focus on legal and institutional determinants of institutional choice is valuable: although the rules of the game are not irrevocable, at any point in time they direct institutional choices. Third, the ecology perspective overcomes the underspecification problems of reform and public choice views by acknowledging variations in district subtypes. Districts are seen as neither monolithic beauty nor beast, but rather as more differentiated types of local government, each with attributes and actions more or less appropriate under particular circumstances.

Yet it is this last point that prompts the first of two criticisms of the metropolitan ecology view of special districts. Although the

perspective notes the importance of studying district subtypes, its theoretical claims and empirical efforts rest largely on the study of a single district subtype, public authorities. Because the ecologic perspective relies on inductive evidence for drawing conclusions about districts, research that encompasses the breadth of district types is imperative. Within this breadth, the perspective fails to illuminate key issues, for example which factors are most critical in accounting for the causes and consequences of various types of special-purpose governments.

The second criticism of the ecologic perspective stems from its claim that special districts are inherently desirable service delivery institutions *because* they are accommodating and adaptive. Most would agree that districts are less radical approaches to service delivery than, for example, metropolitan governments. Nonetheless, districts are not trivial institutional choices. Relative to intergovernmental agreements, contracting, and other impermanent service-delivery approaches, special-purpose governments represent long-term, structural change. One cannot assume that a special district is any more likely to disregard its institutional interests or be any more accommodating to proposals for institutional change than is a general-purpose government. Likewise, one cannot assume that districts' incremental adjustments to metropolitan arrangements are necessarily appropriate solutions in the long term. Although accommodation may be appropriate in the short term, future stability may necessitate radical change.

## STRUCTURALIST PERSPECTIVE

The newest perspective on specialized governance is one I label the structuralist perspective.[88] Developed largely in the urban social sciences since the 1960s (although drawing upon themes advanced in the 1800s), the structuralist perspective advances an alternative explanation for the functioning of metropolitan society. Contrary to mainstream views, which emphasize the interplay between market imperatives and technology in understanding metropolitan functioning, the structuralist perspective proposes a deductive vision based on the underlying logic and imperatives of capitalism.

Proponents of structuralist thought argue that while markets and technology provide a means for shaping metropolitan structure, they do not provide the underlying motivation for metropolitan change and development.[89] Rather, structuralists argue, social, political, and economic relations fundamental to capitalism and capitalist modes of production undergird metropolitan society. To explain metropolitan structure and relations requires focusing on the logic of capitalism, covered in the seminal writings of Karl Marx.[90] Of key interest are the capitalist system's imperative for capital accumulation, antagonistic relations between classes, uneven allocation of power, and the role of the state in shaping development patterns. Early structuralist works focused on the capitalist system's inherent need to accumulate and reproduce capital to maintain the capitalist system itself as well as the dominance of those who controlled capitalist production.[91] Later works embraced the importance of government institutions and human agents whose actions and decisions influenced urban development within the parameters of the capitalist system.[92]

Of particular relevance to metropolitan political economies is the structuralist perspective on the role of local, regional, and national governments, broadly labeled "the state," in facilitating and directing urban development. Mainstream literature, structualists contend, paints the state as a relatively passive, responsive institution that rides the waves of market forces and technological changes.[93] By contrast, the structuralist literature presents the state as a prime collaborator in urban development, intervening and making decisions that reinforce the growth-driven capitalist system of which the state is a part. Although there remains debate over whether the state is more pawn or partner of capitalist interests,[94] the essential role of the state as facilitator of urban growth is a point of consensus.

Consistent with this conceptual framework, structuralist scholars explain metropolitan political organization as a reflection of the production needs of capitalists, aided and abetted by a more or less compliant state. The process of urban decentralization and suburbanization that began in the 1870s and 1880s, for example, is interpreted not as a response to advances in transportation and communication technology, as the orthodox view contends. Rather, decentralization is seen as a legacy of industrial capitalists' decisions to flee the increasingly disruptive and profit-threatening instances of labor unrest fermenting in union-influenced city settings.[95] To seize control of land use, labor, and industrial operations in their new suburban settings, industrialists lobbied state legislators for laws that eased municipal incorporation. Legislators, many of whom wanted to clip the wings of central city bosses and their political machines, responded favorably. Many state legislatures enacted not only permissive incorporation statutes, but also restrictive annexation statutes and laws requiring central cities to extend services to fledgling suburban jurisdictions.[96] Political fragmentation was the logical result. As one observer summarized the incentives for industrialist-initiated incorporations,

> If suburban town boundaries can be drawn to minimize residential population, there will be little pressure for pollution abatement or for high taxes to support social services. Nor will there be effective resistance to using

public budgets to serve industrial infrastructure needs. If the boundary lines can be drawn in a certain manner, the act of incorporation can also help seal out particular kinds of residents whose very presence might upset good labor relations. Workers spatially removed from city vices might lead more diligent, wholesome, and hard-working lives.[97]

The structuralist perspective emphasizes, however, that capitalists do not comprise a monolithic class with unified interests. Rather, the capitalist class comprises numerous factions, including industrial capital (for example, multinational firms), commercial, retail, or merchant capital (local retail firms), development capital (property owners and land developers), finance capital (banks, insurance, and mortgage companies), and construction capital (architecture, engineering, and construction firms).[98] Different capitalist factions may have different interests in and strategies for how to influence urban development and metropolitan political arrangements. These differences depend in part on the power and politics of local, regional, state, and even national governments, and on capitalists' relations with these agencies.[99]

Spencer Olin's case study of regional development in Orange County, California, in the 1960s to 1980s, for example, found that widespread support for metropolitan government from nationally oriented industrial capitalists clashed with widespread opposition to regionalization from local retail capitalists.[100] Although both factions of capital had progrowth agendas, they disagreed over the political organization of the playing field on which growth games would be played. Other structuralist analyses corroborate this factionalization of capital and the peculiarities and complexities of local growth conditions that shape urban development.[101]

## Structuralist View of Special Districts

For the most part, structuralists view special-purpose governments as they do other forms of local government: as mechanisms for capitalist elites to further their economic and development goals. The structuralist assessment of special-purpose governments tends to be harsher than that of general-purpose governments, however. This is primarily because of districts' political isolation, which is considered an objectionable means for bypassing citizen preferences about urban services and governance.

The structuralist literature paints special districts as relatively manipulable, passive institutions created by progrowth interests to realize their goals for development.[102] As evidence, structuralists point to the prevalence of developer-initiated districts as well as the close relationships between developers and districts, often cemented by developer membership on district boards.[103] The perspective further links districts to a progrowth agenda by noting the infrequency with which citizen-based antigrowth or environmental groups initiate special-purpose governments. "[E]nvironmental groups rarely spearhead [the] push for state preemption of municipal regulation through use of public authorities," one observer summarized.[104] This view conflicts with the assertion widely held in development circles that independent development authorities are the product of metropolitanwide consensus about the desirability of prodevelopment policies.[105]

To structuralist scholars, different types of districts exist not because of their geographic flexibility in meeting different consumer preferences, but because different factions of capital require different types of governments to achieve development goals. For example, industrial capitalists with regional markets might support a metropolitan sewer authority that standardized policies and eliminated the need to negotiate with numerous local sewer agencies for permits and connections. By contrast, small-scale development capitalists might prefer a subdivision-sized sewer district that meets their specific needs for controlling local infrastructure. By structuralist logic, whether one or another type of sewer district is inequitable, inefficient, or otherwise contrary to resident needs is irrelevant.[106]

Another group of structuralist scholars qualify the notion that special-purpose governments are passive pawns of development elites. These critics emphasize that districts, once created, pursue their own institutional interests, albeit ones typically consistent with a progrowth agenda.[107] For example, institutional survival itself prompts districts to expand their customer base—and impress future lenders—by extending roads, transit lines, water and sewer systems, utility networks, and airport runways, with little concern about economic or environmental considerations.[108] In addition, a special-purpose government may take advantage of the "technocratic lexicon [that] legitimates the insulation of the agency."[109] Enticed by the potential for institutional freedom, districts perpetuate the perception that they are "outside of politics," thereby playing a moral trump card to increase their distance from citizens and the participatory process.[110]

Other proponents of the structuralist perspective note that districts serve not only their own and developer interests, but also the interests of the local state. Special-purpose governments enable local officials to quietly satisfy prodevelopment clients without unduly jeopardizing relations with a voting public likely to oppose projects that increase resident taxes and threaten the quality of life.[111] By sloughing off potentially controversial development projects to independent districts in a better position to consummate development, local officials win on several fronts: they protect themselves from tough political decisions, win voter approval by focusing energy and resources on basic public services, and improve developer chances of realizing a favorable project outcome.[112]

Although structuralists focus more on the causes than on the consequences of specialized governance, it is possible to make inferences about the latter. Structuralists join metropolitan ecologists in claiming that low political visibility enables districts to inflate their budgets to higher levels than citizens desire, with little concern about either the social costs of investment or the threat of meaningful constituent protest. In broader terms, structuralists argue that specialized service delivery may increase spending by general-purpose governments. Freed from responsibility for district-provided services, general-purpose governments curry favor by providing high-quality, often costly health, welfare, police, fire, parks and recreation, libraries, and other services that satisfy short-term needs regardless of long-term fiscal stress.[113]

With respect to policy consequences, structuralists suggest that reliance on politically insulated districts yields public-service solutions that reflect developer or state priorities rather than those of the voting public. Special-purpose governments are constrained by a hierarchy of allegiances: first to the banks and bond market investors who fund capital projects; next to the imperatives of institutional survival; and last to constituent service demands. Only to the extent that local consumers share the progrowth sentiments typical of finance capitalists and institutional survival would district policies coincide with the public interest. That it does not, structuralists suggest, is evident from citizen protests that often accompany public disclosure of district projects.[114]

## Critique of the Structuralist View

The structuralist perspective offers an important balance to the reform, public choice, and ecologic views of special-purpose governance. Structuralist assertions about the critical role played by capitalist and pro-development interests in the creation and use of special districts are widely accepted. Most analysts, including those outside the structuralist camp, would agree that districts tend toward a progrowth agenda, are routinely used by growth elites to control and shape development, and often collaborate with other local, regional, and national interests on development policy.

Nonetheless, whereas the structuralist perspective appropriately emphasizes the progrowth leanings of special-purpose governments, it fails to acknowledge that not all districts have such interests. By training their sights solely on development-oriented districts, structuralists neglect the many health, fire protection, libraries, recreation, and other nondevelopment districts initiated by residents. The perspective also glosses over the reality that many development-oriented districts are initiated by residents. These oversights result in theoretical explanations that miss the richer, more complex reality of special-purpose governments.

A corollary weakness of the structuralist perspective is its core assertion that special districts are necessarily pawns of prodevelopment interests. This presumption blinds analysts to districts' potential to slow or manage growth. Institutional imperatives notwithstanding, there is nothing inherent to districts that prevents them from supporting antigrowth platforms and implementing antigrowth policies. There is ample evidence that districts enact moratoria, institute slow-growth policies, and otherwise play a central role in growth management.[115] Likewise, there is nothing inherent to districts that prevents them from implementing policies sympathetic to regional redistribution or social equalization. Indeed, metropolitanwide agencies are conceptually ideal for standardizing service levels and expanding the tax base to enable intrametropolitan transfers. By neglecting these possibilities, the structuralist view distorts districts' actual and potential role in metropolitan political economies.

Finally, structuralists' methodological approach to special-purpose governments is problematic. The perspective implies that because every metropolitan area context is unique, the causes and consequences of special districts in metropolitan political economies cannot be generalized. The literature provides the unsatisfying impression that when a case study of a metropolitan area or special-purpose government does not sustain structuralist claims of districts' prodevelopment proclivities, the methodological stance is that each case is distinctive. This prevents scholars from pursuing useful social science generalizations, such as the conditions under which developers turn to districts rather than other institutional choices for service delivery, or why some urban regimes rely heavily on districts while others do not.

## CONCLUSION

The four major theoretical perspectives reviewed in this chapter, institutional reform, public choice, metropolitan ecology, and structuralist, often disagree about the roles, causes, and consequences of special-purpose governments. Much of this disagreement originates in the fundamentally different theoretical assumptions these perspectives make about individual and group behaviors with respect to issues of governance.

The institutional reform and public choice perspectives are the most directly antithetical. The reform perspective bases its stridently negative view of decentralized political structures and special districts on a belief in the greater validity of community goals over those of individuals. Special-purpose governments, as contributors to decentralization are not welcomed, though the perspective predicts they will emerge where municipal fragmentation is considerable and the need for service delivery integration is most imperative. Reformers argue that by compartmentalizing service provision, districts hinder coordination, lead to service duplication, and thwart resource allocations consistent with citizen preferences. The aftermath is increased total public outlays and spending priorities incompatible with resident service preferences.

The public choice perspective takes an opposing view. Based on faith in market mechanisms and a belief in the rationality of welfare-maximizing individuals, the public choice perspective supports decentralized political structures as choice-maximizing, vigorously competitive and, hence, cost-effective arrangements for metropolitan service delivery. Special-purpose governments, as service providers and as protectors of the economic viability of small communities, contribute to healthy interjurisdictional competition and are therefore desirable additions to the metropolitan political economy. Far from thwarting expression of citizen preferences, choice scholars argue, districts directly respond to these preferences. The variety of district subtypes attests to districts' success in satisfying heterogeneous demands for services. Although the level of public outlays and the shares of total resources allocated to particular services may change with district service delivery, such adjustments are consonant with citizen preferences.

Straddling the theoretical divide between these two perspectives is the metropolitan ecology view. Sympathetic to both reform's emphasis on the importance of regional equity and public choice's focus on the importance of preserving small-scale democracies, ecologists hold an understandably mixed view of fragmented but responsive decentralized political arrangements. The ecologic perspective's ambivalence extends to special districts, which meet a wide variety of functional and geographic service needs but do so in politically insulated, interest-group-dominated environments. Ecologists contend that districts will increase total public outlays, in part as a legitimate response to service needs and in part due to fallout from political insulation and excessive administrative leeway. Ecologists further hypothesize that districts' allegiance to financiers and special functional interests instills a bias in favor of large capital projects and other development-oriented services. These allocations, ecologists argue, come at the expense of housekeeping and social services, an outcome often contrary to public priorities.

The structuralist perspective is the most narrowly focused of the four. Based on the premise that opportunities to maximize one's welfare are reserved for dominant economic elites in capitalist societies, structuralists view governmental arrangements, regardless of their organization, as part of a societal framework that enables elites to maintain control over production processes and urban development. Special-purpose governments are merely one dimension of the state's acquiescent relationship with development capitalists. Typically formed by developers, who reap the benefits of politically insulated, financially powerful, and administratively independent agencies, districts skew spending toward the development-oriented services most beneficial to developers, regardless of consumer preferences for basic public and social welfare services.

Each perspective offers insights into the motivations and consequences of specialized governance. No perspective is without conceptual and methodological shortcomings, however. The reform and public choice perspectives tend to underspecify districts, neglecting district subtypes that may not fit their view. The ecologic and structuralist views tend to overspecify districts, drawing their conclusions about special-purpose governments from the study of a relatively narrow set of district subtypes. These shortcomings provide half of the foundation for a new framework for analyzing specialized governance. The other half arises from the small but growing body of empirical evidence on metropolitan political structure and special districts, to which I turn in the next chapter.

## CHAPTER NOTES

1. There is a large body of Progressive Era literature on metropolitan reform. Representative works I draw upon are William Anderson, *American City Government* (New York: Henry Holt and Co., 1925; Chester C. Maxey, "The Political Integration of Metropolitan Communities," *National Municipal Review* 11, no. 8 (1922): 229–52; Thomas H. Reed, *Municipal Government in the United States* (New York: The Century Co., 1926); Thomas H. Reed, "Dual Government for Metropolitan Regions," *National Municipal Review* 16, no. 2 (1927): 118–34; Thomas H. Reed, "The Government of Metropolitan Areas," *Public Management* 12, no. 3 (1930): 75–78; and Studenski, *The Government of Metropolitan Areas.* For contemporary analyses of the institutional reform perspective, see Kenneth Fox, *Better City Government: Innovation in American Urban Politics, 1850–1937* (Philadelphia: Temple University Press, 1977); and M. Christine Boyer, *Dreaming the Rational City* (Cambridge: MIT Press, 1983), chaps. 3, 10.

2. Schiesl, *The Politics of Efficiency*, pp. 2–3.

3. Representative works include Jones, *Metropolitan Government*; Victor Jones, "Local Government Organization in Metropolitan Areas: Its Relation to

Urban Redevelopment," in *The Future of Cities and Urban Redevelopment*, ed. Coleman Woodbury (Chicago: University of Chicago Press, 1953), pp. 481–608; and Robert C. Wood, *1400 Governments: The Political Economy of the New York Metropolitan Region* (Cambridge: Harvard University Press, 1961).

4. See, for example, Lance Liebman, "Metropolitanism and Decentralization," in *Reform of Metropolitan Governments*, ed. Lowdon Wingo (Washington, D.C.: Resources for the Future, 1972), pp. 52–56; Committee for Economic Development, *Reshaping Government in Metropolitan Areas* (New York: Committee for Economic Development, 1970), pp. 16–21; Donald G. Hagman, "Regionalized-Decentralism: A Model for Rapprochement in Los Angeles," *Georgetown Law Journal* 58, nos. 4–5 (1970): 901–53; Royce Hanson, "Toward a New Urban Democracy: Metropolitan Consolidation and Decentralization," *Georgetown Law Journal* 58, nos. 4–5 (1970): pp. 863–99; and Robert G. Dixon, Jr., "Rebuilding the Urban Political System: Some Heresies Concerning Citizen Participation, Community Action, Metros, and One Man-One Vote," *Georgetown Law Journal* 58, nos. 4–5 (1970): pp. 955–86.

5. See, for example, David Rusk, *Cities Without Suburbs* (Washington, D.C.: Woodrow Wilson Center Press, 1993); William R. Barnes and Larry C. Ledebur, *City Distress, Metropolitan Disparities and Economic Growth* (Washington, D.C.: National League of Cities, 1992); I. M. Barlow, *Metropolitan Government* (London: Routledge, 1991); and Anthony Downs, *New Visions for Metropolitan America* (Washington, D.C.: Brookings Institution, 1994).

6. Spillover effects, also known as externalities or third-party effects, occur when the actions of one party affect another party, but there is no compensation between the parties. A common example is air pollution. The fumes generated when I drive my car impose costs on others by lowering air quality, but I pay no compensation to those affected by my harmful behavior. Because I do not bear the full costs, I engage in excessive amounts of driving, thus generating negative spillovers. Conversely, I engage in inefficiently small amounts of activities that generate positive spillover effects, say, planting a beautiful garden, because I am not compensated by others for my socially beneficial behavior. Because effects that occur at political borderlines are especially unlikely due to interjurisdictional complications to involve compensation, spillovers are considered especially problematic in areas with many jurisdictional boundaries, that is, in politically fragmented areas.

7. Charles J. Goetz, "Fiscal Illusion in State and Local Finance," in *Budgets and Bureaucrats: The Sources of Government Growth*, ed. Thomas E. Borcherding (Durham: Duke University Press, 1977), pp. 176–87.

8. Thomas Reed, "Progress in Metropolitan Integration," *Public Administration Review* 9 (1949): 2; and Wood, *1400 Governments*, p. 246 n.

9. Advisory Commission on Intergovernmental Relations (ACIR), *The Problem of Special Districts in American Government* (Washington, D.C.: ACIR, 1964); and Barlow, *Metropolitan Government*, p. 6.

10. J. Bollens, *Special District Governments*, p. 256.

11. Robert G. Smith, *Ad Hoc Governments* (Beverly Hills: Sage, 1974). Also see William A. Robson, *The Government and Misgovernment of London* (London: George Allen & Unwin, 1939). Robson called the proliferation of special-purpose governments "ad hocery."

**12.** Rex D. Honey, "Conflicting Problems in the Political Organization of Space," *Annals of Regional Science* 10, no. 1 (1976): 45–60.

**13.** Stanley Scott and John Corzine, "Special Districts in the San Francisco Bay Area," in *Metropolitan Politics: A Reader*, ed. Michael N. Danielson (Boston: Little, Brown, 1966), p. 258.

**14.** Studenski, *The Government of Metropolitan Areas*; and Jones, *Metropolitan Governments*. For a more recent view, see Advisory Commission on Intergovernmental Relations (ACIR), *Regional Decision Making: New Strategies for Substate Districts*, vol. 1 of *Substate Regionalism and the Federal System* (Washington, D.C.: ACIR, 1973), p. 36.

**15.** J. Bollens, *Special District Governments*, pp. 250–58.

**16.** Anderson, *American City Government*, pp. 82–83.

**17.** Lyle C. Fitch, "Metropolitan Financial Problems," *Annals of the American Academy of Social and Political Science* 314 (November 1957): 66–73.

**18.** David Minge, "Special Districts and the Level of Public Expenditures," *Journal of Urban Law* 53 (1976): 705.

**19.** Committee for Economic Development, *Reshaping Government*, p. 37.

**20.** Jones, "Local Government in Metropolitan Areas," pp. 579–81; ACIR, *The Problem of Special Districts*, pp. 60–62; and, generally, Committee for Economic Development, *Modernizing Local Government* (New York: Committee for Economic Development, 1966).

**21.** John D. Stewart, *The Responsive Local Authority* (London: Charles Knight, 1974), pp. 135–36.

**22.** Lowdon Wingo, "Introduction: Logic and Ideology in Metropolitan Reform," in *Reform of Metropolitan Governments*, ed. Lowdon Wingo (Washington, D.C.: Resources for the Future, 1972), p. 4.

**23.** Jones, "Local Government Organization," pp. 580–86. Source of the phrase "guild autonomy" is Luther Gulick, "Politics, Administration, and the 'New Deal,'" *Annals of the American Academy of Political and Social Science* 169 (September 1933), p. 56.

**24.** Frederick L. Bird, "The Contribution of Authorities to Efficient Municipal Management," *The Authority* (December 1949), p. 5.

**25.** Indeed, formal reform proposals have had little success. As of 1970, following considerable attention to metropolitan reorganization, only 36 of 227 then-designated metropolitan areas (16 percent) had ever held any kind of referendum on metropolitan reform, and only 17 of these reform proposals (7 percent) had been successful. Robert L. Lineberry, "Reforming Metropolitan Governance: Requiem or Reality," *Georgetown Law Journal* 58, nos. 4–5 (1970): 715–17. Also see Joseph F. Zimmerman, "Metropolitan Reform in the U.S.: An Overview," *Public Administration Review* 30, no. 5 (1970): 531–43. Only two major city-county consolidations have occurred since 1970: Lexington-Fayette County, Kentucky (1972) and Anchorage-Greater Anchorage Area Borough, Alaska (1975). On the Lexington-Fayette County case, see W. E. Lyons, *The Politics of City-County Merger: The Lexington-Fayette County Experience* (Lexington: University Press of Kentucky, 1977).

**26.** Portland, Oregon's Metropolitan Service District (Metro), which was formed in 1970 and affirmed by voters in 1992, is an elected agency encompassing three counties and twenty-four municipalities. Metro provides a wide range of functions, including regional planning and policy, transportation planning and allocation of funds, solid waste collection and disposal, recycling, regional air and water quality, operation of the regional zoo, and construction and operation of a convention center. See David Rusk, *Baltimore Unbound: A Strategy for Regional Renewal* (Baltimore: Abell Foundation, 1996), pp. 50–53; and Carl Abbott, *Portland: Planning, Politics, and Growth in a Twentieth-Century City* (Lincoln: University of Nebraska Press, 1983), pp. 254–55, 262–63.

**27.** See, for example, Steven P. Erie, John J. Kirlin, and Francine F. Rabinovitz, "Can Something Be Done? Propositions on the Performance of Metropolitan Institutions," in *Reform of Metropolitan Governments*, ed. Lowdon Wingo (Washington, D.C.: Resources for the Future, 1972), pp. 21–36; Ronan Paddison, *The Fragmented State: The Political Geography of Power* (New York: St. Martin's Press, 1983); Finn Brunn, "Dilemmas of Size: The Rise and Fall of the Greater Copenhagen Council," in *The Government of World Cities: The Future of the Metro Model*, ed. L. J. Sharpe (Chichester: John Wiley and Sons, 1995), pp. 57–76; L. J. Sharpe, "The Abolition of the Greater London Council: Is There a Case for Resurrection?" in *The Government of World Cities: The Future of the Metro Model*, ed. L. J. Sharpe (Chichester: John Wiley and Sons, 1995), pp. 111–30; and Frank Hendriks and Theo A. J. Toonen, "The Rise and Fall of the Rijnmond Authority: An Experiment with Metro Government in the Netherlands," in *The Government of World Cities: The Future of the Metro Model*, ed. L. J. Sharpe (Chichester: John Wiley and Sons, 1995), pp. 147–75.

**28.** For a comprehensive review of the theory and literature of public choice, see Dennis C. Mueller, *Public Choice II* (Cambridge: Cambridge University Press, 1989).

**29.** Richard A. Musgrave and Peggy B. Musgrave, *Public Finance in Theory and Practice.* 5th ed. (New York: McGraw Hill, 1989), chap. 3.

**30.** Paul A. Samuelson, "The Pure Theory of Public Expenditures," *Review of Economics and Statistics* (November 1954): 386–89.

**31.** Charles M. Tiebout, "A Pure Theory of Local Expenditures," *Journal of Political Economy* 64 (1956): 416–24.

**32.** The assumptions for a pure "Tiebout world" are actually more stringent than stated here. They include that residents have perfect information on the tax prices and service levels of public goods in competing communities and that the transaction costs to move are zero.

**33.** See, for example, Vincent Ostrom, Charles M. Tiebout, and Robert Warren, "The Organization of Government in Metropolitan Areas: A Theoretical Inquiry," *American Political Science Review* 55 (1961): 831–42; Robert Warren, "A Municipal Services Market Model of Metropolitan Organization," *Journal of the American Institute of Planners* 30, no. 3 (1964): 193–204; Robert L. Bish, *The Public Economy of Metropolitan Areas* (Chicago: Markham, 1971); Elinor Ostrom, "Metropolitan Reform: Propositions Derived from Two Traditions," *Social Science Quarterly* 53, no. 3 (1972): 474–93; and Robert L. Bish and Vincent Ostrom, *Understanding Urban Government* (Washington, D.C.: American Enterprise Institute, 1973).

**34.** Richard A. Musgrave, *The Theory of Public Finance: A Study in Public Economy* (New York: McGraw-Hill, 1959), p. 15. This notion was first applied to metropolitan political structure in Ostrom, Tiebout, and Warren,

"Organization of Government." For a contemporary discussion, see Advisory Commission on Intergovernmental Relations (ACIR), *The Organization of Local Public Economies* (Washington, D.C.: ACIR, 1987).

   **35.** Werner Z. Hirsch, *The Economics of State and Local Government* (New York: McGraw-Hill, 1970); Juan De Torres, *Government Services in Major Metropolitan Areas: Functions, Costs, Efficiency* (New York: The Conference Board, 1972); and George F. Break, *Intergovernmental Fiscal Relations in the United States* (Washington, D.C.: Brookings Institution, 1967).

   **36.** Robert N. Baird and John H. Landon, "Political Fragmentation, Income Distribution, and the Demand for Government Services," *Nebraska Journal of Economics and Business* 11, no. 4 (1972): 171–84.

   **37.** For example, E. Ostrom cites with favor the works of Aiken and Alford, and Clark, who find a positive correlation between decentralized government structures and public expenditures. See E. Ostrom, "Metropolitan Reform," pp. 491–92; Michael Aiken and Robert R. Alford, "Comparative Urban Research and Community Decision-Making," *New Atlantis* 2 (Winter 1970): 85–110; and Terry N. Clark, "Community Structure, Decision-Making, Budget Expenditure and Urban Renewal in 51 American Communities," in *Community Politics: A Behavioral Approach*, ed. Charles M. Bonjean, Terry N. Clark, and Robert L. Lineberry (New York: Free Press, 1971), pp. 293–314.

   **38.** Geoffrey Brennan and James Buchanan, "Toward a Tax Constitution for Leviathan," *Journal of Public Economics* 8 (1977): 255–73; Geoffrey Brennan and James Buchanan, *The Power to Tax: Analytical Foundations of a Fiscal Constitution* (Cambridge: Cambridge University Press, 1980) p. 184. Also see Advisory Commission on Intergovernmental Relations (ACIR), *Interjurisdictional Tax and Policy Competition: Good or Bad for the Federal System?* (Washington, D.C.: ACIR, 1991); Thomas R. Dye, *American Federalism: Competition Among Governments* (Lexington, Mass.: Lexington Books, 1990); Daphne A. Kenyon and John Kincaid, "Introduction," in *Competition Among States and Local Governments: Efficiency and Equity in American Federalism*, ed. Daphne A. Kenyon and John Kincaid (Washington, D.C.: Urban Institute, 1991), pp. 1–33; and Mark Schneider, *The Competitive City: The Political Economy of Suburbia* (Pittsburgh: University of Pittsburgh Press, 1989).

   **39.** Ostrom, Tiebout, and Warren, "The Organization of Government," pp. 834–36.

   **40.** Robert B. Hawkins, Jr., *Self-Government by District: Myth and Reality* (Stanford: Hoover Institution Press, 1976), p. 110.

   **41.** Warren, "A Municipal Services Market Model," pp. 197–98.

   **42.** Gordon Tullock, "Federalism: Problems of Scale," *Public Choice* 6 (Spring 1969): 19–29.

   **43.** The Advisory Commission on Intergovernmental Relations has twenty-six members: nine representing federal government (three executive branch officials, three senators, three representatives), fourteen representing state and local government (four governors, three state legislators, three county officials, four mayors), and three private citizens representing the public. The president appoints twenty of twenty-six members, all except the senators and representatives who are selected by the president of the Senate and the Speaker of the House, respectively. The commission became a permanent federal agency in 1959. Its future status is uncertain pending federal budget decisions.

44. See ACIR, *The Problem of Special Districts*, pp. 75–81; ACIR, *Regional Decision Making*, pp. 33–45; Advisory Commission on Intergovernmental Relations (ACIR), *The Challenge of Local Government Reorganization* (Washington, D.C.: ACIR, 1974); and Advisory Commission on Intergovernmental Relations (ACIR), *State and Local Roles in the Federal System* (Washington, D.C.: ACIR, 1982), 254–56, 360.

45. ACIR, *The Organization of Local Public Economies*, pp. 55–56.

46. Roger B. Parks and Ronald J. Oakerson, "Metropolitan Organization and Governance: A Local Public Economy Approach," *Urban Affairs Quarterly* 25, no. 1 (1989): 22–23.

47. ACIR, *The Organization of Local Public Economies*, pp. 24–25.

48. Steven Brint, *In an Age of Experts: The Changing Role of Professionals in Politics and Public Life* (Princeton, N.J.: Princeton University Press, 1994), p. 42.

49. See Gregory R. Weiher, *The Fractured Metropolis: Political Fragmentation and Metropolitan Segregation* (Albany: State University of New York Press, 1991), pp. 145–63.

50. Wallace E. Oates, "Searching for Leviathan: A Reply and Some Further Reflections," *American Economic Review* 79, no. 3 (1989): 578–83.

51. See, for example, the focus on voice options in Advisory Commission on Intergovernmental Relations (ACIR), *Metropolitan Organization: The Allegheny County Case* (Washington, D.C.: ACIR, 1992); and Advisory Commission on Intergovernmental Relations (ACIR), *Metropolitan Organization: The St. Louis Case* (Washington, D.C.: ACIR, 1988). The seminal statement on citizen options for expressing dissatisfaction with government is Albert O. Hirschman, *Exit, Voice and Loyalty* (Cambridge: Harvard University Press, 1970).

52. Robert E. Park, Ernest W. Burgess, and Robert D. McKenzie, eds. *The City* (Chicago: University of Chicago Press, 1925); see also Robert E. Park, "Human Ecology," *American Journal of Sociology* 42, no. 2 (1936): 1–15; and Amos Hawley, *Human Ecology: A Theory of Community Structure* (New York: Ronald Press, 1950).

53. Robert E. Park, quoted in John R. Logan and Harvey L. Molotch, *Urban Fortunes: The Political Economy of Place* (Berkeley: University of California Press, 1987), p. 6; see also commentary on the human ecology school in Peter Hall, *Cities of Tomorrow* (Oxford: Basil Blackwell, 1988), chap. 8.

54. See, for example, Arthur Maass, ed., *Area and Power: A Theory of Local Government* (Glencoe, Ill.: Free Press, 1959); Scott Greer, *Governing the Metropolis* (New York: John Wiley and Sons, 1962); Robert C. Wood, *Suburbia: Its People and Their Politics* (Boston: Houghton Mifflin, 1958); and Oliver P. Williams, Harold Herman, Charles S. Liebman, and Thomas H. Dye, *Suburban Differences and Metropolitan Policies: A Philadelphia Story* (Philadelphia: University of Pennsylvania Press, 1965).

55. Edward C. Banfield and Morton Grodzins, "Some Flaws in the Logic of Metropolitan Reorganization," in *Metropolitan Politics: A Reader*, ed. Michael N. Danielson (Boston: Little, Brown, 1966), pp. 142–52; Roscoe C. Martin and Douglas Price, "The Metropolis and Its Problems Reexamined," in *Metropolitan*

*Politics: A Reader,* ed. Michael N. Danielson (Boston: Little, Brown, 1966), pp. 135–42; and H. Paul Friesema, *Metropolitan Political Structure: Intergovernmental Relations and Political Integration in the Quad-Cities* (Iowa City: University of Iowa Press, 1971).

56. Greer, *Governing the Metropolis,* pp. 124–25.

57. Charles R. Adrian, "Suburbia and the Folklore of Metropology," in *Metropolitan Politics: A Reader,* ed. Michael N. Danielson (Boston: Little, Brown, 1966), pp. 172–80; and Robert C. Wood, "A Division of Powers," in *Area and Power: A Theory of Local Government,* ed. Arthur J. Maass (Glencoe, Ill.: Free Press, 1959), pp. 60–64.

58. John C. Bollens and Henry J. Schmandt, *The Metropolis: Its People, Politics, and Economic Life,* 3rd ed. (New York: Harper and Row, 1975), pp. 250–57; Zimmerman, "Metropolitan Reform"; and York Willbern, "Unigov: Local Reorganization in Indianapolis," in *Regional Governance: Promise and Performance,* ed. Advisory Commission on Intergovernmental Relations (ACIR) (Washington, D.C.: ACIR, 1973), pp. 59–64.

59. The Lakewood Plan, named after the city in Los Angeles County in which it was instituted in 1954, refers to arrangements in which municipalities provide no or few services on their own but contract for a package of services from county and special-purpose governments. Winston W. Crouch and Beatrice Dinerman, *Southern California Metropolis* (Berkeley: University of California Press, 1963), chap. 8. For a critique, see Miller, *Cities by Contract.*

60. Michael N. Danielson, "The Adaptive Metropolis: The Politics of Accommodation," in *Metropolitan Politics: A Reader,* ed. Michael N. Danielson (Boston: Little, Brown, 1966), pp. 231–33.

61. Paul Ylvisaker, "Why Mayors Oppose Metropolitan Government," in *Metropolitan Politics: A Reader,* ed. Michael N. Danielson (Boston: Little, Brown, 1966), pp. 180–88; Henry J. Schmandt, *Metropolitan Reform in St. Louis: A Case Study* (New York: Holt, Rinehart and Winston, 1961); Scott Greer, *Metropolitics: A Study of Political Culture* (New York: John Wiley and Sons, 1963); and Rex D. Honey "Versatility Versus Continuity—The Dilemma of Jurisdictional Change," in *Pluralism and Political Geography,* ed. Nurit Kliot and Stanley Waterman (New York: St. Martin's Press, 1983), pp. 232–41.

62. Norton E. Long, "Who Makes Decisions in Metropolitan Areas?" in *Metropolitan Politics: A Reader,* ed. Michael N. Danielson (Boston: Little, Brown, 1966), p. 105.

63. Charles E. Lindblom, "The Science of 'Muddling Through,'" *Public Administration Review* 19, no. 1 (1959): 79–88; and Charles E. Lindblom, "Still Muddling, Not Yet Through," *Public Administration Review* 39, no. 6 (1979): 517–26. For an application, see Martin Meyerson and Edward C. Banfield, *Politics, Planning, and the Public Interest* (Glencoe, Ill.: Free Press, 1955).

64. This literature is voluminous. Representative works include Anthony Downs, *Opening Up the Suburbs: An Urban Strategy for America* (New Haven: Yale University Press, 1973); Michael N. Danielson, *The Politics of Exclusion* (New York: Columbia University Press, 1976); Constance Perin, *Everything in its Place: Social Order and Land Use in America* (Princeton, N.J.: Princeton University Press, 1977); Oliver P. Williams, *Metropolitan Political Analysis: A Social Access*

*Approach* (New York: Free Press, 1971); and Oliver P. Williams and Kent Eklund, "Segregation in a Fragmented Context: 1950–1970," in *Urbanization and Conflict in Market Societies*, ed. Kevin R. Cox (Chicago: Maaroufa, 1978), pp. 213–28. Empirical studies include Richard Child Hill, "Separate and Unequal: Government Inequality in the Metropolis," *American Political Science Review* 68 (December 1974): 1557–68; Kenneth Newton, "American Urban Politics: Social Class, Political Structure and Public Goods," *Urban Affairs Quarterly* 11, no. 2 (1975): 241–64; and Mark Schneider and John R. Logan, "Suburban Racial Segregation and Black Access to Local Public Resources," *Social Science Quarterly* 63 (December 1982): 762–70.

65. See, for example, Gerald D. Suttles, *The Social Construction of Communities*, (Chicago: University of Chicago Press, 1972); Brian J. L. Berry, *The Human Consequences of Urbanization* (New York: St. Martin's Press, 1973); and Mark La Gory, "The Organization of Space and the Character of the Urban Experience," *Publius* 18, no. 4 (1988): 71–90.

66. Wood, *Suburbia*, pp. 208–25; Julius Margolis, "Fiscal Issues in the Reform of Metropolitan Governance," in *Reform as Reorganization*, ed. Lowdon Wingo (Washington, D.C.: Resources for the Future, 1974), pp. 48–53; and, generally, Robert J. Bennett, *The Geography of Public Finance* (London: Methuen, 1980).

67. Max Neiman, "From Plato's Philosopher King to Bish's Tough Purchasing Agent: The Premature Public Choice Paradigm," *Journal of the American Institute of Planners* 41 (1975): 55–73; Michael N. Danielson, "Differentiation, Segregation and Fragmentation in the American Metropolis," in *Governance and Population: The Governmental Implications of Population Change*, ed. A. E. Keir Nash (Washington, D.C.: U.S. Government Printing Office, 1972), pp. 145–50; Perin, *Everything in its Place*, chaps. 1, 3; and Edward D. Soja, "The Political Organization of Space in Metropolitan Areas," in *The Manipulated City: Perspectives on Spatial Structure and Social Issues in Urban America*, ed. Stephen Gale and Eric G. Moore (Chicago: Maaroufa, 1975).

68. Michael N. Danielson, Alan M. Hershey, and John M. Bayne, *One Nation, So Many Governments* (Lexington, Mass.: Lexington Books, 1977); R. D. Norton, *City Life-Cycles and American Urban Policy* (New York: Academic Press, 1979), pp. 65–66, 86–94; Stein, "Federally Supported Substate Regional Governments," pp. 74–81; Danielson, "Differentiation, Segregation and Fragmentation"; Teaford, *City and Suburb*, chaps. 2–3; and Adrian, *A History of American City Government*, pp. 78–94. A good overview of the range of state and federal interventions in metropolitan affairs remains Norman Beckman, "How Metropolitan are Federal and State Policies?" *Public Administration Review* 26, no. 2 (1966): 96–106.

69. Michael Libonati, "Reconstructing Local Government," *The Urban Lawyer* 19, no. 3 (1987): 645–50; Gordon L. Clark, *Judges and the Cities: Interpreting Local Autonomy* (Chicago: University of Chicago Press, 1985), pp. 77–81; Gerald E. Frug, "The City as Legal Concept," *Harvard Law Review* 93, no. 6 (1980): 1058–154; and Richard Briffault, "Our Localism: The Structure of Local Government Law," parts 1 and 2, *Columbia Law Review* 90, no. 1 (1990): 1–115 and no. 3 (1990): 346–454. The legal doctrine known as Dillon's Rule holds that local

governments may exercise only those powers and functions expressly authorized or implied by state legislatures and, more broadly, that the state may alter or retract these powers, impose new rules and mandates, and even abolish local government units altogether without recourse by localities.

70. Some view the state as a relatively heavy-handed manipulator of metropolitan political structure. See, for example, David C. Nice, "An Intergovernmental Perspective on Urban Fragmentation," *Social Science Quarterly* 64, no. 1 (1983): 111–18; G. Ross Stephens, "State Centralization and the Erosion of Local Autonomy," *The Journal of Politics* 36 (February 1974): 44–76; and Charles R. Warren, *The States and Urban Strategies: A Comparative Analysis* (Washington, D.C.: U.S. Department of Housing and Urban Development, 1980). Others view states as relatively benign respondents to local concerns. See, for example, Charles Press, "State Government in Urban Areas: Petty Tyrants, Meddlers, or Something Else?" *Urban Interest* 2 (Fall 1980): 12–21; Vincent L. Marando and Mavis Mann Reeves, "State Responsiveness and Local Government Reorganization," *Social Science Quarterly* 69, no. 4 (1988): 996–1004; and Parris N. Glendening and Mavis Mann Reeves, *Pragmatic Federalism: An Intergovernmental View of American Government*, 2nd ed. (Pacific Palisades, Calif.: Palisades Publishers, 1984).

71. See, for example, Briffault, "Our Localism," pp. 375–78; Danielson, "The Adaptive Metropolis," p. 233; and Richard M. Cion, "Accommodation *Par Excellence*: The Lakewood Plan," in *Metropolitan Politics: A Reader*, ed. Michael N. Danielson (Boston: Little, Brown, 1966), pp. 272–81.

72. Doig, " 'A Murderous Fellow,' " pp. 296–98; Danielson, "The Adaptive Metropolis," pp. 234–35.

73. Danielson, "The Adaptive Metropolis," p. 234; Wood, "A Division of Powers," pp. 58–61; and Hamilton and Wells, *Federalism, Power, and Political Economy*, pp. 134–35.

74. Wood, "A Division of Powers," pp. 62–63.

75. Scott A. Bollens, "Examining the Link between State Policy and the Creation of Local Special Districts," *State and Local Government Review* 18, no. 3 (1986): 117–24; Marando and Reeves, "State Responsiveness"; Danielson, Hershey, and Bayne, *One Nation, So Many Governments*, pp. 69–72; and Advisory Commission on Intergovernmental Relations (ACIR), *State Limitations on Local Taxes and Expenditures* (Washington, D.C.: ACIR, 1977).

76. Advisory Commission on Intergovernmental Relations (ACIR), *The Federal Influence on State and Local Roles in the Federal System* (Washington, D.C.: ACIR, 1981); and Stein, "Federally Supported Substate Regional Governments."

77. Michael N. Danielson and Jameson W. Doig, *New York: The Politics of Urban Regional Development* (Berkeley: University of California Press, 1982), pp. 160–61, 184; and Walsh and Leigland, "The Only Planning Game in Town," pp. 6–7.

78. Minge, "Special Districts," p. 704; Walsh, *The Public's Business*, chap. 7; and Royce Hanson, "Land Development and Metropolitan Reform," in *Reform as Reorganization*, ed. Lowdon Wingo (Washington, D.C.: Resources for the Future, 1974), pp. 17, 26.

79. Walsh, "Public Authorities," pp. 213–14.

80. Stewart, *The Responsive Local Authority*, p. 136. For cases alleging such alterations, see Morrill, "State and Local Government Commissions," pp. 297–308; and Kent S. Butler and Dowell Myers, "Boomtime in Austin, Texas," *Journal of the American Planning Association* 50 (Autumn 1984): 447–58.

81. Hamilton and Wells, *Federalism, Power and Politics*, pp. 135; and Walsh, *The Public's Business*, pp. 337–41.

82. Danielson and Doig, *Urban Regional Development*, pp. 158–59, 199.

83. Walsh, *The Public's Business*, pp. 162–65, 335–37; also see Doig, " 'A Murderous Fellow,' " p. 300.

84. S. Bollens, "Examining the Link," pp. 118, 123.

85. Doig, " 'A Murderous Fellow,' " p. 301.

86. Walsh, "Public Authorities," p. 217.

87. See, for example, S. Bollens, "Examining the Link," pp. 122–23; Doig, " 'A Murderous Fellow,' " pp. 301; Walsh, *The Public's Business*, pp. 343–46; and James Leigland, "External Controls on Public Authorities and Other Special Purpose Governments," in *Public Authorities and Public Policy*, ed. Jerry Mitchell (Westport, Conn.: Greenwood, 1992), pp. 31–47.

88. There is no widely agreed upon label for this perspective, which encompasses Marxist, neo-Marxist, critical political economy, critical leftist, structuralist, and other viewpoints. I use "structuralist" as a convenient shorthand for a view that emphasizes structural conditions of society, without implying that the authors mentioned would so label their work.

89. Mark Gottdiener, "Understanding Metropolitan Deconcentration: A Clash of Paradigms," *Social Science Quarterly* 64, no. 2 (1983): 231. Also see Michael K. Heiman, *The Quiet Evolution: Power, Planning and Profits in New York State* (New York: Praeger, 1989), pp. 4–16; and Joe R. Feagin, *Free Enterprise City: Houston in Political-Economic Perspective* (New Brunswick, N.J.: Rutgers University Press, 1988), pp. 22–34.

90. The central work is Karl Marx, *Capital*, 3 vols. (New York: International Publishers Edition, 1967).

91. For example, Manuel Castells, *The Urban Question* (London: Edward Arnold, 1977); and David Harvey, *Social Justice and the City* (Baltimore: Johns Hopkins University Press, 1973).

92. For example, Anthony Giddens, *Central Problems in Social Theory* (Berkeley: University of California Press, 1979); Mark Gottdiener, *The Social Production of Urban Space* (Austin: University of Texas Press, 1985); and Michael Peter Smith, *The City and Social Theory* (New York: St. Martin's Press, 1979).

93. See, for example, Brian J. L. Berry and John Kasarda, *Contemporary Urban Ecology* (New York: Macmillan, 1977); and Amos Hawley, *Urban Society*, 2nd ed. (New York: Wiley, 1981). As discussed, however, metropolitan ecologists generally do assert an activist role for state institutions in urban development.

94. Some analysts assert a relatively weak role for the state, seeing it as acquiescent to a powerful business elite. See, for example, James O'Connor, *The Fiscal Crisis of the State* (New York: St. Martin's Press, 1973); Clarence N. Stone, "Systemic Power in Community Decision Making," *American Political Science Review* 74 (1980): 978–90; Gordon L. Clark and Michael Dear, *State*

*Apparatus* (Boston: Allen and Unwin, 1984); and, generally, Gregory D. Squires, ed. *Unequal Partnerships: The Political Economy of Urban Redevelopment in Postwar America* (New Brunswick, N.J.: Rutgers University Press, 1989). Others posit a more autonomous state that together with business interests comprise an urban regime that pursues strategies for growth. See, for example, Susan S. Fainstein et al., *Restructuring the City* (New York: Longman, 1983); Stephen L. Elkin, *City and Regime in the American Republic* (Chicago: University of Chicago Press, 1987); Ronald K. Vogel, *Urban Political Economy, Broward County, Florida* (Gainesville: University Press of Florida, 1992); and Clarence N. Stone and Heywood T. Sanders, eds., *The Politics of Urban Development* (Lawrence: University Press of Kansas, 1987).

**95.** Gordon, "Capitalist Development."

**96.** Markusen, "Class and Urban Social Expenditure," pp. 95–102.

**97.** Logan and Molotch, *Urban Fortunes*, p. 185.

**98.** Feagin, *Free Enterprise City*, pp. 30–32.

**99.** Kevin R. Cox and Frank Z. Nartowicz, "Jurisdictional Fragmentation in the American Metropolis: Alternative Perspectives," *International Journal of Urban and Regional Research* 4, no. 2 (1990): 196–211; Andrew E. G. Jonas, "Urban Growth Coalitions and Urban Development Policy: Postwar Growth and the Politics of Annexation in Metropolitan Columbus," *Urban Geography* 12, no. 3 (1991): 192–225; and Thomas M. Beckley, "Leftist Critique of the Quiet Revolution in Land Use Control: Two Cases of Agency Formation," *Journal of Planning Education and Research* 12, no. 1 (1992): 55–66.

**100.** Spencer Olin, "Intraclass Conflict and the Politics of a Fragmented Region," in *Postsuburban California: The Transformation of Orange County Since World War II*, ed. Rob Kling, Spencer Olin, and Mark Poster (Berkeley: University of California Press, 1991), pp. 223–53.

**101.** See, for example, Beckley, "Leftist Critique"; Cynthia Horan, "Beyond Governing Coalitions: Analyzing Urban Regimes in the 1990s," *Journal of Urban Affairs* 13, no. 2 (1991): 119–35; and Robert Kerstein, "Growth Politics in Tampa and Hillsborough County: Strains in the Privatistic Regimes," *Journal of Urban Affairs* 13, no. 1 (1991): 55–75.

**102.** Cox and Nartowicz, "Jurisdictional Fragmentation," pp. 203–4; and Richard A. Walker and Michael K. Heiman, "Quiet Revolution for Whom?" *Annals of the Association of American Geographers* 71, no. 1 (1981): 69, 82–83.

**103.** Frances Fox Piven and Roger Friedland, "Public Choice and Private Power: A Theory of Fiscal Crisis," in *Public Service Provision and Urban Development*, ed. Andrew Kirby, Paul Knox, and Steven Pinch (New York: St. Martin's Press, 1984), p. 412; and Heiman, *The Quiet Evolution*, chap. 4. For case studies of close developer-district ties, see Perrenod, *Special Districts, Special Purposes*; and Robert Gottlieb and Margaret FitzSimmons, *Thirst for Growth: Water Agencies as Hidden Government in California* (Tucson: University of Arizona Press, 1991), pp. 130–31.

**104.** Heiman, *The Quiet Evolution*, p. 21. For an example of special districts as agents of development, see Ronald K. Vogel and Bert E. Swanson, "The Growth Machine Versus the Antigrowth Coalition," *Urban Affairs Quarterly* 25, no. 1 (1989), p. 74.

**105.** Paul E. Peterson, *City Limits* (Chicago: University of Chicago Press, 1981), pp. 133–36.

**106.** Feagin makes this point in reference to the hundreds of municipal utilities districts surrounding Houston, Texas. Feagin, *Free Enterprise City*, pp. 163–64. Also see Perrenod, *Special Districts, Special Purposes*, pp. 28–29, 33–34.

**107.** Gottlieb and FitzSimmons, *Thirst for Growth*, pp. 211–14; and Heiman, *The Quiet Evolution*, chap. 4.

**108.** Logan and Molotch, *Urban Fortunes*, pp. 73–74; and Piven and Friedland, "Public Choice and Private Power," p. 412.

**109.** Piven and Friedland, "Public Choice and Private Power," pp. 412–13. Also see generally, Frank Fischer *Technocracy and the Politics of Expertise* (Newbury Park, Calif.: Sage, 1990), pp. 18–21; and Eva Etzioni-Halevy, *Bureaucracy and Democracy* (London: Routledge and Kegan Paul, 1983), pp. 54–62.

**110.** That policy experts are not, in fact, apolitical, is the conclusion of numerous studies. For a discussion and review, see Brint, *In an Age of Experts*, pp. 129–32.

**111.** Piven and Friedland, "Public Choice and Private Power," pp. 412–13; and Markusen, "Class and Urban Social Expenditure," p. 108.

**112.** Sanders, "Building the Convention City," pp. 139, 154–55; and Piven and Friedland, "Public Choice and Private Power," pp. 412–13.

**113.** Piven and Friedland, "Public Choice and Private Power," pp. 414–15.

**114.** Heiman, *The Quiet Evolution*, p. 21; and Gottlieb and FitzSimmons, *Thirst for Growth*, pp. 105–7, 141–45.

**115.** See, for example, Nels R. Leutwiler, "Playing Taps for Urban Growth Control: Restricting Public Utility Access to Manage Growth," *State and Local Government Review* 19, no. 1 (1987): 8–14; and Julie Hayward Biggs, "No Drip, No Flush, No Growth: How Cities Can Control Growth Beyond Their Boundaries by Refusing to Extend Utility Services," *Urban Lawyer* 22, no. 2 (1990): 285–305.

# 3

## Existing Evidence

Metropolitan political arrangements in general and specialized governments in particular are of interest primarily because analysts believe they matter. As the review of the theoretical literature indicates, claims abound that one or another arrangement of local governments is more efficient, more economical, more responsive, more accountable, more equitable, and more attractive to residents and potential investors. In this chapter I review the nature and validity of empirical evidence on how local government arrangements and the choice to rely on specialized governments may matter to metropolitan political economies.

The state of knowledge on these topics is far less developed than theoretical claims suggest. Although researchers have intensified their efforts over the past two decades, there are relatively few systematic studies of the causes and consequences of local government arrangements in metropolitan regions. As recently as the mid-1980s two analysts of local government structure lamented, "Despite the pleas for reform and change in the institutional structure of local governments . . . the definitive answer to the basic question, 'What difference does it make?,' has yet to be found."[1] Empirical research on special-purpose governments is even less common. One observer recently noted: "Although authorities have been in existence for decades, their performance remains a relatively unexplored area. Few efforts have been made to examine systematically the[ir] social, economic, or political impact."[2]

The empirical review reveals some trends, but relatively few conclusive findings. The absence of consensus is due in part to the paucity of studies, but also to the difficulty in drawing conclusions from studies that vary considerably in focus, scale, and methodology. Empirical analysis is inherently more provisional and messy than theoretical argument. Still, much empirical analysis of political structure and special-purpose governments suffers from methodological shortcomings, many of which could be remedied by careful research choices.

I begin the review by examining the evidence for the significance of local government arrangements in general. This reveals how special-purpose governments fit into the broader findings on local government

**66**

structure, and also provides a context for the subsequent survey of studies that focus on special-purpose governments.

## DO LOCAL GOVERNMENT ARRANGEMENTS MATTER?

### Correlates of Metropolitan Arrangements

The most basic research on local government arrangements asks why some metropolitan regions are more politically fragmented than others and what factors correlate with levels of fragmentation. The earliest and most comprehensive, though statistically elementary, study was conducted in 1962 by political scientists Thomas R. Dye and Brett W. Hawkins.[3] Dye and Hawkins, who sought to add empirical fuel to the emerging public choice critique of institutional-reform thought, examined simple correlation coefficients to identify the factors most closely associated with levels of political fragmentation in metropolitan areas. They found that absolute fragmentation levels (the number of local government units—counties, municipalities, townships, school districts, and special districts—per metropolitan area) were greatest in the larger, older, and, to a lesser extent, more affluent and less domi-nated by a central city of the 212 metropolitan areas existing in 1962.[4] More important, Hawkins and Dye argued, there was no statistically significant correlation between absolute fragmentation levels and sev-eral potential correlates, including the percentage of nonwhite city population and city-suburban differentials in socioeconomic status (in-come, white collar occupation, and educational attainment). Hawkins and Dye concluded that there was little evidence to support the claims of institutional reformers that politically fragmented metropolitan areas were associated with greater intrametropolitan disparities.

Using data from the 1972 Census of Governments, geographers Don-ald J. Zeigler and Stanley D. Brunn used a slightly more sophisticated measure of political fragmentation to examine metropolitan patterns of political structure.[5] Zeigler and Brunn calculated an index of geo-political fragmentation by dividing the number of local governments per 10,000 persons by the percentage of total metropolitan area pop-ulation residing in the central city. Low values of geopolitical frag-mentation signified the more city centered or politically integrated areas, while high values signified the least city centered or politically fragmented metropolitan areas. Zeigler and Brunn found that political structure was a regional phenomenon: the most geopolitically frag-mented metropolitan areas were concentrated in the northeast and north central regions of the United States, with the notable exception of southern New England (primarily Connecticut), which had low levels of geopolitical fragmentation. The least fragmented metropolitan areas were in the south and southwest where county government predominated or state statutes facilitated central city annexations (and, hence, city centrality). With relevance to economic growth policy, Zeigler and Brunn found that the most geopolitically fragmented metropolitan areas had relatively slow or declining growth rates. Contrary to Hawkins and Dye, they also found that metropolitan areas whose central cities most severely lagged behind their suburbs socioeconomically tended to be more geopolitically fragmented. Although Zeigler and Brunn did not make causal claims, they suggested that geopolitical fragmentation exacerbated the troubles of needy central cities and hampered regional solutions to fiscal inequalities.[6]

Subsequent research extended these early empirical efforts. In a careful empirical analysis of the correlates of political structure for 296 metropolitan areas in 1982, economist Michael A. Nelson found a significant positive association between absolute political fragmentation and the heterogeneity of household preferences.[7] Nelson concluded that there was ample support for the public choice assertion that diverse service preferences will be associated with more highly fragmented metropolitan political structures.

Nelson also provided the first systematic test of the relationship between political fragmentation levels and the permissiveness of legal statutes. In particular, Nelson found a significant positive relationship between the permissiveness of incorporation and the number of local governments in an area, an outcome consistent with the claims of metropolitan ecologists. The relationship between the restrictiveness of annexation statutes and the number of local governments turned out to be positive as hypothesized, but statistically insignificant, suggesting a complex link between legal levers and structural outcomes.[8]

Political scientist Nancy Burns shed light on that complexity in her analysis of the determinants of new municipal formations in metropolitan and nonmetropolitan counties in the postwar period.[9] Contrary to Nelson and much conventional wisdom, Burns found a positive and significant relationship between permissive annexation statutes and the proliferation of municipalities. Legal statutes facilitating annexation led not to more politically integrated areas, Burns concluded, but rather to defensive incorporations by communities seeking to escape unwanted annexation to existing cities.[10]

Another explanation was offered by political scientist David C. Nice who argued that permissive turn-of-the-century incorporation statutes—and consequent municipal fragmentation—were the result of collusion between rural and suburban state legislators who sought to dilute the political power of central cities.[11] Using state-level data,

Nice found that permissive annexation statutes, low levels of metropolitan-nonmetropolitan conflict, and low levels of municipal fragmentation were positively associated.[12] Apparently, argued Nice, states that felt less threatened by central cities, that is those that had fewer and less dominant metropolitan areas, were more likely to assist central cities through permissive annexation provisions. By contrast, when central cities and metropolitan areas were more dominant, rural and suburban legislators felt more threatened and consequently made annexations much harder to accomplish. Descriptively, these relationships are consistent with patterns and practices in the less metropolitanized southern and western regions, which are characterized by permissive annexation statutes and lower political fragmentation, and the comparatively metropolitanized northeastern and north central regions, which are characterized by restrictive annexation statutes and high levels of political fragmentation.[13]

## Fiscal and Policy Implications

A second thrust of empirical work focuses on the fiscal and policy consequences of local government arrangements. These studies are of two types. The first, undertaken primarily by economists, is the sizeable corpus of "Leviathan studies" that examine the link between political fragmentation and the size of government, the latter typically measured as total public outlays per capita. The second type, conducted by both economists and political scientists, entails service delivery studies that examine the effects of local government arrangements on the effectiveness of public service delivery. I highlight the findings of each type only briefly here; comprehensive reviews of these literatures are available elsewhere.[14]

The results of Leviathan studies are mixed, due primarily to different researcher choices regarding methodology, unit of analysis, and the selection and measurement of dependent and control variables. Consistent with institutional reform hypotheses, some studies find a positive link between political fragmentation levels and total local government expenditures per capita.[15] Other studies, consistent with the public choice perspective, find the opposite: the more politically fragmented the area, the lower the per capita costs of government.[16] Still other studies find no association between government costs and fragmentation levels or find mixed results for different public services.[17]

Of particular relevance to specialized governance is the high consistency of results when researchers examine the cost implications of political fragmentation for special-purpose and general-purpose governments separately. In most instances, findings indicate that a multiplicity of general-purpose governments is associated with lower per capita spending, while a multiplicity of special-purpose governments is associated with higher per capita spending. I elaborate on this finding later in this chapter.

Studies linking local government organization to service delivery outcomes are likewise inconclusive. Several studies on the implications of city-county consolidation find higher per capita costs of public services and a reduction in fiscal disparities across jurisdictions.[18] Higher costs are attributed to the "equalizing up" phenomenon whereby a service's highest preconsolidation spending level becomes the postconsolidation spending floor. Reduced fiscal disparities allegedly result from the imposition of a single areawide tax rate in a consolidated metropolitan area.

Other assessments of local government reorganizations report a variety of intended and unintended postreform effects. Although there is some evidence that city-county consolidations reduce intrametropolitan service disparities, consolidation also appears to bring scant gains or actual declines in economies of scale, levels of citizen participation, and resident service satisfaction.[19] By contrast, some studies shed more positive light on service performance, notably in terms of service satisfaction, service quality, and economic performance.[20] Overall, the record remains inconclusive.

At the individual service level, public choice scholars offer evidence that more complex government arrangements are associated with greater service efficiency.[21] The reasons for greater efficiency, however, appear only indirectly related to structural factors. For example, a review of studies concluded that the number and size of police protection and education agencies are less relevant to service delivery outcomes than are internal procedures used to mobilize and allocate resources.[22] The cases of solid waste and fire protection services yielded some evidence of economies of scale (above 15,000 persons and 5,000 persons, respectively), but important differences in production mode—public, private, contract, or volunteer—hamper detection of the independent effect, if any, of local government arrangements.[23] More recent analyses of police, fire, streets, and education services conducted by the Advisory Commission on Intergovernmental Relations in two politically complex metropolitan counties, Allegheny County (Pittsburgh, Penn.) and St. Louis County (St. Louis, Mo.), found that local government multiplicity and efficiency are compatible, though not linked causally. The commission concluded that other factors, for example the legal separation of St. Louis City from St. Louis County in that metropolitan area, were more critical determinants of government effectiveness than were levels of political fragmentation.[24]

## DOES SPECIALIZED GOVERNANCE MATTER?

The small body of empirical research focusing on special-purpose governments can be divided into three categories. The first includes empirical analyses of the correlates of special districts in metropolitan areas. The second category includes studies of the fiscal and policy consequences of specialized governance. The third includes case studies examining a broad range of issues associated with the causes and consequences of special-purpose governments, typically at the individual district level.

### Correlates of Special Districts

A number of studies, summarized in table 3–1, investigate the correlates of special-purpose governments.[25] Although each has a distinct methodology, there are notable similarities. With the exception of the study by Burns, the studies are all cross-sectional analyses of the number of special districts in a metropolitan area at a single time. With the exception of the study by Hawkins and Dye, the studies all examine the influence of state policy on the number of special districts in an area, a relationship of particular interest to metropolitan ecologists. Most studies also test the relationship between demographic and demand-related variables hypothesized by public choice scholars to be correlates of government formation.

What evidence do these studies yield about the correlates of special-purpose governments? The most consistent finding is the significance of state policy variables on the number of special districts in a state or metropolitan area. Studies find that home rule powers and state-imposed constraints on municipal revenue raising and boundary change correlate in predictable ways with the number of special-purpose governments in an area. In general, the more stringent the constraints on municipal powers, the greater the number of special districts. One obvious, though not widely tested, correlate, the presence of state enabling legislation for special-purpose governments, had a particularly strong positive association with the number of special districts formed in an area.[26]

The studies also reveal that population and demand-driven factors influence the distribution of special-purpose governments, although not always in obvious ways. In their 1985 study of Illinois counties, for example, David L. Chicoine and Norman Walzer found that the number of special districts per 10,000 residents was inversely associated with population growth, a finding affirmed in Nelson's more comprehensive study of 296 metropolitan areas.[27] Researchers in both studies

**TABLE 3-1** Summary of Studies on the Correlates of Special-Purpose Governments

| Study | Findings |
| --- | --- |
| 212 U.S. metropolitan areas, 1962 (Hawkins and Dye, 1971) | Simple correlation coefficient of .72 between number of districts and number of municipalities. Insignificant correlation between districts per capita and municipalities per capita. |
| U.S. metropolitan areas in southern states, 1972–1977 (MacManus, 1981) | Weak positive relationship between number of new taxing districts and state restrictions on municipal property taxing. |
| 101 Illinois counties, 1977 (Chicoine and Walzer, 1985) | Counties without municipal debt and tax limitations have fewer taxing units (all government types, including districts) than counties with municipal limits. |
| 50 U.S. states (S. Bollens, 1986) | Positive relationship between permissive state enabling laws and number of districts. |
| 50 U.S. states (Marando and Reeves, 1988) | Formation of new multijurisdictional districts reflects local demands rather than state interests and policies. |
| 296 U.S. metropolitan areas, 1986 (Nelson, 1990) | Significant positive relationship between number of districts (including school districts) and (1) household income variance, (2) municipal tax limits, (3) municipal home rule authority, (4) population size, and (5) land area. Significant negative relationship with (1) age variation, and (2) stringency of incorporation laws. |
| 200 U.S. counties, 1952–1987 (Burns, 1994) | Significant positive relationship between number of new districts per decade and (1) population growth, (2) population size, (3) number of development firms interacted with number of black population, and (4) leniency of district formation laws, annexation laws, and tax limits. |

reasoned that population increases and the consequent increases in demands for services contribute to special-district formation, but that the pace of population growth outstrips new government formation. Consistent with public choice hypotheses and his findings for municipalities, Nelson found a positive association between the heterogeneity of household preferences and the number of special districts in a metropolitan area.[28]

Tests of hypotheses implied by institutional reform and structuralist scholars are less common. Hawkins and Dye revealed little support for the institutional reform contention that special-purpose governments form as an antidote to municipal fragmentation. Although they found a positive relationship between the absolute number of special districts and municipal governments in a metropolitan area, the relationship proved insignificant when comparing relative numbers of districts per capita to municipal fragmentation levels. Of particular relevance was Hawkins and Dye's finding that special districts were no more common in metropolitan areas with high central-city dominance than in those with low dominance, a finding that suggested special-purpose governments were equally useful in city and suburban environments.[29]

Only the study by Burns tested the structuralist hypothesis that special district formations are positively linked to the strength of pro-growth elites. For a sample of 200 metropolitan and nonmetropolitan counties, Burns found a positive relationship between the number of development firms in a county and the formation of special districts. Because this relationship is significant only for the 1950–1960 period and occurs only when there are relatively high levels of nonwhite residents, however, the presence of development firms is a limited explanation for district formation. Detailed analysis of district formations by function led Burns to conclude that developers and large nonwhite population groups found common ground in creation of housing and community development authorities in the 1950s.[30]

## Fiscal and Policy Implications

A number of studies, summarized in table 3–2, test the effects of special-purpose governance on local government expenditures.[31] Like the research on district correlates, the studies vary in methodology but have similarities. All except the studies by Minge and Krohm examine the cost effects of special district multiplicity, with most directly testing the Leviathan hypothesis that interjurisdictional competition (gauged by the number of special-purpose governments in an area) acts as a brake on public sector spending. Minge and Krohm compare spending outcomes between special districts and general-purpose governments.

The results of the Leviathan studies show unusual concordance, though notably in a direction contrary to theoretical expectations. Findings contest the hypothesis that the greater the number of special-purpose governments, the greater the level of interjurisdictional competition, and, by extension, the lower the costs of local government. Rather, the studies consistently find that the greater the number of

**TABLE 3-2** Summary of Studies on the Fiscal Consequences of Special-Purpose Governments

| Study | Findings |
| --- | --- |
| Sewer and fire protection districts in California (Krohm, 1973) | District-provided fire protection costs more than municipal provision. No significant cost difference between municipal and district provision for sewer services. |
| 16 cemetery districts in Wyoming, 1960, 1973 (Minge, 1976) | District provision results in significantly higher expenditures than does municipal provision. |
| U.S. metropolitan areas in southern states, 1972–1977 (MacManus, 1981) | Weak support for a negative relationship between growth in number of taxing districts and (1) growth of property tax revenues, and (2) growth of total local government expenditures. |
| 41–51 pooled counties in California, Oregon, Texas, West Virginia, and Kentucky, 1967–1977 (DiLorenzo, 1981) | Restrictions on district formation in California and Oregon raise per capita fire and water expenditures more than in control states. Restrictions not significant for housing and sewage disposal expenditures. |
| 36 Oregon counties, 1977 (Deno and Mehay, 1985) | Boundary commission policies to limit creation and encourage consolidation of districts slow growth in district numbers, but have only weak effect on total local government and fire protection expenditures. |
| 101 Illinois counties, 1977 (Chicoine and Walzer, 1985) | Significant positive relationship between number of districts and local government expenditures for library and parks and recreation; insignificant relationship between districts per capita and total expenditures. |
| 48 U.S. states, 1977 and 1982 (Nelson, 1987) | Insignificant relationship between number of districts and total local government expenditures. |
| 2,900 U.S. counties and 280 metropolitan areas, 1977 (Eberts and Gronberg, 1988) | Significant positive relationship between number of districts and total local government expenditures and revenues. |
| 3,022 U.S. counties, 1981–1982 (Zax, 1989) | Significant positive relationship between number of districts and total local government expenditures and revenues. |

special districts in an area, the *higher* the per capita costs of local government.[32] Researchers conclude that the higher costs associated with specialized governance result either because special districts exploit their local service monopoly by increasing costs or because a multiplicity of special-purpose governments in an area frustrates realization of economies of scale.

Consistent with public choice logic, Chicoine and Walzer offer an alternative explanation for the positive relationship between special-purpose governments and local government costs. They suggest that the higher costs associated with district service delivery reflect the satisfaction of consumer demands for more or higher quality services, demands that are met by special districts.[33]

The absence of comparable cases and the failure to control for nonstructural factors also affecting spending levels preclude drawing conclusions about spending differences between general-purpose and special-purpose governments. David Minge found that cemetery districts in Wyoming cost more to run than equivalent services from municipal providers.[34] Minge attributed the results to the inflationary effects of functional specialization and institutional separation, such as duplication of service, administrative overhead, and low political visibility, thus affirming claims of metropolitan ecologists, structuralists, and institutional reformers. Greg Krohm's results were mixed in a similar study comparing costs of special-purpose versus general-purpose delivery of fire protection and sewer services. He found higher costs for district fire protection services, but no significant difference in spending for municipal versus district sewer services. Krohm speculated in the sewer case that functional expertise might account for lower costs associated with special-purpose service delivery.[35]

The empirical literature offers virtually no aggregate studies examining how special-purpose governments may alter the allocation of resources across spending categories. The closest match is a 1987 study of public works authorities conducted by the Institute for Public Administration (IPA).[36] IPA concluded from its review of the literature that "districts and authorities ... as a class ... lean toward the more revenue producing services," but that there was "no general evidence that districts and authorities make better developmental decisions than other forms of community organization."[37]

## Case Studies of Specialized Governance

The case study literature on special districts is the most voluminous and ungeneralizable of the three categories of empirical research. Several prominent districts, including the Port Authority of New York and

New Jersey, the Metropolitan Water District of Southern California and the Washington Public Power Supply System, have been the subject of books, articles, editorials, and dissertations.[38] Also ample is book, newspaper, and journal coverage of specific topics related to special-purpose governments, for example transit authority operations or investigations into alleged financial abuses by public authorities.[39] Many special-purpose governments publish annual reports of their finances and accomplishments, as do many state agencies.[40] I make no attempt to comprehensively review this large literature, although I draw directly and indirectly on many of these studies.

Table 3–3 summarizes a sampling of cases that focus on the fiscal and policy implications of special-purpose governments. Variations in study design and scope notwithstanding, the cases on cost implications confirm the overall fiscal significance of special-district activity in metropolitan areas, although specific findings on costs and efficiencies yield mixed results.[41] Most broadly, Bradley M. Braun's examination of the economic impacts of Florida's Canaveral Port Authority quantified the authority's sizable impacts on job and productivity growth in the region. In a more focused study comparing the fiscal impacts of special districts and private service providers, James Halteman concluded that special districts were less cost-efficient than the comparison agencies because of administrative inefficiencies. Economist Richard B. Peiser came to a similar conclusion in comparing the fiscal effects of the relatively small, independent municipal utilities districts of Houston Metropolitan Area and the regional utility companies in Dallas Metropolitan Area. He found that the smaller utilities districts were potentially cheaper and more efficient than the larger utility companies in the short run, but were less efficient and manageable over the long term. The Advisory Commission on Intergovernmental Relations (ACIR) reached the opposite conclusion in its 1988 study of fire protection services in St. Louis County. Though previous studies suggested the possibility of economies of scale for fire services up to a population of 100,000, ACIR found for the twenty-four independent fire districts serving 710,000 St. Louis County residents "no evidence of size economies . . . on a property-protected basis."[42] ACIR interpreted this finding as evidence of the economic viability of St. Louis County's small and numerous fire protection units.

Other case studies address the potential policy implications of special-purpose governance.[43] The most fundamental finding is that special districts influence public policy in ways often inconsistent with public goals, particularly with respect to growth and development. Although some studies, such as that by Templer, document districts' ability to *slow* growth, most underscore the metropolitan ecology and

**TABLE 3-3** Summary of Case Studies on the Fiscal and Policy Consequences of Special-Purpose Governments

| Study | Findings |
| --- | --- |
| Central and Southern Florida Flood Control District (CSFFCD); Dade County Port Authority (DCPA) (Carter, 1974) | District activity stimulates growth. CSFFCD lessened risk on developing lands near Everglades. DCPA directed growth through location of its facilities, especially airports. |
| Municipal authorities in Pennsylvania (Halteman, 1979) | Cost of water provision higher for municipal authorities than for private water companies. |
| Municipal utilities districts (MUDs) and regional utility companies (RUCs) in Dallas and Houston (Tex.) metropolitan areas (Peiser, 1983) | RUCs more efficient than MUDs in terms of economies of scale. RUCs constrain supply of developable land. MUDs may lower land prices, promote urban sprawl, and, because of competition, keep costs down in short run. |
| Water districts and MUDs in Houston Metropolitan Area (Perrenod, 1984) | Rapid increase in number of water districts and MUDs coincides with increased use of groundwater, and rate of land subsidence and flooding. |
| 22 water conservation districts in Texas (Templer, 1984) | Districts effective in slowing development due to broad powers to regulate groundwater pumping locations and well production. |
| MUDs in Austin (Tex.) Metropolitan Area (Butler and Myers, 1984) | Developers' ability to secure development approvals through MUDs hinders ability of local municipalities to implement growth management plans. |
| Local governments in St. Louis (Mo.) County (ACIR, 1989) | Political fragmentation not associated with inefficiency due to economies of scale in the case of fire protection, which is largely district provided. |
| Canaveral (Fla.) Port Authority (Braun, 1990) | CPA activities have significant economic impact on region: 31,265 jobs (one-fifth of region's employment), $709 million in production, $225 million in wages. |

structuralist contention that districts foster prodevelopment agendas. Geographer Richard L. Morrill's study of Metro, Seattle (Wash.) Metropolitan Area's sewer and transit agency, argued that Metro's extensive powers "appeared to give [it] *de facto* planning authority over development, a power not authorized by voters."[44] An earlier study by planners Kent S. Butler and Dowell Myers likewise argued that the considerable power of independent municipal utilities districts in the Austin (Texas) Metropolitan Area undermined the ability of Austin officials to implement growth management policies. The authors argued that the utilities districts promoted a pace of growth higher than that approved in public fora. Luther J. Carter's comprehensive and critical assessment of the operations and policies of two Southern Florida districts, the Dade County Port Authority and the Central and South Florida Flood Control District, concluded that "dubious solutions [are] likely to be found" when relatively unaccountable authorities control decisions about major facility locations.[45]

Studies on the cumulative fiscal and policy effects of the trend toward specialized governance generally take a dim view of special districts. Perhaps the most thorough study of this type is Virginia Marion Perrenod's examination of the impacts of municipal utilities and water districts in Houston Metropolitan Area in the 1970s. Perrenod concluded that the unchecked proliferation of these districts was directly linked to serious slope subsidence and groundwater depletion in the area.[46] In a similar vein, Robert Gottlieb and Margaret FitzSimmons found that by the late 1980s the relatively isolated and unaccountable major water districts in Southern California had expanded lines and services to such an extent that they posed a serious threat to public health and environmental quality in the region.[47]

In the broadest terms, then, the existing empirical evidence indicates that specialized governance matters, that it is qualitatively different from general-purpose governance, and that it often generates impacts that are neither intended nor necessarily desired. Beyond these general findings, the body of research on special-purpose governments is insufficient in volume and consistency to draw firm conclusions. The results of many cross-sectional studies are mixed, an artifact in part of research designs with different questions, geographic scales, variables, and methodologies. Of greater concern, however, is that much of this empirical research suffers from conceptual and methodological shortcomings, which diminishes its applicability and reliability.

## METHODOLOGICAL SHORTCOMINGS

The most conspicuous methodological flaw plaguing studies of local government arrangements is equating special-purpose and general-purpose governments under the broad rubric *local government*. By definition, researchers focusing on special-purpose governments successfully dodge this methodological pitfall. Yet many researchers pass this first hurdle only to succumb to one or more of three problematic practices of special districts research. These practices are (1) equating school districts and special districts, (2) disregarding the spatial characteristics of special districts, and (3) using simple tallies of districts rather than measures of their actual influence to gauge the importance of districts to metropolitan political economies.

## School Districts as Special Districts

Although school districts can be considered, by virtue of their independence and functional specialization, a subset of special-purpose governments, their inclusion with nonschool districts introduces bias into analyses of district finances, employment, and numbers. The basic methodological problem is that school district employment and finances typically dwarf those of all other metropolitan-based special districts combined (and often represent over 50 percent of *total* local government expenditures and employment). As a consequence, researchers who include school district employment and finances with nonschool district tallies are effectively analyzing school district operations and shedding scant light on nonschool districts.

Because different states organize education services differently, including school districts also presents problems of cross-state comparisons. The District of Columbia and four states, North Carolina, Tennessee, Virginia, and Maryland, rely on general-purpose governments (or dependent school districts operated by general-purpose governments) to provide education services. If school districts are not separated from nonschool special districts, analyses of special-purpose governments will indicate that states without independent school districts have misleadingly low district numbers and expenditures relative to states with independent school districts. In addition, because education spending in the five places with dependent school districts is included under the finances of general-purpose governments, ratios of special district to total local government expenditures in these states would be artificially low. In either case, the inclusion of school districts with nonschool districts clouds the picture of special-purpose governments.

## Disregarding Spatial Characteristics

A second methodological problem is that traditional measures of special-purpose governments—for example, special districts per capita—disregard districts' spatial characteristics. The size and arrangement of district governments are critical to metropolitan functioning. Of particular relevance is the degree to which districts overlap general-purpose governments. Special-purpose governments whose boundaries are coterminous with those of a municipality or county actually sustain the underlying general-purpose government structure. By contrast, districts whose boundaries are noncoterminous with a municipality or county adapt to area service needs. Because districts that adapt and those that sustain political structure are likely to have distinct purposes and implications, failure to account for spatial differences can lead to faulty conclusions.

## Equating Numbers with Importance

The third methodological problem is perhaps the most common and serious. Nearly all empirical studies of special-purpose governance (and studies of metropolitan political structure more generally) use absolute or relative measures of special districts to gauge their importance to a study area. Although such count-based measures are adequate for analyses of district formation—examining the number of governments formed in the last decade, for example—they are inadequate gauges of district importance.

There are several specific problems. The gap between the number and importance of special-purpose governments stems from the significant number of "paper districts" that have neither employees nor expenditures. An inventory of road districts in a metropolitan area, for example, might include many that remain on the books long after their road improvement activities have ceased. In addition, because simple tallies equate very different district subtypes—for example, a metropolitan, multifunction port authority with a subdivision-sized, single-function lighting district—count-based measures as a gauge of importance are likely to be misleading. Count-based measures are also susceptible to the problem of "excess capacity." At the time of formation a district typically has sufficient capacity to accommodate an increase in service demand without formation of a new district. As a consequence, increases in a district's expenditures or relative influence on area service delivery are not reflected in stable district numbers.

Several examples illustrate the significance of these pitfalls. In terms of simple counts, metropolitan areas in relatively district-sparse Ohio appear to rely less on special-purpose governments than do metropolitan areas in neighboring Indiana, which has comparatively high district counts. Closer examination, however, reveals that districts in Ohio tend to be metropolitanwide authorities providing major urban services such as transit, airports, sewer, and health, while districts in Indiana tend to be small and have relatively minor total expenditure levels. Similarly, with over 160 special-purpose governments, Boston Metropolitan Area appears to rely heavily on specialized entities. A closer look reveals that over 80 percent of these districts are municipally based housing authorities, suggesting that district influence is functionally narrow within the region.[48] To avoid drawing faulty conclusions about district importance, researchers need information on both the functional breadth and financial significance of a region's portfolio of special-purpose governments.

## STRUCTURAL PROBLEMS OF DISTRICT RESEARCH

The methodological shortcomings can be readily overcome through careful research choices. Other structural problems of district research are less tractable. The two most serious of these are data availability and data reliability.

### Data Availability

The bane of research on special-purpose governments is the lack of comparable data. Until recently, states rarely gathered information on special districts, making time-series data nearly nonexistent. States that do collect data on districts vary with respect to the range of information and the quality of its assembly. Some states, notably California and Texas, require districts to report financial and employment information to a state clearinghouse. In most other states, reporting requirements and compliance are spotty. Even if all states diligently collected data, however, cross-state variations in what constitutes a special-purpose government and the equally varied definitions used by individual states to classify special-purpose governments as independent or dependent hamper the use of state-collected data for national studies.

As a result, researchers generally turn to the only national source of data on special districts, the censuses of governments, conducted every five years since 1952 by the U.S. Bureau of the Census. Censuses of governments report the number of local government units by type in each county, plus selected data on their functions, employment, and finances. The data are gathered primarily through voluntary survey responses from individual governments and also from secondary sources at the state and local government level.

Despite its national coverage, there are several data availability concerns with the censuses of governments. Slightly over 10,000 local governments did not respond to requests for information in the 1992 *Census of Governments*, of which 5,172 (52 percent) were special districts.[49] Nonresponding districts represented 16.4 percent of the total tally of special districts; most were considered active. Confirmed inactive districts were dropped from the final counts of governments. In addition, the data in censuses of governments prior to 1972 are less complete than data in subsequent releases, which provide additional information in computer-readable format. Most detrimental to historical analyses is the lack of pre-1972 data on the number, finances, and employment levels of special-purpose governments by function and county.

## Data Reliability

Census of governments data that *are* available are subject to criticism for reliability and usefulness.[50] Specific charges include undercounting independent districts, reclassifying districts as independent or dependent, and overcounting inactive districts.

At the center of the undercounting problem is the Bureau of the Census's determination of an entity's status as independent, the criterion upon which the Bureau includes or excludes districts in national counts. Because classification as independent requires autonomy from parent governments, many otherwise sovereign agencies are excluded from special district totals because their parent government either appoints the district's officers, approves its plans, or scrutinizes its budget. This results in counts that, in the words of one critic, are "neither meaningful nor accurate reflections of reality."[51]

Data from certain states are particularly prone to the undercounting dilemma. In New York State, for example, where few of the dozens of public authorities providing public services meet the independence criteria of the Bureau of the Census, counts may be particularly misleading. According to the Census Bureau, over 93 percent of all special districts in New York's metropolitan areas are fire protection districts. Major public authorities, which include transit, housing, water, and facilities authorities, are not counted. This occurs because data collection procedures for New York State entailed central collection by state officials who reported only fire, consolidated health, and an additional handful of districts created by special legislation.[52] Studies conducted in other states sometimes report significant discrepancies between detailed field counts of independent districts and Census Bureau data for the same geographic area.[53]

An associated methodological complication is the Census Bureau's periodic reclassification of specific district types according to their status as independent. Although most between-census changes in the number of special-purpose governments are due to new formations or dissolutions, some are reclassifications, which can compromise comparability over time. Between the 1972 and 1982 censuses of governments, for example, over 500 dependent municipal trust districts in Oklahoma were reclassified as independent, then again reclassified as dependent after 1982, resulting in an artificial jump and drop in the number of special districts in that state. Hundreds of municipal utilities authorities in Pennsylvania were similarly reclassified from dependent to independent in 1962, while a smaller but relatively important number of drainage and levee districts in Louisiana were reclassified as dependent after 1972. Since the *1987 Census of Governments*, the Bureau of the Census reclassified eighty-four municipal library districts in Missouri and fifty solid waste authorities in West Virginia as independent, among others. The Census Bureau also reclassified as dependent eighty-one housing authorities and ten county industrial pollution control authorities in New Jersey.[54] Each reclassification jeopardizes the accuracy of comparisons across censuses.

Overcounting problems stem from inclusion of inactive districts in government counts. Nearly one-third (2,573 of 8,341) of the districts responding to a question about employees in the *1987 Census of Governments* reported no paid employees. Because some districts function as financing agencies or indirectly provide service through contracts, the absence of paid employees, though suggestive, is neither a necessary nor a sufficient condition for determining district activity.[55] The absence of expenditures, however, may be more incriminating evidence of district inactivity. Of the 12,580 districts reporting financial data in the *1987 Census of Governments*, around one-fifth (2,675, or 21 percent) reported zero expenditures for the previous fiscal year, a proportion suggesting the potential scope of an overcounting problem.

Short of collecting new data and creating new data sets, remedies for undercounting, reclassification, and overcounting problems are limited. There are partial remedies, however. Researchers may determine and disclose their own decision rules to deal with reclassifications. For example, researchers could assume that a reclassified district was consistently dependent or independent over time. For overcounting problems researchers could establish criteria for inactivity, based perhaps on a combination of employee and expenditure characteristics, then drop from the data set any districts ruled inactive. Undercounting issues are most problematic. Beyond the time-consuming and costly collection of new data—an undertaking itself hampered by sparse and inconsistent data series—there is little recourse for undercounted districts. The most promising remedy is to focus on financial activity rather than numbers when examining district influence in a metropolitan area.

These methodological drawbacks notwithstanding, data from the Bureau of the Census are the only national-level information source on special-purpose governments. Although census of governments data sets may not contain all entities considered by states as special-purpose governments (or may contain some not so considered by states), the census data are the most appropriate, thorough, timely, and internally consistent "devil we know" for aggregate studies of special-purpose governments.

## CONCLUSION

Empirical evidence on the correlates and consequences of special-purpose governments in metropolitan areas is growing but still modest. Although scholars broadly agree that specialized governance is increasingly important to the metropolitan political economy, there is little consensus about specific causes and fiscal and policy consequences. Inconclusive findings stem in part from variations in research design, variable choices, and measurement. Yet even when researchers employ similar methodologies and yield comparable outcomes, researchers' methodological approach to special districts often suffers from flaws that cast doubt on findings. Most serious and common among these pitfalls is the use of simple count-based tallies of special-purpose governments as a measure of the importance of districts in an area. Other pitfalls include combining school districts and nonschool districts under the rubric "special districts" and overlooking the distinctiveness of the spatial scale and arrangement of districts within a metropolitan area. Most of these problems can be addressed through careful research design. Less tractable are structural problems associated with the availability and reliability of data on special-purpose governments. Despite concerns about undercounting, overcounting, and reclassifying districts over time, however, the more useful data sources for comprehensive analysis of special-purpose governments are the censuses of governments compiled every five years by the U.S. Bureau of the Census.

## CHAPTER NOTES

**1.** David L. Chicoine and Norman Walzer, *Governmental Structure and Local Public Finance* (Boston: Oelgeschlager, Gunn & Hain, 1985), p. 35.

**2.** Mitchell, "Policy Functions and Issues for Public Authorities," p. 11.

**3.** Brett W. Hawkins and Thomas R. Dye, "Metropolitan 'Fragmentation': A Research Note," in *Politics in the Metropolis*, 2nd ed., ed. Thomas R. Dye and Brett W. Hawkins (Columbus, Ohio: Charles E. Merrill, 1971), pp. 493–99.

**4.** Central-city domination was measured as the percentage of total metropolitan population living in central cities, which were defined as jurisdictions with a population of 50,000 or more. The researchers noted that when fragmentation was measured on a relative basis as the number of government units per 100,000 capita, correlations were weaker and often reversed in direction.

There was a slight tendency for smaller, younger, and more racially and socio-economically homogeneous metropolitan areas to have more total local governments per capita.

**5.** Donald J. Zeigler and Stanley D. Brunn, "Geopolitical Fragmentation and the Pattern of Growth and Need: Defining the Cleavage Between Sunbelt and Frostbelt Metropolises," in *The American Metropolitan System: Present and Future*, ed. Stanley D. Brunn and James O. Wheeler (New York: V. H. Winston and Sons, 1980), pp. 77–92.

**6.** Ibid., p. 90.

**7.** Michael A. Nelson, "Decentralization of the Subnational Public Sector: An Empirical Analysis of the Determinants of Local Government Structure in Metropolitan Areas in the U.S.," *Southern Economic Journal* 57, no. 2 (1990): 443–57. Heterogeneity of household preferences was measured by intrametropolitan variation in household incomes.

**8.** Ibid., p. 453.

**9.** Nancy Burns, *The Formation of American Local Governments* (New York: Oxford University Press, 1994).

**10.** Ibid., p. 80.

**11.** Nice, "An Intergovernmental Perspective," pp. 111–18.

**12.** Nice borrowed his measure of metropolitan/nonmetropolitan conflict from Daniel Elazar who defined it vaguely as conflict between metropolitan and nonmetropolitan residents who hold divergent views of urban conditions. See Daniel J. Elazar, *American Federalism: A View from the States* (New York: Thomas Y. Crowell, 1966), pp. 182–85. On this basis, Elazar classified twenty-two states as having high metropolitan-nonmetropolitan conflict. Closer examination reveals that these states are merely those with the highest degrees of metropolitanization.

**13.** For alternative views, see Vincent L. Marando and Mavis Mann Reeves, "States and Metropolitan Structural Reorganization," in *Subnational Politics in the 1980s: Organization, Reorganization and Economic Development*, ed. Louis A. Picard and Raphael Zariski (New York: Praeger, 1987), pp. 73–88; and Marando and Reeves, "State Responsiveness."

**14.** For a review of Leviathan studies, see Oates, "Searching for Leviathan." For a review of service delivery studies, see Vincent Ostrom, Robert Bish, and Elinor Ostrom, *Local Government in the United States* (San Francisco: ICS Press, 1988), pp. 139–87; and George A. Boyne, "Local Government Structure and Performance: Lessons from America?" *Public Administration* 70 (Autumn 1992): 333–57.

**15.** Baird and Landon, "Political Fragmentation," pp. 180–84; Andrew M. Isserman, "Interjurisdictional Spillovers, Political Fragmentation and the Level of Local Public Services: A Re-examination," *Urban Studies* 13 (1976): 1–12; Chicoine and Walzer, *Governmental Structure*, pp. 174–75; Kevin F. Forbes and Ernest M. Zampelli, "Is Leviathan a Mythical Beast?" *American Economic Review* 79, no. 3 (1989): 568–77; and Drew Dolan, "Fragmentation: Does it Drive Up the Costs of Government?" *Urban Affairs Quarterly* 26, no. 1 (1990): 28–45.

**16.** Robert F. Adams, "On the Variation in the Consumption of Public Services," *Review of Economics and Statistics* 47, no. 4 (1965): 400–405; Thomas J. DiLorenzo, "Economic Competition and Political Competition: An Empirical

Note," *Public Choice* 40 (1983): 203–9; David L. Sjoquist, "The Effect of the Number of Local Governments on Central City Expenditures," *National Tax Journal* 35, no. 1 (1982): 79–87; Mark Schneider, "Fragmentation and the Growth of Local Government," *Public Choice* 48 (1986): 255–63; and Randal W. Eberts and Timothy J. Gronberg, "Can Competition Among Local Governments Constrain Government Spending?" *Economic Review* (Federal Reserve Bank of Cleveland) 24, no. 1 (1988): 2–9.

17. Hawkins and Dye, "Metropolitan 'Fragmentation,' " pp. 498–99; Richard E. Wagner and Warren E. Weber, "Competition, Monopoly, and the Organization of Government in Metropolitan Areas," *Journal of Law and Economics* 18 (December 1975): 661–84; Jeffrey S. Zax, "Is There a Leviathan in Your Neighborhood?" *American Economic Review* 79, no. 3 (1989): 560–67; and Schneider, *The Competitive City*.

18. Gail C. A. Cook, "Toronto Metropolitan Finance: Selected Objectives and Results," in *Metropolitan Financing and Growth Management Policies*, ed. George F. Break (Madison: University of Wisconsin Press, 1978), 133–52; and Richard D. Gustely, "The Allocational and Distributional Impacts of Governmental Consolidation: The Dade County Experience," *Urban Affairs Quarterly* 12, no. 3 (1977): 349–64.

19. Erie, Kirlin, and Rabinovitz, "Can Something Be Done?" pp. 21–36; and Bruce D. Rogers and C. McCurdy Lipsey, "Metropolitan Reform: Citizen Evaluations of Performances in Nashville-Davidson County, Tennessee," *Publius* 4, no. 4 (1974): 19–34.

20. See, for example, W. E. Lyons and David Lowery, "Governmental Fragmentation Versus Consolidation: Five Public Choice Myths About How to Create Informed, Involved, And Happy Citizens," *Public Administration Review* 49, no. 6 (1989): 533–43; Chicoine and Walzer, *Governmental Structure*, pp. 204–9; James A. Christenson and Carolyn E. Sachs "The Impact of Government Size and Number of Administrative Units on the Quality of Public Services," *Administrative Science Quarterly* 25, no. 1 (1980): 89–101; Kathryn A. Foster, "Exploring the Links Between Political Structure and Metropolitan Growth," *Political Geography* 12, no. 6 (1993): 523–47; and David Rusk, *Cities Without Suburbs*, pp. 91–98.

21. Elinor Ostrom, ed., *The Delivery of Urban Services: Outcomes of Change*, Urban Affairs Annual Reviews, vol. 10 (Beverly Hills: Sage, 1976); and Ronald J. Oakerson, "Size, Function, and Structure: Jurisdictional Size Effects on Public Sector Performance," *Proceedings of the National Rural Studies Committee* (Corvallis: Western Rural Development Center, Oregon State University, 1992), pp. 84–93.

22. Ostrom, Bish, and Ostrom, *Local Government*, pp. 171–72. On police services, see Roger B. Parks, "Metropolitan Structure and Systemic Performance," in *Policy Implementation in Federal and Unitary Systems*, ed. Kenneth Hanf and Theo A. J. Toonen (Dordrecht, The Netherlands: Martinus Nijhoff, 1985), pp. 161–91. On education, see John E. Chubb and Terry M. Moe, *Politics, Markets, and America's Schools* (Washington, D.C.: Brookings Institution, 1990), 104–6.

23. On solid waste service delivery, see E. S. Savas, *The Organization and Efficiency of Solid Waste Collection* (Lexington, Mass.: Lexington Books, 1977). On

fire protection, see Philip B. Coulter, Lois MacGillivray, and William Edward Vickery, "Municipal Fire Protection Performance in Urban Areas: Environmental and Organizational Influences on Effectiveness and Productivity Measures," in *The Delivery of Urban Services: Outcomes of Change*, ed. Elinor Ostrom (Beverly Hills: Sage, 1976), pp. 231–60.

**24.** Advisory Commission on Intergovernmental Relations (ACIR), *Metropolitan Organization: Comparison of the Allegheny and St. Louis Case Studies* (Washington, D.C.: ACIR, 1993), pp. 21–22.

**25.** The summarized studies are Hawkins and Dye, "Metropolitan 'Fragmentation' "; Susan A. MacManus, "Special District Governments: A Note on Their Use as Property Tax Relief Mechanisms in the 1970s," *Journal of Politics* 43, no. 12 (1981): 1207–14; Chicoine and Walzer, *Governmental Structure*, pp. 80–81; S. Bollens, "Examining the Link"; Marando and Reeves, "State Responsiveness"; Nelson, "Decentralization of the Subnational Public Sector"; and Burns, *The Formation of American Local Governments*.

**26.** Burns, *The Formation of American Local Governments*, p. 97.

**27.** Chicoine and Walzer, *Governmental Structure*, pp. 80–81; and Nelson, "Decentralization of the Subnational Public Sector," p. 455.

**28.** Nelson, "Decentralization of the Subnational Public Sector," pp. 452, 454.

**29.** Hawkins and Dye, "Metropolitan 'Fragmentation,' " pp. 494–95.

**30.** Burns, *The Formation of American Local Governments*, pp. 81–83, 93–95.

**31.** The summarized studies are Greg Krohm, "The Production Efficiency of Single Purpose versus General Purpose Government," in *Findings of the Organizational Structure of Local Government and Cost Effectiveness* (Sacramento: California Office of Planning and Research, 1973); Minge, "Special Districts"; MacManus, "Special District Governments"; Thomas J. DiLorenzo, "The Expenditure Effects of Restricting Competition in Local Public Service Industries: The Case of Special Districts," *Public Choice* 37 (1981): 569–78; Kevin T. Deno and Stephen L. Mehay, "Institutional Constraints on Local Jurisdiction Formation," *Public Finance Quarterly* 13, no. 4 (1985): 450–63; Chicoine and Walzer, *Governmental Structure*, pp. 169–83; Michael A. Nelson, "Searching for Leviathan: Comment and Extension," *American Economic Review* 77, no. 1 (1987): 198–204; Eberts and Gronberg, "Competition Among Local Governments"; and Zax, "Leviathan in Your Neighborhood."

**32.** DiLorenzo and MacManus revealed minor exceptions to this conclusion. DiLorenzo found that institutional restrictions on special-district formation in California and Oregon led to more rapid increases in local government fire and water expenditures compared with increases in states with no restrictions on district formation (Texas, West Virginia, and Kentucky). This effect was negligible for housing and sewer service spending, however. In her study of southern metropolitan areas, MacManus found only weak support for an inverse relationship between district formation rates and the rate of increase in government expenditures and property tax revenues. DiLorenzo, "Expenditure Effects of Restricting Competition," pp. 572–74; and MacManus, "Special District Governments," p. 1212.

**33.** Chicoine and Walzer, *Governmental Structure*, pp. 172–73.

**34.** Minge, "Special Districts," pp. 701–18.

**35.** Krohm, "Production Efficiency," pp. 33–36.

**36.** Institute for Public Administration (IPA), *Special Districts and Public Authorities in Public Works Provision*, draft report (New York: IPA, 1987).

**37.** IPA, *Special Districts and Public Authorities*, pp. IV–31, IV–30.

**38.** Starting points for this literature are the comprehensive bibliographies found in Walsh, *The Public's Business*; Perrenod, *Special Districts, Special Purposes*; Gottlieb and FitzSimmons, *Thirst for Growth*; Mitchell, ed., *Public Authorities and Public Policy*; and Leigland and Lamb, *Who is to Blame?*

**39.** On transit authorities, see, for example, Glacel, *Regional Transit Authorities*; Alexander V. Zaleski, "A New Authority for Massachusetts: Best Solution for a Difficult Task?" *National Civic Review* 74, no. 11 (1985): 531–37; Robert G. Smith, "Reorganization of Regional Transportation Authorities to Maintain Urban/Suburban Constituency Balance," *Public Administration Review* 47, no. 2 (1987): 171–79; and Neil W. Hamilton and Peter R. Hamilton, *Governance of Public Enterprise: A Case Study of Urban Mass Transit* (Lexington, Mass.: Lexington Books, 1981). On alleged financial abuses, see, for example, Diana B. Henriques, *The Machinery of Greed: Public Authority Abuse and What to Do About It* (Lexington, Mass.: Lexington Books, 1986); Axelrod, *Shadow Government*; Joel Garreau, "The Shadow Governments: More than 2,000 Unelected Units Rule in New Communities," *Washington Post* 14 June 1987, sec. A, p. 1; James Carberry, "Special Districts: Forgotten Government," *Riverside (Calif.) Press-Enterprise*, weeklong series, 10–14 March 1968; and Juan Cameron, "Whose Authority?" *Atlantic Monthly* 204, no. 2 (1959): 38–42.

**40.** For example, Florida Advisory Commission on Intergovernmental Relations (ACIR), *Special District Accountability in Florida* (Tallahassee: Florida ACIR, 1987); Texas Advisory Commission on Intergovernmental Relations (ACIR), "Special District Governments in Texas," *Intergovernmental Report* 5, no. 3 (Austin: Texas ACIR, 1977); Hoffman, *Municipal Authorities in Pennsylvania*; and Colorado Division of Local Government, *Special District Service Plans* (Denver: Colorado Division of Local Government, n.d.).

**41.** Case studies with a fiscal focus are Bradley M. Braun, "Measuring the Influence of Public Authorities Through Economic Impact Analysis: The Case of Port Canaveral," *Policy Studies Journal* 18, no. 4 (1990): 1032–44; James Halteman, "Private Water Supply Firms and Municipal Authorities: A Comparative Analysis in Pennsylvania," *State and Local Government Review* 11, no. 1 (1979): 29–34; Peiser, "The Economics of Municipal Utility Districts," pp. 43–57; and ACIR, *The St. Louis Case*, esp. pp. 69–77.

**42.** ACIR, *The St. Louis Case*, p. 72.

**43.** Case studies with a policy focus are Dennis C. Muniak, "Federal Divestiture, Regional Growth, and the Political Economy of Public Authority Creation: The Emergence of the Metropolitan Washington Airports Authority," *Policy Studies Journal* 18, no. 4 (1990): 943–60; Otis W. Templer, "Adjusting to Groundwater Depletion: The Case of Texas and Lessons for the Future of the Southwest," in *Water in the Southwest*, ed. Zachary A. Smith (Albuquerque: University of New Mexico Press, 1989), pp. 247–68; Morrill, "State and Local Government Commissions," pp. 297–308; Butler and Myers, "Boomtime in Austin," pp. 447–58; Luther J. Carter, *The Florida Experience: Land and Water Policy in a Growth*

*State* (Baltimore: Johns Hopkins University Press, 1974); Perrenod, *Special Districts, Special Purposes*; and Gottlieb and FitzSimmons, *Thirst for Growth*.

**44.** Morrill, "State and Local Government Commissions," p. 299.

**45.** Carter, *The Florida Experience*, p. 267.

**46.** Perrenod, *Special Districts, Special Purposes*, pp. 102–8.

**47.** Gottlieb and FitzSimmons, *Thirst for Growth*, pp. 211–18.

**48.** U.S. Bureau of the Census, *1987 Governments File*.

**49.** U.S. Bureau of the Census, *1992 Census of Governments*, vol. 1, no. 1, p. xv.

**50.** See James Leigland, "The Census Bureau's Role in Research on Special Districts: A Critique," *Western Political Quarterly* 43, no. 2 (1990): 367–80; IPA, *Special Districts and Public Authorities*, pp. II–7–9; Walsh, *The Public's Business*, app. B; and Mitchell, "The Policy Activities of Public Authorities."

**51.** Walsh, *The Public's Business*, p. 355.

**52.** U.S. Bureau of the Census, *1982 Census of Governments*, vol. 1, no. 1, app. A, pp. A-180–87. On authorities in New York State, see Walsh and Leigland, "The Only Planning Game in Town"; and Heiman, *The Quiet Evolution*, chap. 4. On authorities in New York City, see Walsh, "Public Authorities," pp. 188–219.

**53.** For example, the Census Bureau reports 421 special districts in Georgia in 1992; the Georgia Department of Community Affairs reports 750 public authorities alone, not counting independent taxing districts. See U.S. Bureau of the Census, *1992 Census of Governments*, vol. 1, no. 1, p. 48; and Wells and Scheff, "Performance Issues for Public Authorities," p. 170. See also Stetzer, *Special Districts in Cook County*, pp. 53–54. Stetzer found that "only in a very rough manner" are special-district tallies for Cook County, Illinois, consistent with Bureau of the Census data.

**54.** U.S. Bureau of the Census, *1992 Census of Governments*, vol. 1, no. 1, p. xv.

**55.** Seymour Sacks, " 'The Census Bureau's Role in Research on Special Districts: A Critique': A Necessary Rejoinder," *Western Political Quarterly* 43, no. 2 (1990): 381–83. But see also James Leigland, "In Defense of a Preoccupation with Numbers, A Response," *Western Political Quarterly* 43, no. 2 (1990): 385–86.

# 4

# A New Conceptual Framework

The theoretical and empirical critiques in the previous two chapters demonstrate the need for improved ways of conceptualizing and analyzing special-purpose governments. I propose in this chapter such a framework, one that draws upon institutional choice theory as a useful basis for understanding specialized governance.

According to institutional choice theory, changes in jurisdictional arrangements occur when institutional innovators—private citizens, local government officials, state legislators, special interest groups, and others—see opportunities to realize profit from such changes. Profit opportunities arise from outside catalysts, such as population growth, new patterns of income distribution, and technological advancements, that alter the demand for or supply of goods and services. Institutional changes are of two types: *changes enabled under existing institutional rules*, such as zoning adjustments, annexations, formation of special districts, contracting arrangements, and service-sharing agreements; and *changes in the institutional environment itself*, that is, changes in the rules of the game that regulate new government formation or boundary adjustments.

The conceptual framework presented in this chapter adapts institutional choice theory to the question of why special-purpose governments are increasingly popular service alternatives. The framework highlights four key notions: first, that the metropolitan area contains a variety of interest groups each with different service delivery goals; second, that special-purpose governments possess distinct attributes that give them a comparative advantage relative to general-purpose governments in helping interest groups realize their goals; third, that legal, institutional, and political parameters set the limits within which specialized governance operates; and fourth, that different geographic and financial subtypes of special districts are distinct institutional choices.

This fourth notion is of particular importance. As I indicated in chapters 2 and 3, much of the theoretical controversy and empirical misconception surrounding special districts stem from treating special

90

districts as a monolithic local government type with a singular motivation and outcome. By systematically differentiating the causes and consequences of district subtypes, the conceptual framework developed here yields a more accurate portrait of specialized governance.

This chapter has two sections. In the first and longest I consider four choices leading to specialized service delivery. In the second section I authenticate the institutional choice process by introducing legal, institutional, and political factors that shape institutional outcomes.

## PRELUDE TO FOUR INSTITUTIONAL CHOICES

Given the numerous institutional options available, why do metropolitan interest groups choose special-purpose governments for service provision? What makes special districts so special?

One way to answer these questions is to consider the typical decision path faced by metropolitan interest groups, as shown in figure 4–1. The decision path starts with a demonstrated service need, then continues through four increasingly specific choices about how to satisfy that need. Shown in the hatched boxes are three interest groups—metropolitan residents, local government officials, and private developers—most commonly faced with service needs and, hence, institutional choices. The arrows leading to boxed choices mark the path culminating in special-purpose governance. Paths not taken are truncated for simplicity in the figure.

To reach the specialized government outcome, interest groups must make three separate decisions: first, to provide the service using public as opposed to private or nonprofit institutions; second, to provide the service at the local as opposed to the state or federal level; and third, to provide the service using special-purpose as opposed to general-purpose government. Having settled on this outcome, metropolitan interest groups then make a fourth decision about the specific geographic and financial subtype of special district to use for service delivery. Although the decision path represents these choices linearly, in practice they are often made simultaneously.

I initially make two simplifying assumptions about institutional choices. The first is that each of the three metropolitan interest groups highlighted in the decision tree has unified service objectives. The second assumption is that the legal environment permits all possible institutional options for service provision. Later in the chapter I relax the second assumption and consider the effects of legal, institutional, and political constraints or incentives on institutional choices.

The following journey along the decision path dwells relatively briefly on the first two institutional choices, then spends more time on

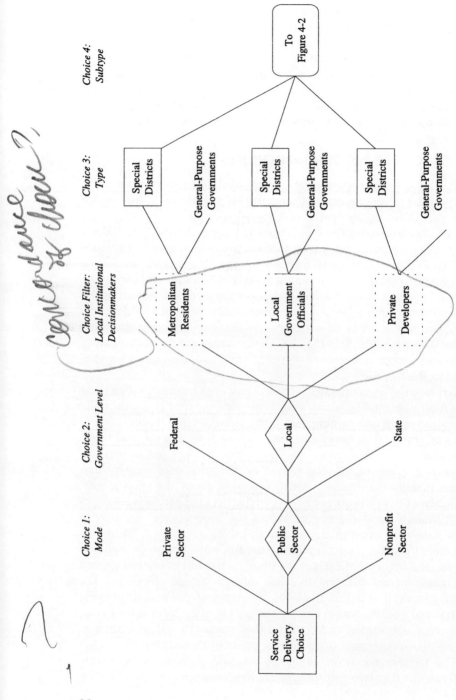

**Figure 4-1** Institutional Choice Decision Tree. The Path to Special-District Service Delivery

the last two, which are most directly concerned with the choice for specialized governance.

## CHOICE 1: WHICH SERVICE MODE?[1]

Different service modes, private, public and nonprofit, have different attributes that make them more or less suited to achieving service-delivery goals.

By virtue of their right to reap the profits of their business acumen and labors, private institutions have the greatest incentives to deliver services efficiently, that is, to provide the type and quality of goods consumers demand at the lowest possible cost. At the same time, the private sector's pursuit of profits has service-delivery repercussions many consider undesirable. These repercussions include dissuading private firms from undertaking unprofitable though socially desirable activities, preventing consumers without sufficient funds from obtaining needed services, and, by taking advantage of incomplete information in the private goods marketplace, inducing firms to substitute lesser quality for higher quality goods without adjusting prices accordingly.

By contrast, because their officials and employees may not collect profits, nonprofit agencies have less incentive to shun unprofitable endeavors or take advantage of customers. The nonprofit sector's access to tax-free revenues frees agencies to offer socially desirable or non-priceable goods that market mechanisms will not provide. The nonprofit sector's exemption from equal-access principles permits it to complement local government by providing services in response to the preferences of donors. By the same token, the absence of a profit motive means nonprofit entities have less incentive to produce services efficiently, thus leading to perceived or actual financial negligence.[2] Because nonprofit institutions depend upon funding from persons or agencies with particular interests, there is no guarantee nonprofits will raise sufficient revenues to meet pressing service needs. Moreover, there is little besides fear of losing donors to prevent a nonprofit from investing in activities irrelevant to their cause or contrary to a broader public interest.

Like nonprofits, public sector institutions lack the profit incentive that would steer them away from financially unpromising, even if socially desirable, services. The public sector also enjoys exemption from property taxes, the right to market tax-free investments to private individuals or corporations, and, typically, the power to levy taxes. Because it has the legal responsibility to ensure equal access to public services, the public sector guarantees service provision to all residents and fosters standardized service and tax policies throughout a jurisdiction. Its reliance on and commitment to democratic governance in the form of public hearings, voting, and lobbying promotes greater responsiveness and accountability to citizens than commonly demanded of the private or nonprofit sectors. The downside of these attributes is threefold. First, without a profit incentive the public sector has little incentive (other than reelection in the case of elected officials) to produce goods and services most efficiently and effectively. Second, equal access constraints mean that the public sector has a legal obligation to provide a service to all if it provides it to one, which often means higher service costs and lower service quality. Third, dependence on the political process may favorably incline the public sector toward the demands of well-organized relative to poorly organized groups, regardless of need.[3]

In light of these differences, why might metropolitan interest groups turn to public sector institutions, the first necessary step to special-district service delivery? The answer rests in the shortcomings of private and nonprofit sectors for providing collective goods and services. Compared to the private sector, the public sector can address market failures. Market failures arise in several instances, notably when the goods demanded are public goods that defy market pricing; a good or service generates spillover effects, which are not taken into account when determining prices and quantities produced; information about the buying and selling of items is hidden, incredible, inaccurate, or costly to obtain; and a good exhibits increasing returns to scale, making it impossible to achieve the market efficiency criterion of setting price equal to marginal cost.[4] Compared to the nonprofit sector, the public sector has two equity-based advantages. First, because nonprofits have no obligation to provide services evenly across a population, only a public sector can guarantee full coverage of services. Second, because nonprofits have allegiance to their donors rather than to the public at large, they are unable to provide and pay for the merit goods that reflect society's moral or philosophical values.[5]

## CHOICE 2: WHICH SERVICE LEVEL?[6]

Once metropolitan interest groups decide to provide a service using public sector institutions, they face the subsequent choice of which government level—federal, state, or local—should take responsibility for delivering the service. This question can be reformulated as one of centralized (federal or state) versus decentralized (local) service delivery.

Analysts of fiscal federalism identify three major functions for government: achieving macroeconomic stabilization, altering the distribution of society's resources to attain a socially desirable outcome, and allocating resources efficiently under conditions of market failure. There is widespread consensus that because of the openness of the economy, citizen mobility, national imperatives, and the inability of local jurisdictions to create money, the first two functions, macroeconomic stabilization and redistribution, should be responsibilities of central governments. The third function, efficient resource allocation, is most amenable to decentralized service delivery, although not all services are most efficiently produced at local levels.

The resource allocation function is of greatest interest for students of special-purpose governments. Analysts widely agree that centralized resource allocation is appropriate for national-level public goods, such as national defense and foreign policy, and state-level public goods, such as state highways or economic development programs, which benefit all affected residents or are appropriately provided at uniform quality throughout the nation or state. Goods or services meeting one or more of four conditions are appropriately provided at decentralized levels. These conditions are (1) when the good or service is a local-level public good, the costs and benefits of which are more or less contained within a defined geographic area, (2) when provision of the good or service at nonuniform levels does not jeopardize the public health, safety, or welfare, (3) when decentralized provision would facilitate resident participation in and scrutiny of local government, and (4) when decentralized provision would increase information, thereby enabling consumers to make more efficient consumption decisions.

As one might imagine, these conditions qualify a wide range of goods and services for decentralized provision. A subsequent challenge is determining the optimal geographic scale *within* the metropolitan context, that is, whether a good or service is best provided at the regional, county, municipal, or submunicipal scale. Analysts agree that there is no single optimum but rather a range of acceptable scales subject to complex tradeoffs.[7] The key tradeoff is between the properties of a good (its economies of scale, spillover effects, and production requirements) and the properties of the metropolitan area and its residents (geographic obstacles to service delivery, settlement patterns, local government arrangements, and resident preferences for specific services). I revisit these tradeoffs in the context of special districts under choice 4.

## CHOICE 3: WHICH SERVICE TYPE?

Assume now that metropolitan interest groups have chosen to deliver services using local-level public institutions. The next institutional choice is the one central to this study: whether services are provided by general-purpose or special-purpose governments.

There are virtually no services that cannot be provided by either general- or special-purpose entities. In practice, of course, certain services, notably police protection and public assistance, are nearly always the responsibility of general-purpose governments. There is no institutional reason, however, why these services could not be part of the special district portfolio. In fact, the states of Connecticut, California, and New York have enabled police protection districts, and numerous states rely on special-purpose governments for social service tasks, including health and housing.[8]

Understanding the institutional choice between special-purpose and general-purpose governments requires addressing two questions: (1) what attributes distinguish special- and general-purpose governments from one another?; and (2) how do these distinctive attributes facilitate or impair metropolitan interest groups from realizing their service delivery goals?

## Distinctive Attributes of Special-Purpose Governments

General- and special-purpose governments share numerous attributes related to public powers, revenue raising, and administration. They are not alike, however, both because they have some uncommon attributes and because their common attributes are often constrained to different degrees by state government.

Six of these distinctions are particularly significant for institutional choice deliberations. These are (1) functional specialization, (2) geographic flexibility, (3) political visibility, (4) financial flexibility, (5) administrative flexibility, and (6) planning and land use control. It is important to note that there is nothing inherently positive or negative about these attributes. As we shall see, whether they are considered institutional strengths or limitations depends on the eye of the interest group beholder.

### 1. Functional Specialization

The most fundamental, indeed definitional, difference between special-purpose and general-purpose governments is their degree of functional specialization. As their names imply, a general-purpose government provides a range of public services, whereas a special district performs a single or limited specified services.[9]

Functional specialization has four potential implications that are relevant to institutional choices. First, functional specialization may hamper coordination of the planning, financing, and delivery of services in metropolitan areas.[10] General-purpose governments have the ability to coordinate capital investment and social programming. They may also "rob Peter to pay Paul" when revised resident priorities, state mandates, new labor contracts, or political events require a redirection of funds from one department budget to another. By contrast, functionally specialized governments have limited leeway to coordinate services or adjust budgets and programs in response to outside imperatives.

Second and on the other hand, functional specialization may safeguard programs from capricious or merely convenient spending adjustments. To the extent that an agency controls its budget and agenda, it controls its fiscal and political well-being. Functional specialization may protect politically vulnerable programs the constituents of which lack the influence or organization necessary to hold their own at budget time. By the same token, specialization might also serve to protect the pet programs of powerful special interest lobbies.

Third, functional specialization, and by extension special-purpose governments, stymies full-line forcing, the practice whereby goods and services are offered as a single package rather than as individual offerings.[11] Full-line forcing has mixed effects. On the one hand, it means that special-purpose governments may be better able to achieve efficiency by more finely tailoring service provision to consumer preferences. On the other hand, specialized governments may threaten the viability of popular or needed services that depend on the budgetary refuge provided by service bundling.

Fourth, functional specialization offers a legal, inexpensive, and easily administered means for meeting minimalist or specialized service demands. Unincorporated communities wishing to provide (and pay for) less than a full menu of general-purpose government services may achieve that goal through special-purpose governments. Districts can also meet the needs of incorporated neighborhoods that seek a level of services, for example garbage collection and public safety, over and above the level provided areawide.[12] By the same token, functionally specialized districts also provide a legal escape from collective funding of specific services, possibly frustrating goals for redistribution.

## 2. Geographic Flexibility

The second key distinction is that general-purpose governments are geographically rigid while special-purpose governments are geographically adaptable. The basis for this distinction is legal: special districts may overlap one another and general-purpose governments, whereas general-purpose governments of the same type must be geographically exclusive.

The two principal implications of geographic flexibility are that it facilitates efficiency and enables redistribution. Geographically flexible units can more readily realize economies of scale or avoid diseconomies of scale. They are also more able to internalize spillovers, which increases fiscal equivalence, the condition whereby those who receive a service pay for it, and those who pay for a service receive it. By contrast, geographically rigid units cannot readily adjust boundaries to accommodate changes in service demand, technology, and new development patterns.[13]

### 3. Political Visibility

A third distinction between general and special-purpose governments is their degree of political visibility. General-purpose governments tend to be highly visible primarily because they play many civic roles and their officials are elected. Because specialized governments have limited purposes and their officials are often appointed, special-purpose governments have relatively low political visibility. Meeting practices provide an instructive example. General-purpose government meetings are relatively regular, frequent, publicized, and reported in the media. By comparison, special district meetings are irregular, infrequent, poorly publicized, and sporadically covered.[14]

Political visibility has mixed implications for service delivery. On the one hand, political visibility is a handmaiden to accountability and responsiveness. To the extent that special-purpose governments are hidden from the public eye, they may be less responsive than are general-purpose governments to resident preferences. On the other hand, high visibility, together with accountability and responsiveness, are not necessarily desirable. Political visibility is a staple of project delay, service compromise, and political stalemate. A general-purpose government committed to satisfying competing demands may suffer political impasse and institutional paralysis to the detriment of public welfare. Moreover, responsiveness is no guarantee of fairness. A government is more likely to respond to organized and powerful special interest groups than to comparatively disorganized and politically weak consumer groups, regardless of the worthiness of purpose.[15] The political insulation of special-purpose districts is thus both bane and blessing. Isolation provides an opportunity to implement programs without political derailment, but also provides a lightning rod for criticism from politicians and a skeptical public accustomed to full disclosure in public agencies.[16]

### 4. Financial Flexibility

General- and special-purpose governments are subject to state-imposed limitations on borrowing, taxing, and spending, as well as formal requirements for accounting, budgeting, and financial reporting. What distinguishes the two government types is the severity of these limitations. Special-purpose governments are generally subject to fewer and less severe fiscal constraints.[17]

Financial restrictiveness has three important implications for service delivery. First, governments faced with ceilings on revenue raising may fall short of meeting citizen demands for services. Combined with the additional mandate to balance annual budgets, as well as grim fiscal trends in rising input costs and declining government aid, most general-purpose governments are under chronic fiscal stress and unable to satisfy local demands for service. By comparison, special-purpose governments may face a more sanguine fiscal picture, in great part because of the milder restrictions on revenue raising.

The second implication has the opposite effect. State limitations presumably reflect taxpayer support for reining in what citizens view as unnecessary government spending. In that regard, the unrestricted special district provides a means for circumventing citizen preferences on public sector spending. Of particular consequence is districts' exemption from voter approval of revenue bond issues, a financial freedom that may seriously undermine the fiscal preferences of citizens.[18]

Third, relatively weak constraints on the revenue-raising capacity of taxing districts represent a legal means to "double dip" from the existing tax base. A general-purpose government brushing up against its tax or borrowing ceiling can form a special-district government to levy hidden taxes in their stead. The result is more tax revenue for government services, an outcome undoubtedly contrary to the antitax preferences that spawned tax ceilings in the first place.

### 5. Administrative Flexibility

General- and special-purpose governments are subject to regulations governing personnel, worker safety, environmental protection, and administrative operations. As with financial constraints, however, administrative flexibility tends to be greater for special-purpose governments. Special districts, notably public authorities, are often exempt from civil service regulations, rules for competitive bidding and procurement, financial reporting procedures, and local building codes.[19]

There are two conflicting implications of administrative constraints. On the one hand, constraints may impede agency responsiveness, performance, innovation, and morale.[20] To the extent special districts are exempt from such constraints they may suffer less from the real and perceived maladies of regulated bureaucracies. Agencies with wide administrative discretion may get the job done more responsively and rapidly than will agencies whose administrative hands are tied.[21]

On the other hand, administrative constraints are designed to enhance government accountability and ensure standardized responses to public requests. In this sense, an administratively constrained general-purpose government may be a better protector of the public trust than is a relatively unconstrained special-purpose agency.[22]

### 6. Planning and Land Use Control

The final key distinction is the greater powers of general-purpose governments with respect to planning and land use control. General-purpose governments possess police powers and eminent domain powers. Although special districts usually possess eminent domain powers, their police powers are generally limited and do not include the power to zone land or enact subdivision or other land use regulations.

The primary implication of land use controls is the power they grant an agency to manage physical and social environments. Although special-purpose governments that provide development-oriented services such as water, sewer, and roads make critical decisions affecting the location and pace of growth, they do not determine the underlying policies of planning and development.[23] By contrast, general-purpose governments can both plan for and provide development-oriented (and development-responsive) services, thereby directly controlling land use policies and outcomes.

## Why Special Districts Get the Nod

The varying strengths and limitations of special- versus general-purpose governments make it clear that neither institutional choice is wholly superior to the other in terms of service delivery. That leaves the question of why special-purpose governments might get the nod as service provider. The answer originates in the different service objectives and preferences of the three metropolitan interest groups most involved in institutional choices: metropolitan residents, local government officials, and private developers. Understanding the rise of special-purpose governance requires understanding why these three interest groups believe special districts may be superior to general-purpose governments for achieving service delivery goals.

### Metropolitan Residents[24]

Metropolitan residents are the buyers and consumers of public services. As such, their foremost service-delivery goal is efficient and responsive service provision. Residents also have a collective preference for the appropriate level of service standardization, that is, the level of intrametropolitan redistribution achieved through tax revenue or service transfers. The challenge for metropolitan residents is how to make the tradeoff among the often conflicting goals of efficiency, equity, and responsiveness in service delivery.[25] Different institutions tend to be better suited to accomplish one or another goal. Thus, support for a local-government alternative depends on how residents prioritize their competing goals and which institutions are most likely to achieve these goals.

Under what conditions might special-purpose government appeal to metropolitan residents? Clues lie in the distinct attributes of special-purpose versus general-purpose governments. In districts' favor are their geographic flexibility and functional specialization, which give them greater capacity to enhance efficiency through more closely tailored service packages. On the debit side, specialized governance asks residents to sacrifice political visibility, accountability, and responsiveness. Somewhat ambiguous is whether metropolitan residents view districts' administrative and financial flexibility as strengths or liabilities. Assuming that flexibility favors efficiency over equity, then residents who endorse such a priority will prefer special-purpose governments over their general-purpose counterparts. Whether residents welcome or lament districts' lack of planning powers is also ambiguous. Those who favor the current development policies of the general-purpose government or managed growth in general will likely approve of strong constraints on special-purpose planning powers. Those who prefer a faster pace of growth or are critical of current policies may support greater planning latitude for special-purpose agencies.

Districts thus have mixed appeal for metropolitan residents. A shorthand rule of thumb for institutional choice can be summarized as: *if residents favor districts' economic advantages more than they reject the associated political sacrifices, they will choose special districts over general-purpose governments and vice versa.*

### Local Government Officials[26]

The most basic goal of local government officials is to get reelected. To do so, local government officials must heed several often competing imperatives: maintain the jurisdiction's fiscal health, preserve its credit in the eyes of financiers and investors, satisfy resident needs, and broker interest group conflicts that may threaten social order and fiscal responsibility.[27] In practical terms, local officials must protect property values, enhance the tax base, foster economic growth, construct and maintain facilities to attract and retain investors, provide services and goods to meet diverse resident preferences, and generally uphold the community quality of life.[28] Because the fortunes of local government employees also depend on healthy local economies and satisfied residents, one could also assume that government employees share the service-delivery goals of local officials.[29]

If a local government currently provides services in-house, the choice to use special-purpose governments represents an unequivocal loss of control over service delivery. There would have to be compelling reasons for local officials to willingly relinquish such control. Do such reasons exist?

The combination of district attributes and local government constraints indeed provides sufficient reasons for local officials to surrender service control to independent special districts. Districts' geographic flexibility and functional specialization foster service efficiencies in ways that general-purpose governments, by virtue of boundary rigidities and equal-access constraints, cannot match. Local officials might also yield service responsibility to avoid an anticipated subpar service performance and its attendant electoral and economic development costs. Officials could partially offset the loss of service control by forming a new district with boundaries coterminous with the underlying jurisdiction, of course. In that way, local officials might dampen loss of policy control through judicious district board appointments and leverage over initial budgets.

Local government officials might also find districts' financial flexibility useful for maintaining service quality, thereby pleasing voters and investors. To officials, a clear asset of special-purpose governments is that they provide a means for circumventing constraints on local taxing and borrowing. In addition, there may be fiscal advantages to sloughing off costly services to financially powerful districts. At the same time, officials must balance these advantages against the potential for districts to crowd out general-purpose governments in competition for scarce private investment in public bonds. To the extent districts block general-purpose governments from private funding—and a number of analysts believe they do—reliance on special districts would exacerbate local fiscal stress to the political dismay of local officials.[30]

Finally, districts' low visibility presents local government officials with unmistakable opportunities for political gain. By transferring service responsibility to districts, local officials may evade politically perilous decisions to raise taxes or incur large amounts of debt. In a similar vein, local officials can dispose of politically difficult decisions about growth by consigning control over development-oriented services to nominally neutral, politically insulated authorities. This enables local officials to simultaneously keep taxes in line, indulge private investors' progrowth interests, and disclaim responsibility for unpopular development projects. Low visibility also enhances districts' potential as abundant sources of political patronage posts, which elected officials may find appealing despite the additional scrutiny it brings.[31]

From the perspective of local government officials, then, each of districts' distinctive features—functional specialization; low political visibility; geographic, administrative, and financial flexibility; and lack of land use controls—may be viewed as service-delivery assets. Districts' most serious debits are their expropriation of officials' control over services and their receipt of private market funds that might otherwise flow to general-purpose governments. For local government officials, the institutional choice rule of thumb is clear-cut, though still qualified: *choose special-purpose governments for service delivery unless their fiscal and coordinative drawbacks outweigh clear economic and political benefits.*

### Private Developers[32]

Private developers' overriding service-delivery goal is to maximize profits through development. As both consumers and producers of public services, developers attempt to attain high profits by using high-quality, low-cost public services and producing cost-effective services for sale. Public sector advantages particularly sought by developers are publicly funded infrastructure networks, speedy development approvals, a regulatory environment conducive to growth, and public assistance in obtaining low-cost land, labor, and capital for production.

Why might developers look to special- rather than general-purpose governments for service delivery? The answer is found in the recognition that nearly every attribute that distinguishes special districts from general-purpose governments facilitates development. Low political visibility endows districts with far greater political latitude than general-purpose governments to approve unpopular development projects. Limited public access and the prevalence of appointed rather than elected board members also works to the advantage of developers who seek to influence development by serving as or having close relations with district board members.[33] Further facilitating development are administrative freedoms that, because they hinder the mobilization of public opposition that might downsize, delay, or halt controversial projects, ultimately expedite development. Functional specialization and geographic flexibility permit developers to gerrymander district boundaries such that the district has ample support within its borders. In addition, developer-created districts tend—at least initially—to be wholly compliant to developer preferences inasmuch as developers often handpick members of the original district board.[34] Finally, districts' financial reach, notably their ability to secure large sums of up-front capital, represents a considerable savings for developers who would otherwise have to pay preconstruction costs out-of-pocket.

To developers, districts' low political visibility, wide administrative discretion, financial reach, geographic flexibility, and functional specialization are clear assets for achieving service-delivery goals. Districts' only serious debit is their limited ability to control the development process. The institutional choice guideline for developers is the strongest of all three interest groups: *choose special-district service delivery routinely, except when direct control over land use is essential to profits or when general-purpose governments are especially friendly to development.*

## CHOICE 4: WHICH DISTRICT SUBTYPE?

If the rubric "special districts" comprised a relatively homogenous set of local governments, the choice just considered would complete the process of institutional choice for special-purpose governments. Districts are not a monolithic government type, however. They come in dozens of varieties, sporting different sizes, functions, governing board characteristics, forms of financing, and powers.

The final institutional choice is the appropriate district subtype, a decision that has two major dimensions, geographic scope and mode of financing.[35] Should the district be regional, coterminous with municipal boundaries, or more finely tailored to subcounty service areas? Should district services be financed collectively using revenues from property taxes or paid for out-of-pocket through user fees? The geographic scope and form of financing of specialized governments are important because they signal different service goals and are likely associated with different service outcomes.

The interaction of geographic and financial attributes is shown in the matrix in figure 4–2. Before examining geographic and financing combinations found in individual cells, I consider first the service motivations and implications of geographic and financial choices (column and row) separately.

### Geographic Scope

Each of the three geographic subtypes of districts—regional, municipally coterminous (hereafter coterminous), and subcounty, nonmunicipally coterminous (hereafter subcounty)—has different purposes and potential impacts.

Districts formed at the county level or higher *regionalize* service delivery. Goals of regionalization include greater equity, accomplished through service standardization, and greater efficiency, accomplished by capturing economies of scale and internalizing spillovers. Certain services, namely those subject to large economies of scale, strong spillovers, and relatively narrow ranges of consumer preferences, are considered particularly appropriate for regional service delivery. These tend to be system maintenance services, such as sewer, utilities, transit, and airports, which are capital-intensive, have high fixed costs, and are

Geographic Scope

| | Regionwide "Regionalizing" | Coterminous with municipality "Capitalizing" | Subcounty "Particularizing" |
|---|---|---|---|
| **Taxing** "Collectivizing" | I. Regionalizing-Collectivizing<br><br>Ex: Metropolitan (St. Louis) Zoological Park & Museum District | III. Capitalizing-Collectivizing<br><br>Ex: Winnetka (Ill.) Public Library District | V. Particularizing-Collectivizing<br><br>Ex: Harris Co. (Tex.) Municipal Utilities District #145 |
| **Nontaxing** "Privatizing" | II. Regionalizing-Privatizing<br><br>Ex: Metropolitan Washington (D.C.) Airports Authority | IV. Capitalizing-Privatizing<br><br>Ex: Portland (Oreg.) Housing Authority | VI. Particularizing-Privatizing<br><br>Ex: Foothill (Calif.) Municipal Water District |

Financing Mode

**Figure 4-2** Special-District Subtypes

105

subject to a narrow range of consumer preferences.[36] Geopolitical theory notwithstanding, any service can be regionalized in the interests of equity and service equalization. In this regard, lifestyle services, such as primary education, libraries, and police patrols, which are typically provided at subcounty levels due to small economies of scale, weak spillovers, and relatively intense and broad consumer preferences, are sometimes provided at a regional scale.[37]

Districts formed with boundaries coincident with an underlying municipal jurisdiction slight regional efficiency and equity goals in favor of *capitalizing* objectives. Municipal officials engage in fiscal capitalizing when they form districts to raise additional revenues from a municipal tax base or private markets. Officials engage in political capitalizing when they form districts to "depoliticize" service delivery or slough off responsibility for services that entail difficult political choices.

Despite geopolitical theories about optimal service scales, the wide range of situations that entail capitalizing motivations yield a wide functional range of coterminous districts. For example, although theory suggests that system maintenance services are more efficiently provided at regional levels, for political and fiscal reasons municipal officials may prefer coterminous districts, which are more conducive to local control. Political and fiscal expediency may also explain why municipal officials would form a special-purpose government to produce lifestyle services.

Neither regionalization nor capitalization motives account for subcounty districts. Rather, subcounty districts, which tend to be relatively small and irregularly sized, are intended to *particularize* services to meet specialized needs. Particularizing districts, which include submunicipal assessment districts and districts in unincorporated areas, seek efficiency through greater responsiveness to relatively homogeneous demands for services within narrowly drawn service-area boundaries. Some particularizing districts also have capitalizing objectives. Foremost among these are the subdivision-sized, developer-created districts formed to take advantage of low political visibility and easy access to up-front development capital.

Given the diversity of preferences within a metropolitan area and the variety of situations amenable to particularizing behavior, it is not surprising that districts of all functions are found at the subcounty scale. Recognition of particularizing goals is necessary to explain why, for example, sewer or water districts, which tend to reach their most efficient levels at a regional scale, are often provided at small, presumably inefficient scales.

## Financing Mode

Like districts of different geographic scope, the two financial subtypes of districts—property-taxing (hereafter taxing) and non–property-taxing (hereafter nontaxing)—have different motivations and potential service-delivery outcomes.

Taxing districts *collectivize* the costs of service delivery. Collectivizing districts spread service costs across all property owners within district boundaries rather than assess individual users for services actually consumed. Collective tax financing inevitably results in redistribution of costs from nonresidents to residents, service users to nonusers, and tax-exempt organizations to taxpaying ones. Collective financing is essential for indivisible or nonchargeable services, such as police protection and public health, although it can be used for a wide range of services.

The service outcomes of collectivized financing are mixed. Most analysts agree that property tax funding sacrifices fiscal equity by separating those who pay from those who benefit. Analysts further agree that tax financing promotes communal responsibility for important social services and likely narrows service disparities.[38]

By contrast, nontaxing districts *privatize* the costs of service delivery. By funding services through revenues from user fees, tolls, rents, and other individualized charges, nontaxing districts rely on private consumers rather than the general public for support. Only services that are divisible and chargeable, such as water, sewer, and utilities, are candidates for user-based financing.

The service outcomes of privatized financing are mixed. Analysts generally agree that privatized financing enhances fiscal equity, encourages the conservation of resources by exposing customers to the actual costs of service provision, and eliminates cross-subsidization of service delivery, all of which increases efficiency.[39] User fee financing raises equity objections on the grounds that lower-income patrons may be unable to purchase needed services, however. This objection has carried less weight in recent years with the adoption of administrative provisions that protect needy residents without sacrificing the efficiency advantages of privatized financing.[40]

## Geographic and Financing Combinations

With these geographic and financial considerations in mind, it is possible to examine the service delivery implications of the six district subtypes identified in figure 4–2.

### I. Regionalizing-Collectivizing Districts.

The regionwide, taxing districts in cell I are the most regionally redistributive of the six subtypes. These districts are typically formed by joint agreement of local (and sometimes state) officials to spread the costs across all metropolitan taxpayers of widely enjoyed or socially beneficial services. In this category are districts providing services with regional benefits such as zoos, convention centers, libraries, parks, and environmental protection. The Metropolitan (St. Louis) Zoological Park and Museum District provides a specific example.

### II. Regionalizing-Privatizing Districts.

When most metropolitan residents hear "special districts" they probably think of the regional public authorities found in cell II. Districts in this category collect revenues from users of district services— bus riders, bridge crossers, tunnel users, highway riders, housing leasers, water consumers, and so forth—regardless of metropolitan residency status. Like their cell I cousins, many of these authorities form by joint agreement of local and state officials to capture economies of scale. Instead of spreading costs across all metropolitan residents, however, cell II districts seek fiscal equity by ensuring that service users rather than nonusers foot the bill. The Metropolitan Washington (D.C.) Airports Authority falls into this category, as do many metropolitan transit, airport, sewer, and utilities authorities that charge individual users tolls, fees, and rents for actual consumption of services.

### III. Capitalizing-Collectivizing Districts.

The special-purpose governments in cell III are taxing, coterminous districts. The large majority are formed by municipal officials to capitalize on districts' administrative flexibility, financial powers, and low political visibility. Cell III governments rely on collective revenues either because the service is nondivisible or has important public benefits. Many fire, recreation, and health and hospital districts fall into this category. The Winnetka (Illinois) Public Library District provides a specific example.

### IV. Capitalizing-Privatizing Districts.

Cell IV contains coterminous, nontaxing districts. Like their cell III counterparts most of these are formed by municipal officials seeking to circumvent debt limitations or slough off fiscally or politically demanding services. Unlike cell III governments, however, capitalizing-privatizing districts rely on revenues from individual consumers, thereby achieving fiscal equity and evading cross-subsidization of services by the general taxpayer. Municipal housing authorities, such as the Portland (Oregon) Housing Authority, are the most common type, of cell IV district. Also in this category are most municipal water, sewer, and utilities districts.

### V. Particularizing-Collectivizing Districts.

Cell V contains special-purpose governments with the seemingly impossible purpose of particularizing and collectivizing service delivery. In actuality, geographically particularized, financially collectivized districts are quite common and less paradoxical than they may seem at first glance. Cell V districts appeal to all three metropolitan interests: local government officials wishing to meet specialized service demands in unincorporated or submunicipal areas, metropolitan residents seeking a finely tailored package of services, and developers wishing to construct infrastructure for subdivision projects. The lion's share of these districts are of two types, fire protection districts serving unincorporated communities and developer-sponsored water, sewer, and utilities districts. An example is the Harris County (Texas) Municipal Utilities District #145, one of hundreds of similar districts in the Houston Metropolitan Area.

### VI. Particularizing-Privatizing Districts.

Cell VI governments are the least redistributive and most fiscally equitable subtype in the matrix. By raising revenues from and providing services to private individuals within delimited subcounty service areas, cell VI districts most closely approximate the private marketplace for goods and services. Like those in cell V, cell VI governments appeal to local officials, developers, and residents of unincorporated communities or submunicipal neighborhoods who seek to accommodate particular service preferences. Among the user-fee-based districts in this cell are subcounty sewer, water, natural resources, and road districts. An example is the Foothill (California) Municipal Water District, which provides water service to a partly incorporated, partly unincorporated service area in southern California.

The importance of recognizing different district subtypes stems from their logically different purposes and outcomes. Consider the possible reasons for and effects of forming districts of different subtypes. A regionwide, toll-financed highway authority and a subdivision-sized, tax-financed road district, for example, are different institutional species, even though both provide road services. In the former case, road users, whether metropolitan residents or nonresidents, pay for and receive services based on their actual use of the toll road. In the latter case, property owners within the district agree to share collectively in the funding and receipt of road services, regardless of how much any single person uses area roads. The reasons why a community might form one rather than the other type of road district differ based on demographics, demand for roads, local political circumstances, and preferences for redistribution or fiscal equity. With respect to consequences, a large, toll-financed authority more readily internalizes spillover effects, coordinates routes, and realizes economies of scale in road services than does a small, collectivized district. The subdivision-sized district also sacrifices a close match between road users and road payers, a gap overcome by toll road financing in the larger district.

In a similar vein, differences emerge when comparing motivations for other district subtypes. Theoretical and empirical understanding of district causes and consequences is jeopardized when analysts neglect relevant differences in district subtypes.

## ADDING COMPLEXITY AND REALISM

Until now the conceptual framework has assumed that no factors limit the initiation or realization of institutional choices. In reality, of course, there are numerous parameters that encourage, discourage, or prevent alterations in institutional arrangements or the rules governing those arrangements. Although these parameters are rarely irrevocable—even state or federal constitutions can be revised to change the rules of the game—as a practical matter they influence institutional choices. Despite the most energetic efforts of metropolitan interest groups to realize their service goals, legal, institutional, and political parameters encourage or discourage specific institutional options.

### Legal Parameters

State constitutions and statutes establish the ground rules for special-district formation and use. Most fundamental is state enabling legislation, which specifies the types and powers of particular districts permitted in a state. No matter how desirable or worthy a specialized government may be for service delivery, if it is not enabled by state law it is not a viable institutional option.

Even when state enabling legislation exists, specific provisions, such as who has the right to initiate a district, the need for voter referenda, and geographic criteria, may limit or encourage certain institutional choices. For example, Arizona statutes permit formation of general improvement districts (GIDs) to provide sewer, water, pest abatement, lighting, road surfacing, cable TV, and other services to unincorporated communities.[41] GIDs have limits, however, among

*Example — rw AZ only*

*good example*

them a four-thousand-acre minimum service area. Regardless of a settlement's need for, say, sewer services, if the settlement encompasses three thousand acres, it lacks legal standing to form a GID. Unless property owners within the area can convince neighboring owners of at least one thousand total acres to join the proposed district, sewer advocates will have to make an alternative institutional choice to obtain sewer services. One option in Arizona is formation of a sanitary district, an entity that has a land area minimum of only 160 acres. Reinforcing the prominence of legal parameters is the further stipulation of Arizona law that only property owners, not residents or elected officials, have standing to initiate formation of either GIDs or sanitary districts.

Legal parameters affecting general-purpose governments also influence the use of special-purpose governments. Such constraints include state-imposed limitations on municipal or county formation, revenue raising, boundary changes, or service provision. The New York State Constitution, for example, prohibits counties, cities, towns, villages, school districts, and even the state itself from issuing bonds without pledging the jurisdiction's full faith and credit to repay indebtedness. Public authorities are the only local government in New York State with the legal right to issue revenue bonds backed solely by facility charges. Not surprisingly, public authorities are extremely attractive mechanisms for fiscal capitalizing, more so than in states that grant wider revenue bond authority.

Federal laws also affect the prevalence of special-purpose governance. Since the 1930s, federal funding for mass transportation, housing and urban renewal, natural resources (soil conservation, drainage, irrigation, and flood control), hospitals, and sewage treatment has often privileged special-purpose over general-purpose governments.[42] By the mid-1960s the proliferation of districts in response to federal preferential treatment prompted the Advisory Commission on Intergovernmental Relations to recommend greater federal emphasis on general-purpose governments and greater oversight of district formations.[43] Despite the urging of the Commission, federal policies for provision of air quality, solid waste removal, airports, housing, and health services continue to encourage special-purpose governments.[44]

Federal income tax laws also influence choices about district types and financing. Tax provisions permitting deduction of local property tax payments but not user fee payments enhance the desirability of tax-funded rather than user-fee–funded services in the eyes of taxpayers. In addition, because the *Tax Reform Act of 1986* severely restricted the tax-exempt status of private purpose industrial development bonds, these bonds and the districts that offered them became far less attractive options for industrial development services.[45]

*How to simplify?*

## Institutional Parameters

A variety of institutional factors influence the use of special-purpose governments. These factors include the number, size, and arrangement of local governments in a metropolitan area; the nature of intergovernmental service agreements; the extent of private and nonprofit involvement in service delivery; patterns of federal and state aid and service provision; and practices that reflect structural characteristics of society, such as discriminatory practices or residential segregation on the basis of income, age, race, ethnicity, religion, or other characteristics.

Some institutional parameters have straightforward implications for specialized governance. If a metropolitan area has few municipalities, the likelihood of coterminous districts is necessarily reduced. If a metropolitan area is fully incorporated, there can be no districts serving unincorporated settlements. If a metropolitan area has many small municipalities, there may be a greater impetus for regional districts to capture economies of scale or internalize spillover effects.

Other institutional parameters have less straightforward implications. In Texas, for example, laws for district formation are permissive and municipalities have extensive extraterritorial powers to annex adjoining unincorporated areas. Not surprisingly, special-purpose governments are more numerous and short-lived than in neighboring Louisiana where district formation is restrictive and counties, rather than municipalities, possess extensive service delivery powers.[46] In the northeast and north-central regions, where many hospitals operate as nonprofits, we would expect fewer hospital districts than in the south and west where nonprofit hospitals play a minor role.[47]

A final set of institutional parameters is practices of the institutional choice process itself. Metropolitan residents, local government officials, and developers affect and are affected by the institutional environment for decision making. Low-income participants may be restricted from playing a pivotal role in institutional choices due to administrative fees and other costs. Disabled residents may find board or council chambers inaccessible despite federal laws outlawing such barriers. Other vital interests may be alienated from the decision process by institutional logistics such as meeting times, parliamentary rules, and limited opportunities for citizen participation. Developers may be thwarted—or aided—by complicated procedures that spread institutional deliberations over multiple agencies, multiple meetings, and multiple months. Centralized political processes with relatively streamlined, bureaucratic, and formalized practices of institutional change may likewise modify institutional choices, depending on the political savvy and organizational acumen of participants.

## Political Parameters

Overlaid on the legal and institutional environments for special-purpose governance are political factors, which also influence institutional choices. These parameters include intergovernmental rivalries, patterns of cooperation or conflict in joint service agreements, local sentiment about growth, political views on specialized governance, and the politics of business-government relations. Although the legal and institutional environments may enable an institutional option, favorable political conditions are often necessary to implement that option. For example, the relative paucity of districts in Michigan is not because the state legislature has not enabled districts, but because elected officials in strong home rule municipalities are wary of surrendering service control to nonelected officials.[48] Similarly, although Arkansas statutes enable over twenty different types of special districts, only about half of these have ever been activated, undoubtedly for a number of political reasons.

Peculiarities of local politics also play a role in the formation of special-purpose governments. Historic enmity between neighboring jurisdictions may preclude service sharing, but be put aside long enough to agree on an independent district for service delivery. Even though political conflicts have blocked city-county consolidations in Pittsburgh, Cleveland, St. Louis, and other metropolitan areas, these and other areas have been comparatively receptive to the less structurally radical regional special district.[49]

## CONCLUSION

By recognizing differences in district subtypes and the multiple motivations and implications of special-purpose governments, the conceptual framework presented in this chapter offers a more useful way to think about special districts than do conventional approaches to specialized governance.

The new framework rests on the reality of multiple metropolitan interest groups, each with different goals for service delivery. Metropolitan residents seek efficient and responsive service delivery. Local government officials seek reelection by offering taxpayers and consumers high-quality, low-cost services and a secure fiscal and social environment. Private developers seek maximum profits by securing public provision of infrastructure, land, and services, and a favorable regulatory environment for development. Within the bounds of legal, institutional, and political parameters, these interest groups make choices amongst institutional options for service provision.

Special-purpose governments often get the nod because they offer a distinct and desirable institutional alternative relative to general-purpose governments. Six attributes in particular distinguish special districts from their general-purpose counterparts: specialized functions, greater geographic flexibility, less restrictive financial constraints, less restrictive administrative constraints, lower political visibility, and weaker control over planning and land use functions. The appeal of special-purpose governments to metropolitan interest groups rests on their belief that district attributes offer a superior means relative to general-purpose government attributes for achieving service goals.

Districts are not a monolithic local government type, however. Different districts vary depending on particular characteristics, such as function, size, and revenue capabilities, which are associated with different motivations and service outcomes. Specifically, countywide or larger districts regionalize service delivery to standardize services and increase efficiency by capturing economies of scale and internalizing externalities. Districts coterminous with a municipality capitalize service delivery, either fiscally or politically, by enhancing revenue-raising capabilities and providing a safe institutional means for making tough political decisions about service delivery. Subcounty districts particularize service delivery by accommodating specialized service needs and the relatively homogeneous preferences of local service consumers. Taxing districts collectivize service delivery by spreading service costs over an entire community, thereby ensuring the availability of the service to all district residents. Finally, nontaxing districts, which rely on user-based financing, privatize service delivery, thereby enhancing efficiency through fiscal equity and encouraging conservation-sensitive decisions about individual consumption levels.

The utility of this framework is its potential to shed far more specific light than conventional conceptions on the causes and consequences of special-purpose governance. Empirical analysis can show the extent to which different district subtypes do, in fact, have different motivations and implications. Such insights offer not only a basis for improved theory, but also guidance for the metropolitan residents, local public officials, and property developers most involved in and affected by specialized governance.

## CHAPTER NOTES

1. This discussion draws on three particularly useful sources on this topic: John D. Donahue, *The Privatization Decision: Public Ends, Private Means* (New York: Basic Books, 1989), chaps. 1–2; Rainey, Understanding and Managing Public Organizations, chap. 1; and Weisbrod, *The Nonprofit Economy*, chap. 2.

2. See Seymour Martin Lipset and William Schneider, *The Confidence Gap: Business, Labor, and Government in the Public Mind*, rev. ed. (Baltimore: Johns Hopkins University Press, 1987), pp. 15–29. Public sector officials do, of course, have a political incentive to avoid service inefficiencies to win reelection.

3. John W. Kingdon, *Agendas, Alternatives, and Public Policies*. (Glenview, Ill.: Scott, Foresman, 1987), pp. 52–57.

4. Increasing returns to scale characterize goods such as utilities, water, sewer, and transit, which generally have large fixed costs. Each additional customer lowers average unit costs by spreading total costs over a larger base. Decreasing average costs implies marginal costs below average cost. Thus, setting price equal to marginal cost implies a selling price lower than average cost, a situation prohibitive to profit-maximizing producers. To ensure provision of such goods requires that government either provide them in-house or regulate production by guaranteeing fair profits and rates of return.

5. Merit goods are those such as seat belts or bike helmets that government compels people to consume for their and society's own good. As John D. Donahue notes, efforts to enforce Prohibition, thank returning World War II veterans for their sacrifices, and put a man on the moon were all merit goods, which thereby warranted collective, rather than individualistic, funding. See Donahue, *The Privatization Decision*, pp. 20–22.

6. I draw on four key sources in this section: David King, *Fiscal Tiers: The Geography of Multi-Level Governments* (London: George Allen & Unwin, 1984); Wallace E. Oates, "Decentralization of the Public Sector: An Overview," in *Decentralization, Local Governments and Markets*, ed. Robert J. Bennett (Oxford: Clarendon, 1990), pp. 43–58; Wallace E. Oates, "An Economist's Perspective on Fiscal Federalism," in *The Political Economy of Fiscal Federalism*, ed. Wallace E. Oates (Lexington, Mass.: Lexington Books, 1977), pp. 3–20; and Samuel H. Beer, "A Political Scientist's View of Fiscal Federalism," in *The Political Economy of Fiscal Federalism*, ed. Wallace E. Oates (Lexington, Mass.: Lexington Books, 1977), pp. 21–46.

7. Honey, "Conflicting Problems."

8. Connecticut Advisory Commission on Intergovernmental Relations (ACIR), *Independent Special Taxing Districts in Connecticut* (Hartford: Connecticut ACIR, 1988); U.S. Bureau of the Census, *1962 Census of Governments*, vol. 1, no. 1, pp. 66–67, table 12; and New York Office of the State Comptroller, *Special Report on Municipal Affairs* (Albany: New York Office of the State Comptroller, 1991). Districts created under general law in Connecticut still have, among other authorized purposes, the power "to appoint and employ watchmen or police officers." As of 1962, California had four tax-financed police protection districts serving unincorporated communities, although no new districts of this type have been enabled since 1959. As of 1962 New York enabled police districts in counties adjacent to first-class cities (a classification fitting New York City only), although none of these districts currently exists. One example among many social services districts is Florida's Boards of Juvenile Welfare, which have powers to levy ad valorem taxes to fund child guidance and mental health services at the county level. U.S. Bureau of the Census, *1992 Census of Governments*, vol. 1, no. 1, app. A.

9. Strictly speaking, the divide is not absolute. There are cases where general purpose governments have especially limited functional responsibilities, for example counties in New England states and townships in some midwestern states. Likewise, some special districts possess latent powers to provide a wide range of functions, although they only rarely exercise these powers. See ACIR, *State and Local Roles*, pp. 239–40, 246–47; and Sokolow et al., *Choices for the Unincorporated Community*, pp. 91–92.

10. But see Elaine B. Sharp, *Urban Politics and Administration* (White Plains, N.Y.: Longman, 1990), pp. 206–7, which acknowledges the "coordinative potential" of metropolitan special districts.

11. For an analytic discussion, see Wagner and Weber, "Competition, Monopoly."

12. The proliferation of downtown business improvement districts (BIDs), dependent entities that are business owners' equivalent of homeowners' associations, increasingly serve this function in medium- and large-sized cities. For more on BIDs, see Richard Bradley, "Downtown Renewal: The Role of Business Improvement Districts," *Public Management* (February 1995): pp. 9–13; and Thomas J. Lueck, "Business Districts Grow at Price of Accountability," *New York Times*, 20 November 1994, pp. 1, 46–47.

13. See, generally, Tullock, "Federalism: Problems of Scale."

14. Walsh, *The Public's Business*, pp. 345, 347. Whether low turnout at district meetings is evidence of "the chicken" of low political visibility or "the egg" of citizen apathy is unclear. Providing some support for the latter is the experience of the Amherst (New York) Industrial Development Agency, an independent authority in the Buffalo region, which recently ended an experiment with monthly evening meetings after a total of five citizens attended seven meetings in 1994. Dick Dawson, "Amherst IDA Discontinues Night Session," *Buffalo News*, 27 February 1995, sec. C, p. 5.

15. See, for example, Clarence N. Stone, "Elite Distemper Versus Problems of Democracy," in *Power Elites and Organizations*, ed. G. William Domhoff and Thomas R. Dye (Newbury Park, Calif.: Sage, 1987), pp. 239–65. For an alternative view see Richard C. Rich, "The Political Economy of Urban Service Distribution," in *The Politics of Urban Public Services*, ed. Richard C. Rich (Lexington, Mass.: D.C. Heath, 1982), pp. 1–17.

16. An example of this tension was evident in the 1994 labor negotiations between the (New York) Metropolitan Transit Authority (MTA) and the Long Island Rail Road, a division of MTA. According to news accounts, then-governor Mario Cuomo undermined the MTA bargaining position by intervening in negotiations, allegedly to the benefit of workers. This was despite the fact that Cuomo is chief executive of the MTA's parent government and appoints the director of MTA. Richard Leone, former chairman of the Port Authority of New York and New Jersey, described it as "a classic example of the conflicts between the needs of elected politicians and the views of publicly minded professionals." Cuomo, he explained, "is the one who has to live with the political consequences" should the railroad workers go on strike, ample rationale, Leone argued, for disregarding the sovereignty of independent authorities. See Tom Redburn, "The M.T.A.'s Engineer," *New York Times*, 26 June 1994, pp. 23, 27.

17. Leigland, "External Controls on Public Authorities." Relatively weak or weakly enforced controls over special-district finances have been cited as sources of financial mismanagement and corruption in Axelrod, *Shadow Government*; and Henriques, *The Machinery of Greed*.

18. The need for voter approval on bond issues originates in the type of revenues that back particular bonds. General obligation or moral obligation bonds, which are backed by the full faith and credit of the issuing authority (typically general-purpose governments with taxing power), require voter approval. Revenue bonds, a staple of special districts, are backed by the future revenues of a project rather than by the general tax base. As a consequence, revenue bonds are often exempt from voter approval.

19. Walsh, *The Public's Business*, pp. 233–55.

20. Rainey, *Understanding and Managing Public Organizations*, chap. 6.

21. Doig, " 'A Murderous Fellow,' " p. 297; and Doig and Mitchell, "Expertise, Democracy," pp. 20–27.

22. This argument received ample press coverage in the aftermath of the February 26, 1993, bombing of the Port Authority of New York and New Jersey's World Trade Center in New York City. The Port Authority's administrative freedoms included exemption from local fire and building code regulations. Although the Port Authority claimed its buildings met or exceeded local codes, and although most experts agreed that one code or another would have made no difference in the outcome of the bombing, political pressures in the wake of the crisis provoked the Port Authority to relinquish its regulatory exemptions. Thomas J. Lueck, "Port Agency to Observe Fire Codes," *New York Times*, 23 March 1993, sec. B, pp. 1–2.

23. Which is not to say that districts may not hold de facto control over local planning and growth initiatives. See Butler and Myers, "Boomtime in Austin"; Gottlieb and FitzSimmons, *Thirst for Growth*; and Heiman, *The Quiet Evolution*, chap. 4.

24. Sources that examine institutional choice through a resident lens include Sokolow et al., *Choices for the Unincorporated Community*; Kaufman, "Administrative Decentralization"; and numerous works in public choice theory, notably Bish, *The Public Economy*; and Ronald J. Oakerson and Roger B. Parks, "Citizen Voice and Public Entrepreneurship: The Organization Dynamic of a Complex Metropolitan County," *Publius* 18, no. 4 (1988): 91–112.

25. Rainey, *Understanding and Managing Public Organizations*, pp. 48–50.

26. Sources that discuss service-delivery issues from the viewpoint of local government officials include Martin Shefter, *Political Crisis/Fiscal Crisis: The Collapse and Revival of New York City* (New York: Basic Books, 1985); Peterson, *City Limits*; Esther Fuchs, *Mayors and Money: Fiscal Policy for New York and Chicago* (Chicago: University of Chicago Press, 1992); Robert M. Stein, *Urban Alternatives: Public and Private Markets in the Provision of Local Services* (Pittsburgh: University of Pittsburgh Press, 1990); and numerous works on local government finance, including selections in Alberta M. Sbragia, ed., *Municipal Money Chase* (Boulder, Colo.: Westview, 1983); and George F. Break. *State and Local Finance* (Madison: University of Wisconsin Press, 1983).

27. Shefter, *Political Crisis/Fiscal Crisis*, pp. 4–6.

28. Piven and Friedland, "Public Choice and Private Power," pp. 405–10;

Jonas, "Urban Growth Coalitions," esp. pp. 201–2; and Schneider, *The Competitive City*, pp. 35–38.

**29.** This is a simplifying assumption. A body of work distinguishes the interests of local government bureaucrats from those of elected officials. This literature argues that bureaucrats seek to maximize their department's budget in order to increase salaries and policy influence. See William A. Niskanen, Jr., *Bureaucracy and Representative Government* (Chicago: Aldine-Atherton, 1971); William A. Niskanen, Jr., "Bureaucrats and Politicians," *Journal of Law and Economics* 18 (1975): 617–43; Gary Miller and Terry M. Moe, "Bureaucrats, Legislators and the Size of Government," *American Political Science Review* 77 (1983): 297–322; and, for reviews, Schneider, *The Competitive City*, pp. 32–35; Mueller, *Public Choice II*, pp. 337–42; and William A. Niskanen, Jr., "A Reflection on *Bureaucracy and Representative Government*," in *The Budget-Maximizing Bureaucrat*, ed. André Blais and Stéphane Dion (Pittsburgh: University of Pittsburgh Press, 1991), pp. 13–32.

**30.** See, for example, Walsh, *The Public's Business*, pp. 59, 63; IPA, *Special Districts and Public Authorities*, pp. VI–2; and Lamb and Rappaport, *Municipal Bonds*, pp. 14–15, 78–79.

**31.** Walsh, *The Public's Business*, pp. 184–87, 205–6, 279–80, 332–34. The use of independent authorities as patronage mills was one reason for a review of specialized governments in New Jersey. See Dan Weissman, "Independent Authorities Coming Under Review," *North Jersey Star-Ledger*, Sunday, 20 November 1994, pp. 1, 20. A recent exposé of specialized governments and commissions in and around Buffalo, New York, accused Buffalo officials of using both the Buffalo Sewer Authority and the Buffalo Municipal Housing Authority as part of the city's patronage system. Richard Kern, "Open Government?" *Alt* 5, no. 1 (February 1995), p. 1.

**32.** Sources with a private-developer outlook on institutional choice include Mitchell, "The Uses of Special Districts"; Mullen, "The Use of Special Assessment Districts"; and, generally, works sponsored by the Urban Land Institute, including Porter, Lin, and Peiser, *Special Districts*; and James C. Nicholas, "The Costs of Growth: A Public vs. Private Sector Conflict or a Public/Private Responsibility," in *Understanding Growth Management: Critical Issues and a Research Agenda*, ed. David J. Brower, David R. Godschalk, and Douglas R. Porter (Washington, D.C.: Urban Land Institute, 1989), pp. 43–58.

**33.** Institute for Local Self Government, *Special Districts or Special Dynasties?: Democracy Denied* (Berkeley: Institute for Local Self Government, 1970); and Heiman, *The Quiet Evolution*, chap. 4. Developers who have close relations with county and municipal officials, of course, may prefer to mine the general-purpose government vein rather than turn to special districts. See Cox and Nartowicz, "Jurisdictional Fragmentation," pp. 202–3.

**34.** Perrenod, *Special Districts, Special Purposes*, p. 23; and Mullen, "The Use of Special Assessment Districts," pp. 373–74.

**35.** A more fundamental choice is obviously a district's function. In the current context, however, choice of function is a relatively trivial decision. If, for example, a metropolitan interest group sought library service from special-purpose governments, the group would presumably choose a library district rather than, say, an airport authority. Function is important when examining institutional choice outcomes, however, and in subsequent chapters district function takes center stage in analyses.

36. Honey, "Conflicting Problems"; and L. J. Sharpe, "The Future of Metropolitan Government," in *The Government of World Cities: The Future of the Metro Model*, ed. L. J. Sharpe (Chichester: John Wiley and Sons, 1995), pp. 15–16.

37. The disaggregation of services into system maintenance and lifestyle categories is from Williams, *Metropolitan Political Analysis*, pp. 88–91.

38. See, for example, Colman, "A Quiet Revolution," pp. 8–15; and John H. Bowman, Susan MacManus, and John L. Mikesell, "Mobilizing Resources for Public Services: Financing Urban Governments," *Journal of Urban Affairs* 14, nos. 3–4 (1992): 325–26.

39. See, for example, Colman, "A Quiet Revolution," pp. 8–10; and Ronald C. Fisher, *State and Local Public Finance* (Glenview, Ill.: Scott, Foresman, 1988), pp. 326–35.

40. An example would be school lunch subsidies for low-income patrons. See Bowman, MacManus, and Mikesell, "Mobilizing Resources for Public Services, p. 326; and Colman, "A Quiet Revolution," pp. 13–15, 20–21. For an alternative view, see Richard M. Bird and Enid Slack, "Urban Finance and User Charges," in *State and Local Finance*, ed. George F. Break (Madison: University of Wisconsin Press, 1983), pp. 230–35.

41. U.S. Bureau of the Census, *1982 Census of Governments*, vol. 1, no. 1. *Government Organization* (Washington, D.C.: U.S. Government Printing Office, 1983), pp. 114–16.

42. ACIR, *Regional Decision Making*, p. 22.

43. Advisory Commission on Intergovernmental Relations (ACIR), *Impact of Federal Urban Development Programs on Local Government Organization and Planning* (Washington, D.C.: ACIR, 1964), p. 23; and ACIR, *The Problem of Special Districts*, p. 75.

44. Stein, "Federally Supported Substate Regional Governments," pp. 74–81.

45. Lamb and Rappaport, *Municipal Bonds*, chap. 11; Fisher, *State and Local Finance*, pp. 248–52; and IPA, *Special Districts and Public Authorities*, pp. IV-5–9.

46. Feagin, *Free Enterprise City*, pp. 163–64; and, generally, Jose Jorge Anchondo, *Special Districts: A Growing Form of Government in Texas Metropolitan Areas* (Austin: Texas Advisory Commission on Intergovernmental Relations, 1985).

47. Weisbrod, *The Nonprofit Economy*, pp. 83–84, table A-21.

48. C. Grady Drago (Executive Director of the Michigan Commission on Intergovernmental Relations), telephone conversation with author, 24 January 1992.

49. Jon C. Teaford, *The Twentieth Century American City*, 2nd ed. (Baltimore: Johns Hopkins University Press, 1993), pp. 72–73, 108; Jones, *Metropolitan Government*, p. 92; and Zimmerman, "Metropolitan Reform in the U.S.," pp. 536, 540.

# 5*

# What Accounts for
# Specialized Governance?

U.S. metropolitan areas offer an excellent testing ground for investigating the utility of the conceptual framework and various theoretical explanations for specialized governance. Although the number of special-purpose governments in metropolitan areas has grown at a rapid and steady pace for several decades, the use of specialized governments has been uneven. Some metropolitan areas rely on special districts to a high degree for a variety of services. Others do not. These observations provide the basis for a systematic analysis of alternative theories about special districts. How can we account for the wide variation in the prevalence of special districts across metropolitan areas? Why do some metropolitan areas embrace special-purpose governments while other areas do not?

The literature on metropolitan political economies offers several explanations for why interest groups might turn to special districts for service delivery. Institutional-reform scholars emphasize the need for districts, specifically metropolitanwide ones, to rationalize a politically fragmented region. Public choice scholars stress the diversity of resident demands for service, which are well met by geographically and functionally varied districts. Metropolitan ecologists point to the influence of legal and institutional encouragements and constraints on local governments, which make special districts a particularly attractive government option to many interest groups. Structuralist scholars highlight districts' administrative and political appeal to property developers.

The conceptual framework's disaggregation of special-purpose governments into geographic and financial subtypes offers a more sophisticated way to think about and investigate these competing explanations. Most fundamentally, if it is true that districts of different

*Parts of this chapter originally appeared in Kathryn A. Foster, "Specialization in Government: The Uneven Use of Special Districts in Metropolitan Areas," *Urban Affairs Review* 31, no. 3 (1996): 283–313. © 1996 by Sage Publications, Inc. Reprinted by permission of Sage Publications, Inc.

geographic scales and financing modes have different purposes and outcomes, then we should expect different reasons for their use. In this chapter I examine empirically the determinants of reliance on special districts, focusing on the utility of alternative theoretical explanations for the prevalence of special-purpose governments in U.S. metropolitan areas.

## THE DISTRIBUTION OF DISTRICTS

The hallmark of specialized governance in the United States is the uneven distribution of special districts across metropolitan areas, as summarized in table 5–1. In 1992 the number of districts in metropolitan areas ranged from 0 to 665.[1] The mean number of districts per metropolitan area, forty-three, is significantly higher than the median value of twenty-three, revealing the upwardly skewed distribution of districts. Indeed, fifty-one district-heavy metropolitan areas, those with more than 70 districts apiece, account for over half of the 13,343 special districts. The large majority of metropolitan areas, nearly 75 percent, have fewer than fifty special districts.[2]

A ranked list of the twenty highest and lowest metropolitan areas based on the number of special districts in 1992 reveals the importance of population size and state location to the distribution of districts (table 5–2). Although the relationship between population size and number of districts is evident, it is not absolute. Several district-light metropolitan areas, notably New Orleans and Baton Rouge, have much

---

**TABLE 5-1**  Summary Characteristics of Special Districts, 1992 ($N = 312$ metropolitan areas)

| | |
|---|---|
| Total number of special districts | 13,343 |
| Median districts per metropolitan area | 23 |
| Mean districts per metropolitan area | 43 |
| Standard deviation | 63 |
| Range | |
|    minimum | 0 (Monroe, La.) |
|    maximum | 665 (Houston, Tex.) |
| Number of metropolitan areas with | |
|    fewer than 50 districts | 233 |
| Number of metropolitan areas with | |
|    more than 70 districts | 51 |

**Source**:  Calculated from data in U.S. Bureau of the Census, *1992 Census of Governments*, vol. 1, no. 1, pp. 44–83, table 28.

**TABLE 5-2** Metropolitan Areas Ranked by Number of Special Districts, 1992

| *Top Twenty* | | *Bottom Twenty* | |
|---|---|---|---|
| *Metropolitan Area* | *Number of Districts* | *Metropolitan Area* | *Number of Districts* |
| 1. Houston, Tex. | 665 | 1. Monroe, La. | 0 |
| 2. Denver, Colo. | 358 | 2. Danville, Va. | 1 |
| 3. Chicago, Ill. | 357 | 2. Alexandria, La. | 1 |
| 4. Pittsburgh, Pa. | 324 | 2. Shreveport, La. | 1 |
| 5. St. Louis, Mo. | 318 | 2. Lafayette, La. | 1 |
| 6. Philadelphia, Pa. | 318 | 2. Iowa City, Iowa | 1 |
| 7. Sacramento, Calif. | 238 | 7. New Orleans, La. | 2 |
| 8. Kansas City, Mo. | 207 | 7. Dubuque, Iowa | 2 |
| 9. Riverside-San Bernardino, Calif. | 186 | 7. Rochester, Minn. | 2 |
| 10. Boston, Mass. | 167 | 7. Jackson, Mich. | 2 |
| 11. Los Angeles-Long Beach, Calif. | 156 | 11. Lynchburg, Va. | 3 |
| 12. Seattle, Wash. | 149 | 11. Baton Rouge, La. | 3 |
| 13. Scranton, Pa. | 143 | 11. Houma-Thibodoux, La. | 3 |
| 14. Indianapolis, Ind. | 136 | 11. Laredo, Tex. | 3 |
| 15. Nassau-Suffolk, N.Y. | 136 | 11. Niagara Falls, N.Y. | 3 |
| 16. Harrisburg, Pa. | 124 | 11. Santa Fe, N. Mex. | 3 |
| 17. Omaha, Nebr. | 118 | 11. Hagerstown, Md. | 3 |
| 18. Albany, N.Y. | 116 | 11. Wilmington, N.C. | 3 |
| 19. Oakland, Calif. | 114 | 11. Jacksonville, N.C. | 3 |
| 20. Fresno, Calif. | 111 | 11. Owensboro, Ky. | 3 |

**Source**: Calculated from data in U.S. Bureau of the Census, *1992 Census of Governments*, vol. 1, no. 1, pp. 44–83, table 28.

larger populations than several district-heavy metropolitan areas, such as Scranton and Harrisburg. Likewise, although cross-state differences are apparent—Louisiana and Virginia, for example, are not heavy users of special districts—the presence on both lists of metropolitan areas in Texas (Houston and Laredo) and New York (Nassau-Suffolk and Niagara Falls) implies that state differences are also not absolute. The overview nonetheless suggests two important factors, size and state location, influence the distribution of districts across metropolitan areas.

The summary statistics and rankings of special-purpose governments say nothing about the distribution of geographic and financial subtypes of districts. Data classifying districts by geographic scope and financing mode are not yet available by county for 1992, but can be

TABLE 5-3 Geographic and Financial Attributes of Special Districts, 1987
(N = 8,456 districts reporting both geographic and financial attributes)

| | Percentage of Total: | | | |
| --- | --- | --- | --- | --- |
| | Regionwide | Coterminous | Subcounty | Row Percent |
| With Property-Taxing Powers | 10.3 | 8.8 | 40.5 | 59.6 |
| Without Property-Taxing Powers | 13.0 | 12.3 | 15.1 | 40.4 |
| Column Percent | 23.3 | 21.1 | 55.6 | 100.0 |

Source: U.S. Bureau of the Census, 1987 Governments File.

calculated for 1987 from the data files of the *1987 Census of Governments* (table 5–3).[3] The data indicate that the majority of districts, nearly 56 percent, are subcounty governments, which commonly particularize service delivery in unincorporated urban fringe communities. Nearly one-quarter regionalize services at the countywide or larger scale. The remaining one-fifth have borders coterminous with a municipality, a geographic scope most useful to local officials seeking to capitalize on districts' financial, administrative, and political attributes. On the financial side, nearly 60 percent have access to property-taxing powers for collectivizing revenue raising. The remaining 40 percent are nontaxing districts, which rely on user fees, bond revenues, or other nontax revenue sources.[4] As a result, the most common type of special-purpose government in metropolitan areas, comprising 41 percent of the total reporting, is a subcounty taxing district. Most of these are fire protection, water, sewer, or utilities districts serving urban fringe areas of the metropolis.

## THEORETICAL HYPOTHESES

What accounts for the uneven distribution of special-purpose governments across metropolitan areas? How useful are alternative theoretical perspectives in explaining the uneven distribution?

Because different district subtypes are likely to have different motivations, the first step in answering these questions is linking specific theoretical hypotheses to specific district subtypes, as shown in table 5–4.[5] Regionwide districts, whether taxing or nontaxing, are most closely linked to fragmentation-driven hypotheses of institutional reformers. Subcounty districts, which typically serve unincorporated communities, are linked to numerous hypotheses, namely the demand-

**TABLE 5-4**  Theoretical Hypotheses and District Subtypes

| Theoretical Perspective | Hypothesized Reasons for District Use | Relevant District Subtypes |
|---|---|---|
| Institutional reform | 1. to ameliorate inefficiencies of political fragmentation | regionwide |
| | 2. to enable small municipalities to capture economies of scale | regionwide |
| Public choice | 1. to tailor services in unincorporated settlements | subcounty |
| | 2. to meet service demands in rapidly growing areas | subcounty, coterminous, regionwide |
| | 3. to tailor services to diverse resident preferences | subcounty, coterminous |
| Metropolitan ecology | 1. to circumvent constraints on municipal boundary change: | |
| | annexation | subcounty |
| | incorporation | subcounty |
| | 2. to circumvent constraints on municipal revenue raising: | taxing |
| | property tax constraints | taxing |
| | debt constraints | nontaxing |
| | 3. to circumvent constraints on municipal home-rule powers | coterminous |
| Structuralist | 1. to meet needs of property developers | subcounty; development-oriented |

driven public choice theories, ecologic hypotheses about boundary constraints, and structuralist theories linking property-developer goals to district formation. Coterminous districts relate primarily to other metropolitan ecology hypotheses, namely those concerned with the restrictiveness of constraints on municipal home-rule powers and revenue raising. Structuralist hypotheses about developer interests also pertain to the subset of districts providing development-oriented services like water, sewer, and roads, regardless of the district's geographic scope or mode of financing.

To assess empirically the importance of various factors on the distribution of districts, I test a model that includes variables representing these alternative theoretical explanations. The cross-sectional model tests the cumulative outcome as of 1987 of institutional choices to form special-purpose governments. The dependent variables are the number of districts of particular geographic and financial subtypes in a metropolitan area.[6]

To investigate the distribution of districts by subtype, the model includes local government structure variables associated with institutional reform contentions, service demand variables for public choice hypotheses, legal factors associated with metropolitan ecology theories, and developer-oriented variables to assess the structuralist claims. The model also includes several control variables to account for metropolitan or state characteristics not identified with a particular theoretical perspective. Although reducing complex theories to a few measurable variables risks oversimplification, aggregate analyses are useful for revealing general patterns.

## Explanatory Variables

### Local Government Structure

Two variables account for the institutional reform claim that districts form to instill order on a chaotic, fragmented local government structure.[7] The first is the number of municipal governments in the metropolitan area. According to reformers, the larger the number of municipalities in the metropolitan area, the greater the need for special districts, specifically regionwide districts, to overcome the alleged inefficiencies and coordination problems caused by political fragmentation.

The second local government structure variable, the average population size of suburban municipalities, addresses reformers' concern with small local government units. Because small local governments are allegedly less efficient and administratively capable than larger jurisdictions, there should be more districts, especially regionwide ones, where the average population size of suburbs is smaller.

### Service Demand

Three variables measure the public choice view of districts as institutional responses to diverse citizen demands for public services.[8] The first variable, growth in metropolitan population since 1970, reflects the notion that faster growing metropolitan areas place greater service demands on public agencies than do slower growing or stable metropolitan areas. Because special districts are relatively easy to form and functionally versatile, they should be most prevalent in rapid growth environments where development needs often outpace the service-delivery capabilities of general-purpose governments.

The second demand variable, the percent of metropolitan population in unincorporated areas, addresses the public choice assertion that special-purpose governments are especially well-suited to meet the service needs of unincorporated communities. According to public choice logic, unincorporated communities that desire a full range of municipal public services will incorporate. Communities that remain unincorporated presumably desire a narrower range of services, a preference well met by forming a special district for those specific services. By this reasoning there should be more special districts, especially subcounty ones, in metropolitan areas that have a higher proportion of population residing in unincorporated areas.

The third service demand variable, income diversity, measures the heterogeneity of preferences for public services within a metropolitan area.[9] Because persons with different income levels tend to demand different service bundles, metropolitan areas with greater income variability require the greater variety of service options that special districts are well-suited to provide.[10] If this reasoning is correct, there should be more districts in metropolitan areas with heterogeneous as opposed to homogeneous preferences.

### Legal Factors

The third set of variables tests metropolitan ecology assertions about the influence of legal factors on the distribution of special districts.[11] The use of legal variables in empirical analysis is a challenge for two reasons. First, although state-based legal measures provide a gross gauge of the local-government policy environment, they cannot account for potentially significant interstate or intrastate variations in implementation of state policy by courts or local officials. Such variations are virtually impossible to account for in quantitative models. Second, legal statutes change over time. If we knew the formation dates of special districts it would be possible to link a state's policy environment in existence at district conception with formation of the district. Data in the *1987 Census of Governments* on district formation dates is spotty, however. Overall, 40 percent of districts (5,022 of 12,580) did not report a formation date, and the failure to report in some metropolitan areas was upward of 75 percent.

In the model that follows I measure legal factors as either binary or categorical variables for years in the 1970s or early 1980s. This choice is premised on the assumption that although legal parameters change, they do not often do so to the extent that states alter their relative categorical assignment. Because the legal variables in the model measure state policy governing local-government formation and powers, their values are identical for all metropolitan areas within a single state.[12]

The first three legal variables measure constraints on municipal political status and boundary change. The restrictiveness of municipal incorporation and municipal annexation are binary variables gauging the potential for unincorporated settlements to receive services by either incorporating as a new municipality or being annexed by an existing municipality (a value of 1 reflects the more restrictive case). Incorporation is considered restricted where state law requires communities to achieve a minimum population threshold before incorporation can proceed. Municipal annexation is considered restricted where state law requires both a referendum and majority vote in the area to be annexed before annexation can proceed.[13] States that restrict either municipal incorporation or annexation should have more special districts, particularly districts serving unincorporated communities. Because annexation and incorporation limitations operating singly may be offset by service alternatives other than special districts, I also include an interactive variable measuring the joint presence of annexation and incorporation restrictions. When annexation is restricted communities may pursue incorporation; when incorporation is restricted communities may seek to be annexed. When incorporation and annexation are *simultaneously* restricted districts should be most prevalent.

Two categorical variables measure the severity of state-imposed constraints on municipal revenue raising. The first classifies the restrictiveness of limitations on municipal property-taxing powers as either weak, moderate, or heavy.[14] The restrictiveness of limitations on municipal borrowing powers similarly gauges the ability of a municipality to incur debt.[15] In both instances, ecologists predict more special districts in metropolitan areas where municipalities face more restrictive fiscal environments. To the extent municipalities turn to districts to circumvent financial constraints, there should be more taxing districts where tax limitations are most severe and more nontaxing districts where debt limitations are most severe.

The final legal variable gauges the level of municipal home-rule powers, specifically with respect to functional autonomy.[16] Because a municipality with greater functional authority has more discretion with respect to service delivery, the more permissive the municipal powers, the fewer special-purpose governments expected. By contrast, the more restrictive the functional powers, the more special-purpose governments expected.

### Development Interests

The model includes a single variable accounting for the structuralist hypothesis that property-development interests encourage district formation. Case studies use qualitative measures to assess the strength of development interests in an area.[17] Measuring the strength of the development interests at the aggregate level, however, is difficult. I follow Nancy Burns by using as a proxy the number of developer firm equivalents per 10,000 capita in the metropolitan area.[18] The structuralist view contends that development interests initiate or encourage special districts because these institutions are relatively receptive to growth. By this logic there should be more special districts in areas with a higher presence of developer firms.

### Control Variables

The model includes three variables that control for metropolitan or state attributes.[19] Metropolitan population size controls for the positive influence of population size on urban service demand and the consequent need for service providers. Larger populations might use more special districts simply because larger areas require more facilities of wider variety. Because the effect of increasing population size should decrease as metropolitan population increases, I use the log of population rather than its absolute value.

Metropolitan area age, measured as the number of years prior to 1995 that an area was designated metropolitan by the Bureau of the Census, controls for the different functional responsibilities associated with metropolitan areas in different life-cycle stages. Prior research has demonstrated a positive relationship between metropolitan age and the functional breadth of municipalities.[20] Municipalities in younger metropolitan areas tend to provide fewer services than older centers. In addition, because the variety and acceptance level of special districts has increased over time, newer metropolitan areas may more readily accept special-purpose governments as viable service-delivery institutions. For these reasons, younger metropolitan areas are expected to have more districts than older metropolitan areas.

The final control variable measures the legal potential for special districts. This is measured by an index tallying the breadth of district functional types authorized by state general enabling legislation.[21] The logic of this variable is straightforward: metropolitan areas in states authorizing a large number of district functional types will have more districts than will metropolitan areas in states enabling a limited number of district types.

## FINDINGS

### Preliminary Diagnostics

Diagnostic tests revealed weak to mild associations between the explanatory variables, well below levels suggesting problems of multicollinearity. The only exception was the .73 correlation between metropolitan age and log of population size. Because of the theoretical importance of these variables, both were retained in estimations.

To eliminate potential but unknown nonreporting bias, the estimations omit the sixty-nine metropolitan areas in which fewer than 60 percent of districts reported geographic information. Very few districts failed to report financial data, making adjustments unnecessary for the estimations by financial subtype.

Cook's D tests identified three metropolitan areas, Denver, Philadelphia, and Houston, with distortionary influence on the regionwide, coterminous, and subcounty district estimations, respectively. Houston Metropolitan Area, with its exceptionally high number of municipal utilities districts, also had a distortionary influence on the estimation for taxing districts. Distortionary observations were omitted from the appropriate estimations.

A simple analysis of variance (ANOVA) model was estimated to assess the influence of state location only on the distribution of districts. The purpose was to ascertain the degree to which state factors, which encompass historical, legal, cultural, and policy differences that vary by state, influence the prevalence of districts.[22] The ANOVA model yielded an adjusted-$R^2$ value of .13, signifying that state factors alone account for 13 percent of the variation in district distribution across metropolitan areas. State location is obviously an important consideration. The final estimations include state-based legal factors, although not separate variables for each state due to variable limitations.

Preliminary estimations using ordinary least squares revealed the presence of heteroscedasticity, with the variance of error terms positively related to metropolitan size and local-government multiplicity. This was expected, given the skewed distribution of the dependent variables in which some metropolitan areas have many special-purpose governments, but many metropolitan areas have relatively few of any given subtype. In all cases, running a double log model (which uses log transformations of the dependent and explanatory variables) greatly reduces heteroscedasticity. The results of the double log models are reported below.

## Geographic and Financial Subtypes

How useful are the alternative hypotheses for explaining the distribution of districts across metropolitan areas? Are different district subtypes associated with different motivations, as the conceptual framework suggests?

Model estimations, shown for geographic subtypes in table 5–5 and financial subtypes in table 5–6, reveal the complexity of factors

**TABLE 5-5**  Distribution of Geographic Subtypes of Districts, 1987

|  | Dependent Variables: | | |
| --- | --- | --- | --- |
|  | Regionwide Districts | Coterminous Districts | Subcounty Districts |
| Variable | Coefficient[a] | Coefficient[a] | Coefficient[a] |
| Local government structure | | | |
| Number of municipalities, | .37** | .32** | .13 |
| 1987 | (5.34) | (5.32) | (1.98) |
| Average suburban popula- | −.07 | .13** | .08 |
| tion, 1980 | (1.38) | (2.73) | (1.54) |
| Service demand | | | |
| Unincorporated popu- | .28** | −.15** | .06 |
| lation, 1980 (%) | (4.67) | (−2.79) | (0.93) |
| Metropolitan population | −.05 | .01 | .07 |
| growth, 1970-1987 (%) | (−0.63) | (0.12) | (0.84) |
| Distribution of household | −.02 | −.00 | .07 |
| income, 1980 | (−0.32) | (−0.03) | (1.34) |
| Legal factors | | | |
| Annexation limits | −.31** | −.03 | −.22* |
|  | (−3.31) | (−0.39) | (−2.46) |
| Incorporation limits | −.05 | −.35** | −.19* |
|  | (−0.53) | (−4.03) | (−1.98) |
| Annexation/incorporation | .16 | .14 | .17 |
| limits (interaction) | (1.23) | (1.21) | (1.36) |
| Moderate debt limits[b] | .05 | .13* | .20** |
|  | (0.87) | (2.52) | (3.40) |
| Heavy debt limits[b] | .05 | .01 | .15** |
|  | (0.94) | (0.25) | (2.65) |
| Moderate property tax limits[c] | −.12* | −.20** | −.12* |
|  | (−2.17) | (−4.03) | (−2.15) |

associated with district prevalence. For most district subtypes, legal and institutional factors associated with the metropolitan ecology perspective account better for the uneven distribution of districts than do local government, service demand, and development factors. Still, the results indicate considerable slippage between hypothesized relationships and the experience of metropolitan areas.

Specific findings associated with theoretical hypotheses are instructive for assessing the utility of alternative perspectives and for shedding light on what does and does not appear to matter for the distribution of special-purpose governments across metropolitan areas.

### Institutional Reform Hypotheses

Consistent with the predictions of institutional reformers, there are indeed more regionwide special districts in metropolitan areas that

TABLE 5-5 *continued*

| | Dependent Variables: | | |
|---|---|---|---|
| | *Regionwide Districts* | *Coterminous Districts* | *Subcounty Districts* |
| *Variable* | Coefficient[a] | Coefficient[a] | Coefficient[a] |
| Heavy property tax limits[c] | −.17* | −.38** | −.28** |
| | (−2.34) | (−6.16) | (−4.04) |
| Limited home-rule powers[d] | .11 | .20* | .32** |
| | (1.19) | (2.53) | (3.58) |
| Broad home-rule powers[d] | .26** | .10 | .47** |
| | (2.68) | (1.22) | (4.95) |
| Developer interests | | | |
| Developer firms index, 1982 | −.09 | −.04 | −0.09 |
| | (−1.43) | (−0.63) | (−1.50) |
| Control variables | | | |
| Log of metropolitan | .32** | .23** | .39** |
| population, 1987 | (3.42) | (2.79) | (4.23) |
| Metropolitan area age | .04 | −.04 | .01 |
| | (0.47) | (−0.57) | (0.16) |
| District functional breadth | .65** | .32** | .55** |
| index, 1982 | (9.52) | (5.39) | (8.30) |
| Constant | .—** | .— | .—** |
| | (−3.46) | (−0.78) | (−5.21) |
| Adjusted $R^2$ | .51 | .62 | .53 |
| $n$ | 239 | 239 | 239 |

a. Standardized regression coefficient (betas). Numbers in parentheses are *t*-statistics.
b. Base case = weak debt limits.
c. Base case = weak property-taxing limits.
d. Base case = neutral home-rule powers.
*$p < .05$   **$p < .01$

have more municipalities. To the probable dismay of reformers, however, the positive link between municipal jurisdictions and districts pertains not only to the regional authorities reformers tolerate, but also to the coterminous and subcounty districts reformers condemn. Municipal fragmentation is as likely to sustain fragmented political structures through formation of small-scale districts as it is to regionalize political structures through formation of countywide or larger districts.

Contrary to reform predictions, metropolitan areas with a smaller average suburban size are no more likely than areas with a larger average suburban size to have regionwide special districts. Average suburban size is, in fact, unrelated for the most part to numbers of districts. The only exception is coterminous districts, which are more common where average suburban size is larger. The tendency of small

TABLE 5-6   Distribution of Financial Subtypes of Districts, 1987

| Variable | Dependent Variables: | |
| --- | --- | --- |
| | Taxing Districts | Nontaxing Districts |
| | Coefficient[a] | Coefficient[a] |
| Local government structure | | |
| Number of municipalities, 1987 | −.06 | .27** |
| | (−1.01) | (4.92) |
| Average suburban population, | .07 | .01 |
| 1980 | (1.57) | (0.13) |
| Service demand | | |
| Unincorporated population, | .03 | .03 |
| 1980 (%) | (0.63) | (0.63) |
| Metropolitan population | .10 | −.02 |
| growth, 1970–1987 (%) | (1.31) | (−0.25) |
| Distribution of household | .20** | −.04 |
| income, 1980 | (4.22) | (−0.86) |
| Legal factors | | |
| Annexation limits | −.32* | −.25** |
| | (−3.88) | (−3.55) |
| Incorporation limits | .00 | −.36** |
| | (0.02) | (−4.81) |
| Annexation/incorporation | .13 | .32** |
| limits (interaction) | (1.17) | (3.24) |
| Moderate debt limits[b] | .17** | .04 |
| | (3.03) | (0.88) |
| Heavy debt limits[b] | .15** | −.02 |
| | (3.01) | (−0.35) |
| Moderate property tax limits[c] | −.06 | −.16** |
| | (−1.11) | (−3.65) |

localities to form districts evidently lags behind that of larger munici-palities, contrary to reform claims. Perhaps this is because areas with smaller suburbs satisfy service needs through private homeowners' associations, or by contracting with county or other municipal govern-ments for service, rather than by forming specialized governments.[23] Unfortunately, Bureau of the Census data do not account for these increasingly common nondistrict service alternatives.

## Public Choice Hypotheses

Empirical support for the demand-driven hypotheses of the public choice perspective is surprisingly weak. Contrary to predictions, popu-

TABLE 5-6 *continued*

| | Dependent Variables: | |
| | --- | --- |
| | *Taxing Districts* | *Nontaxing Districts* |
| *Variable* | *Coefficient*[a] | *Coefficient*[a] |
| Heavy property tax limits[c] | −.07 | −.39** |
| | (1.15) | (−7.60) |
| Limited home-rule powers[d] | .29** | .06 |
| | (3.96) | (1.00) |
| Broad home-rule powers[d] | .54** | −.03 |
| | (6.97) | (−0.37) |
| Developer interests | | |
| Developer firms index, | −.15* | −.03 |
| 1982 | (−2.51) | (−0.37) |
| Control variables | | |
| Log of metropolitan | .39** | .44** |
| population, 1987 | (4.51) | (5.94) |
| Metropolitan area age | −.01 | −.01 |
| | (−0.08) | (−0.11) |
| District functional breadth | .55** | .48** |
| index, 1982 | (9.37) | (9.41) |
| Constant | .—** | .— |
| | (−8.03) | (−0.94) |
| Adjusted $R^2$ | .48 | .61 |
| $n$ | 307 | 308 |

a. Standardized regression coefficient (betas). Numbers in parentheses are *t*-statistics.
b. Base case = weak debt limits.
c. Base case = weak property-taxing limits.
d. Base case = neutral home-rule powers.
*$p < .05$      **$p < .01$

lation growth rates have an insignificant influence on the number of districts in metropolitan areas. Fast-growing metropolitan areas are not more likely than slow-growing areas to have special-purpose governments. This finding reinforces the reality of multiple motivations for districts. Slow-growing areas, which often suffer depleted fiscs, turn to financially powerful and politically isolated districts to exploit their revenue-raising abilities. Fast-growing areas turn to easy-to-form, geographically flexible districts to meet rapidly expanding service demands. The statistical fallout of these offsetting tendencies is the insignificant relationship between population growth and the distribution of special-purpose governments.

Probably for similar reasons, metropolitan areas with more diverse service demands, as measured by the distribution of incomes, are not associated with higher numbers of special districts. Homogeneous and heterogeneous areas both find districts that meet these areas' service needs. Taxing districts, which are more common when income heterogeneity is high, are again the only exception to this pattern. This finding implies a "Tiebout world" where internally homogeneous, externally distinct communities finance services using collective means such as taxing districts. Why a similar relationship does not exist for nontaxing districts is unclear.

Of broader significance to the distribution of special-purpose governments is the percentage of unincorporated population in a metropolitan area. There is an understandable inverse relationship between unincorporated population share and the number of coterminous districts. Unincorporated communities cannot, of course, form districts coterminous with a municipality. Beyond this finding, however, the influence of unincorporated territory is not as the public choice perspective suggests. Public choice theorists contend that unincorporated settlements will prefer the offerings of a tailored package of special-purpose governments to the standardized offerings of a county government. The findings suggest otherwise. The greater the share of unincorporated population in an area, the more regionwide, but *not* the more subcounty districts in the area. This implies that a county's use of regionwide districts to standardize service delivery throughout an unincorporated area overwhelms an unincorporated community's use of subcounty districts to achieve a tailored service package. Assuming that individual unincorporated communities have different demands for services, this finding contradicts public choice theories.

### Metropolitan Ecology Hypotheses
Although there is ample evidence that legal factors are significant determinants of district prevalence, the nature of influence is often not as metropolitan ecologists predict. For example, although ecologists are correct that constraints on municipal boundary changes influence the number of districts in an area, they are not correct about how. Districts of all types tend to be less common where annexation or incorporation limits operate alone. Where boundary options are constrained, communities apparently turn first to nondistrict service options—perhaps annexation in the case of incorporation limits and incorporation in the case of annexation limits—before turning to special-purpose governments. This implies a "second best" role for districts, consistent with the institutional-reform school of thought.[24] More in line with ecologist reasoning is that the simultaneous presence of

annexation and incorporation restrictions is associated with greater numbers of districts. Except for nontaxing districts, however, these relationships fall shy of statistical significance at the .05 level.

There is also some evidence that constraints on municipal revenue raising influence the numbers of special districts, but, again, not in the ways that ecologists predict. Debt limits are not associated with higher numbers of debt-dependent (nontaxing) districts. This suggests that restrictions on borrowing do not, as ecologists predict, necessarily prompt municipalities to use debt-funded districts as a substitute. Rather, debt constraints prompt greater reliance on taxing districts at both the municipal and subcounty scales. Special districts seem to represent an alternative, rather than a substitute, institutional means of achieving service delivery in areas in which municipalities face debt restrictions.

The findings with respect to property-taxing constraints also challenge expectations. Faced with tax constraints, local officials form fewer, rather than more, special districts, not only at the municipal level, but also at the regional and subcounty scale. Moreover, metropolitan areas in which municipalities face tax restrictions have significantly fewer nontaxing districts, although insignificantly fewer taxing districts. These unexpected negative relationships between tax constraints and district subtypes may have two explanations. First, municipal officials may fear that the antitax sentiment that results in municipal tax constraints signals a pervasive distaste for taxation by any local government type. In other words, tax limitations have their intended effect: they hold down service levels and the consequent need for revenues by holding down the number of providers. As a result, taxing *districts* are no more desirable than taxing *municipalities*, and, hence, are not formed. Second, the inverse relationship between tax constraints and specialized governments may be a statistical artifact of ahistorical, cross-sectional analysis. For example, the high-district states of Illinois and Pennsylvania had relatively weak taxing constraints in the late 1970s when the tax index was measured, thus contributing to the inverse relationship revealed by the analysis. Until the early 1970s, however, local governments in both of these states faced severe taxing constraints, which were widely seen as a motivation for district formation.[25] Thus the link between taxing limits and district formation may operate as ecologists predict; the cross-sectional analysis in this study, however, fails to capture it.

Contrary to expectations, broad home-rule powers are associated with greater numbers of regionwide and subcounty districts, but not coterminous ones. Broad municipal powers apparently equip local officials with the necessary discretion and authority either to provide the service in-house or to join with other jurisdictions to regionalize services through special districts.[26] The positive relationship between limited home-rule powers and coterminous and subcounty districts suggests that limited autonomy is likewise a strong motivation for districts. Within the municipality, districts represent a means for local officials to maintain service offerings while circumventing limited functional powers. Outside the municipality, limited home-rule powers may prompt residents of unincorporated communities to petition for local districts rather than turn to weak neighboring municipalities to obtain desired services.

### Structuralist Hypotheses

Despite ample case-study evidence suggesting a positive relationship between property-development interests and reliance on special-purpose governments, reviewed in chapter 3, model results do not sustain the structuralist hypothesis that there is such a link. There are several possible explanations. It is plausible, though unlikely, that a district's potential as an institutional means to thwart growth prompts prodevelopment stakeholders to resist district formation.[27]

More likely, however, is that the absence of a significant relationship says less about the veracity of the original hypothesis than about two factors related to measurement and developer behavior. First, as noted, measuring development interests at the aggregate level is extremely problematic. The mere presence of developer and subdivider firms in an area, no matter how measured, cannot capture relevant information about developer focus and strategies, the local market for real estate, or local sentiments toward growth. Second, property developers need not form special districts to achieve progrowth goals. Indeed, as structuralist scholars have suggested, prodevelopment interests support any local government arrangement that fosters development.[28] Many county and municipal governments promote, or are receptive to, infrastructure development and growth in general.[29] Of significance in recent years has been the enthusiastic embrace by suburban developers of private, subdivision-sized homeowners' associations, which, like districts, may wield considerable regulatory and financial control over service decisions.[30] The availability of alternative prodevelopment institutional choices means special districts may, but need not necessarily, be a familiar institution in areas where prodevelopment sentiment is high.

### Metropolitan Controls

Two of the three control variables are especially important in accounting for the prevalence of district subtypes. As expected, there tends to be more of all types of special-purpose governments in more populated metropolitan areas. The demand for districts is clearly associated with the greater complexity and service needs found in larger areas.

Less expected is that metropolitan area age has no independent effect on district prevalence after controlling for population size. Within any population size class, neither older nor newer metropolitan areas are significantly more apt to form districts. This is likely due to the multiple and offsetting motivations for districts that render them useful to metropolitan areas of all ages. For example, officials in older metropolitan areas may turn to financially powerful and easily formed districts to overhaul aging infrastructure systems just as readily as officials of younger metropolitan areas turn to districts to help finance and develop new infrastructure systems.

The control variable with greatest relative influence on district distribution is the functional breadth of districts enabled in state legislation. There are simply more districts of all geographic and financial subtypes in metropolitan areas located in states that permit more different functional types of districts. This finding underscores the too-often-neglected reality that legal potential is a necessary condition for special districts. The rules of the local-government game influence its outcome.

The overall analysis reveals considerable slippage between hypothesized relationships and the experience of metropolitan areas, as summarized in table 5–7. In most cases, factors hypothesized to influence the distribution of districts were indeed significant, but often in ways contrary to predictions. The factors advanced by the public choice and structuralist perspectives had limited influence in unexpected ways. Factors proposed by the institutional-reform and metropolitan ecology perspectives fared somewhat better, either because the hypothesized factors were more often significant or because the nature of significance proved closer to predictions. The only variables that were consistently influential in the ways anticipated, however, were two control variables: metropolitan population size and functional breadth of districts enabled. From a theoretical viewpoint, the findings partially support the claims of the metropolitan ecologist perspective, support in a limited way those of the institutional-reform perspective, and fail to support the claims of the public choice and structuralist perspectives.

## Functional Subtypes of Districts

So far, I have ignored the distribution of districts by functional subtype. My assumption has been that separate analysis of district distribution by function is not warranted: would the determinants of, say, library

**TABLE 5-7**  Summary of Results on the Distribution of District Subtypes

| Theoretical Perspective | Factor | Significance of Factor[a] | Relationship as Predicted? |
|---|---|---|---|
| Institutional reform | Number of municipalities | High | Yes for regionwide districts; no for others |
|  | Smaller-sized suburbs | Limited | No |
| Public choice | Percentage unincorporated population | Partial | No |
|  | Metropolitan population growth | None | No |
|  | Heterogeneity of population | Limited | No |
| Metropolitan ecology | Annexation limits | High | No |
|  | Incorporation limits | Partial | No |
|  | Annexation/incorporation limits | Limited | Yes |
|  | Debt limits | Partial | Yes |
|  | Property tax limits | High | No |
|  | Limited home-rule powers | Partial | Yes |
|  | Broad home-rule powers | Partial | No |
| Structuralist | Development interests | Limited | No |
| Control variables | Metropolitan population size | High | Yes |
|  | Metropolitan area age | None | No |
|  | Functional breadth | High | Yes |

**a.** High = significant for at least four of five district subtypes; Partial = significant for two or three district subtypes; Limited = significant for one district subtype; None = significant for no district subtypes.

districts in Charlotte, North Carolina, be expected to differ from those in Raleigh, North Carolina, for example? Yet for at least two issues this assumption may not be justified. The first pertains to the influence of state legal frameworks on the distribution of districts. The second pertains to the influence of development interests, which may matter for development-oriented, although not necessarily other, districts.

The greater disaggregation of the dependent variable associated with functional subtypes prevents using regression techniques to investigate these potential influences. As the data in table 5–8 indicate, a large majority of metropolitan areas have no districts of specific functional types. Except for housing, natural resources, and water districts,

TABLE 5-8   Metropolitan Areas with No Districts of Selected Functions
($N$ = 311 metropolitan areas)

| Function | Areas with No Districts of Function | Percentage of Total Metropolitan Areas |
|---|---|---|
| Utilities (Gas and Electric) | 227 | 83.6 |
| Highway | 259 | 83.3 |
| Ports | 257 | 82.6 |
| Library | 227 | 73.0 |
| Airport | 226 | 72.7 |
| Parks and Recreation | 206 | 66.2 |
| Transit | 202 | 65.0 |
| Multifunctional Water-Sewer | 191 | 61.4 |
| Fire Protection | 165 | 53.0 |
| Health and Hospitals | 158 | 50.8 |
| Sewer | 158 | 50.8 |
| Water | 133 | 42.8 |
| Housing and Community Development | 48 | 15.4 |
| Natural Resources | 39 | 12.5 |

Source:   U.S. Bureau of the Census, *1987 Governments File.*

fewer than half of the metropolitan areas have even one district of specific functions. For a few functions, namely ports, highways, and utilities, fewer than 20 percent of the metropolitan areas have any districts of that function.

Even when metropolitan areas do rely on special-purpose governments for a particular function, the area rarely has a large number of them (table 5–9). A low number of districts is most common when the function is typically provided on a regional scale, as is the case with airport, transit, port, or utilities. The methodological implication is insufficient variability in the dependent variable to permit regression analysis.

As a consequence, I use simple ANOVA models to examine the influence of state location on the distribution of districts by function. Explanatory variables are dummy variables representing state location, which captures the effect of legal, institutional, cultural, or other factors and practices that vary systematically by state.[31]

The data in table 5–10 reveal that state location is often a significant determinant of the distribution of districts by functional subtype. For sewer, housing, highway, and fire protection districts, state location accounts for over 30 percent of the variation in the number of districts

**TABLE 5-9**   Mean Number of Districts per Metropolitan Area, by Function

| Function | Areas with at Least One District of Function | Mean Districts per Metropolitan Area[a] |
|---|---|---|
| Airport | 85 | 1.3 |
| Utilities (Gas and Electric) | 51 | 1.5 |
| Transit | 109 | 1.5 |
| Ports | 54 | 1.6 |
| Health and Hospitals | 153 | 2.9 |
| Highway | 52 | 4.0 |
| Library | 84 | 4.0 |
| Multifunction Water-Sewer | 120 | 4.3 |
| Parks and Recreation | 105 | 5.1 |
| Housing and Community Development | 263 | 5.4 |
| Natural Resources | 272 | 6.4 |
| Sewer | 153 | 6.6 |
| Water | 178 | 8.0 |
| Fire Protection | 146 | 15.7 |

**Source**:   U.S. Bureau of the Census, *1987 Governments File*.
**a.** Means calculated only for metropolitan areas with at least one district of selected function.

in metropolitan areas. State location accounts for about one-quarter of that variation for another six district subtypes: airport, transit, health and hospital, library, water, and natural resources districts. For only three district subtypes, ports, utilities, and parks and recreation, is state location a relatively weak influence on district prevalence. Analysis of district prevalence indicates clusters of districts by function: library (districts most numerous in metropolitan areas in Illinois and Indiana), fire protection (New York), sewer (Pennsylvania), natural resources (California), housing and community development (New England states), highways (Missouri), and health and hospitals (California). State-based practices and habits are clearly important determinants of district use.

The second relevant analysis for functional subtypes of districts is whether there is a positive relationship between developer presence and prevalence of development-oriented districts in a metropolitan area, as structuralist scholars hypothesize. Although analysis of district distribution by geographic and financial subtypes of districts did not find a significant effect of developer presence, such a relationship might exist for districts providing development-oriented services like water, sewer, and roads.

**TABLE 5-10**  Effect of State Location on Distribution of Districts, by Function

| Function | Adjusted $R^2$ |
|---|---|
| Sewer | .38 |
| Housing and Community Development | .38 |
| Fire Protection | .34 |
| Highway | .34 |
| Airport | .27 |
| Transit | .27 |
| Health and Hospital | .25 |
| Library | .25 |
| Water | .24 |
| Natural Resource | .24 |
| Port | .14 |
| Parks and Recreation | .11 |
| Utilities (Gas and Electric) | .08 |

**Note**:  Results are for an analysis of variance (ANOVA) model using state location as the sole explanatory variable (see text and note 22).

As the data in table 5–11 indicate, there is only weak statistical support for a positive relationship between the presence of development firms and the number of water, sewer, highway, or multifunction water-sewer districts in an area. The correlations are weak, proving significant at the .10 significance level only for water and multifunction water-sewer districts. Given the considerable case study support for such a link between developers and districts, the lack of statistical support may signal methodological problems accounting for developer presence, rather than the absence of an actual relationship in practice.

**TABLE 5-11**  Effect of Developer Presence on Number of Development-Oriented Districts

| Function | Pearson's r |
|---|---|
| Water | .12* |
| Multifunction Water-Sewer | .11* |
| Sewer | .04 |
| Highway | .04 |

**Note**:  See text and note 15 for explanation of developer presence.
*$p < .10$

## CONCLUSION

Empirical analysis of the determinants of special districts suggests three conclusions. The first is that no single theoretical explanation can account for the uneven distribution of districts across metropolitan areas. District prevalence results from a combination of factors, the most influential of which is the breadth of state laws enabling districts, a factor not linked directly to any theoretical perspective. Beyond this factor, there is at least some support for three of the four theoretical perspectives considered. The only exception is the structuralist perspective, which advances hypotheses about developer influence that are difficult to model in the aggregate and in which public agencies and private homeowners' associations may be substitutes for districts. In short, the breadth of district determinants suggests that no single theoretical explanation alone or best accounts for the presence of special-purpose governments in metropolitan areas.

The second conclusion is validation of the conceptual framework with respect to the complexity of special-purpose governments. Different geographic, financial, and functional subtypes of districts interact differently with factors proposed to influence district use. Understanding districts requires recognizing that *special districts* is a plural concept that embraces specific subtypes of districts, each with different motivations and purposes. As the frequent occurrence of findings contrary to theoretical predictions confirms, scholars and policy experts must be more precise when thinking theoretically and methodologically about specialized governments.

Third, the analyses underscore the importance of the legal environment as a key factor of district prevalence. Although demand-driven factors matter in accounting for district use, they do so within the parameters of a legal environment that enables districts. Put simply, states that permit more kinds of special districts have more special districts. Other metropolitan- and state-level legal and institutional factors—namely the number of municipal governments in an area and state-imposed rules governing municipal powers and revenue-raising capabilities—also influence district prevalence. Whatever influence nonlegal factors have is reflected, modified, and directed through a legal framework that permits, prohibits, encourages, or discourages particular government arrangements.

This last conclusion has particular relevance for policy. Although technological, cultural, economic, and demographic forces may be largely beyond the control of policymakers, legal levers are well within their grasp. By manipulating these levers—for example, by establishing the restrictiveness or permissiveness of local government formation and powers—policymakers set the ground rules for and ultimately predispose which government and service-delivery arrangements are possible and likely. Whether laws are in place to enable or encourage the outcomes policymakers desire is within the purview of public officials.

An important qualification of this conclusion is that legal structures, although clearly consequential, do not alone drive the institutional choices of public officials, residents, or developers. State-based legal attributes cannot explain intrastate differences in the distribution of districts. Faced with an identical set of legal parameters, government actors in different metropolitan areas within the same state may make different choices about local-government structure and the implementation of public services. For example, the foundation for work by W. E. Lyons, David Lowery, and Ruth Hoogland DeHoog rests on the very different political structures found in two metropolitan areas in Kentucky: Louisville, which is highly politically decentralized, and Lexington-Fayette County, a consolidated city-county government.[32] In a similar vein, Richard Peiser concluded that the variant use of municipal utilities districts within Texas—Houston Metropolitan Area has hundreds while Dallas Metropolitan Area has a handful, for example—was due to multiple local factors, including the hilliness of the land, water-table levels, settlement patterns, zoning regulations, and characteristics of the development community.[33] Although a permissive legal framework is necessary, it is clearly not sufficient for enabling local-government activity.

## CHAPTER NOTES

1. Data are for 312 metropolitan areas and primary metropolitan statistical areas (not including Honolulu, Hawaii, and Anchorage, Alaska) with boundaries defined as of 1987.

2. Compiled from data in U.S. Bureau of the Census, *1992 Census of Governments*, vol. 1, no.1, pp. 44–83, table 28.

3. Because of peculiarities in the data file of the *1987 Census of Governments*, Alexandria (La.) Metropolitan Area was not included in subsequent analysis. Because this metropolitan area had a single special-purpose government, the impact of its exclusion is negligible.

4. Because cross-tabulated data in table 5–3 account only for districts reporting both geographic and financial information, they do not represent completely the distribution of districts by financial mode. Analysis of the 12,088 districts (of 12,580) reporting financial data in 1987 reveals a slight nonreporting bias in favor of taxing districts: 55 percent of the total districts reporting have property-taxing powers versus 60 percent in the subset shown in table 5–3. In other words, nontaxing districts were less apt to report their geographic scope

than were taxing districts. The smaller number of districts accounted for in the cross-tabulated data is due to less-frequent reporting of geographic data: only 8,597, or approximately two-thirds, of districts indicated their geographic scope.

5. Most empirical analyses fail to distinguish districts by type. The few exceptions are MacManus, "Special District Governments," and Chicoine and Walzer, "Governmental Structure," both of which limit analyses to taxing districts; and Marando and Reeves, "State Responsiveness," which examines multijurisdictional districts only.

6. Although simple tallies of districts are not appropriate indicators of the degree to which metropolitan areas rely on special districts, they are appropriate for accounting for the distribution of districts. Subsequent analyses of the cost and policy outcomes of districts use reliance measures rather than tallies, pursuant to the discussion in chapter 3.

7. Sources for these variables are as follows. For number of municipalities: U.S. Bureau of the Census, *1987 Census of Governments*, vol. 1, no. 1. "Municipalities" includes all townships or town governments in the New England states, New York, New Jersey, and Pennsylvania, and also townships with greater than 2,500 persons in Michigan and Wisconsin. In these instances, townships generally function as full-service municipalities performing a wide range of urban functions. See ACIR, *State and Local Roles*, chap. 4. For average suburban population size: for municipal data, U.S. Bureau of the Census, *1987 Census of Governments*, vol. 1, no. 1; and for population estimates as of October 1986, U.S. Bureau of the Census, *1988 City and County Data Book* (Washington, D.C.: U.S. Government Printing Office, 1988), app. E. Figures were adjusted to omit population in centers with greater than 50,000 population.

8. Sources for variables are as follows. For population growth, 1970–1987: U.S. Bureau of the Census, *1988 City and County Data Book*, app. E; U.S. Bureau of the Census, *1972 Census of Governments*, vol. 1, no. 1; and U.S. Bureau of the Census, *1970 Census of Population*, vol. 1, pt. 1, sec. 1. *General Population Characteristics* (Washington, D.C.: U.S. Government Printing Office, 1972). For percent unincorporated: calculated from data in U.S. Bureau of the Census, *1982 Census of Governments*, vol. 1, no. 1. For income dispersion: calculated from original data provided by Michael A. Nelson, as used in Nelson, "Decentralization of the Subnational Public Sector," and modified using data in U.S. Bureau of the Census, *1980 Census of Population and Housing*, vol. 1, chap. C. *General Social and Economic Characteristics* (Washington, D.C.: U.S. Government Printing Office, 1983), various state issues, tables 124, 180.

9. Following Nelson, I measure income diversity as the standard deviation of 1979 household income across nine income classes. I modified Nelson's data by choosing midpoint values for the lowest and highest income classes as $4,000 and $70,000, respectively (Nelson used $5,000 and $50,000), and calculated income diversity scores for metropolitan areas not included in Nelson's study. See Nelson, "Decentralization of the Subnational Public Sector," p. 449.

10. For most goods higher income is associated with greater demand, although the income elasticity of demand for public goods may be positive or negative depending on the nature of the good. See Robert P. Inman, "The

Fiscal Performance of Local Governments: An Interpretive Review," in *Current Issues in Urban Economics*, ed. Peter Mieszkowski and Mahlon Straszheim (Baltimore: Johns Hopkins University Press, 1979), pp. 270–321; and Fisher, *State and Local Public Finance*, pp. 283–301.

11. Sources for these variables is as follows. For home-rule powers, annexation limits, and incorporation limits: Melvin B. Hill, Jr., *State Laws Governing Local Government Structure and Administration* (Athens: Institute of Government, University of Georgia, 1978). For debt and tax constraints: Susan A. MacManus, "State Government: The Overseer of Municipal Finance," in *The Municipal Money Chase*, ed. Alberta M. Sbragia (Boulder, Colo: Westview, 1983), pp. 155–59, table 6.3.

12. Following Schneider and Marando and Reeves, I do not include federal policies affecting local governments, on the assumption that federal policy effects are sufficiently uniform across metropolitan areas. See Schneider, *The Competitive City*, p. 223, n. 5; and Marando and Reeves, "State Responsiveness," p. 998.

13. Hill, *State Laws*, p. 12.

14. This measure is from MacManus, "The Overseer of Municipal Finance," pp. 155–59, table 6.3. The index accounts for sources of legal constraints (none, statutory, constitutional); millage rate limitations (none, 1–10 mills, over 10 mills); property tax levy limits (no or yes); full disclosure law requiring notice and public hearing of tax increases above a set formula (no or yes); and assessment constraints controlling the rate of increase in property assessment (no or yes). MacManus classified states as having either none, minimal, moderate, or heavy restrictions on the basis of points assigned to restrictions. I combined the none and minimal category into a single category.

15. The borrowing constraints index pertains to general obligation bonds only and accounts for the existence of rate limits (no or yes); the source of legal constraints (none, statutory, constitutional, or both); and the power to exceed debt limits (unlimited, restricted by vote requirement, none). Based on point assignments, states are classified as having either minimal, moderate, or heavy restrictions. MacManus, "The Overseer of Municipal Finance," pp. 155–59, table 6.3.

16. These data follow Hill, who classifies municipalities as having either broad, neutral, or limited home-rule powers according to provisions in state constitutions and statutes. Broad functional home-rule authority means "local governments have been given a great deal of autonomy in carrying out local functions, that local governmental powers are broad and allow for wide local discretion." Limited functional home-rule authority means that "local governments have been given little autonomy in carrying out local functions, that local governmental powers are greatly circumscribed and allow for limited local discretion." Hill, *State Laws*, p. 12.

17. See, for example, Fainstein et al., *Restructuring the City*; Stone and Sanders, eds., *The Politics of Urban Development*; Scott Cummings, ed., *Business Elites and Urban Development* (Albany: State University of New York Press, 1988); and Vogel, *Urban Political Economy*.

18. Burns, *The Formation of American Local Governments*, p. 127. Burns used a simple tally of the number of real estate developers to gauge developer

strength. To better account for variation across these firms, I weighted the already categorized data in U.S. Bureau of the Census, *County Business Patterns, 1982*. In particular, I counted each developer/subdivider firm (three-digit SIC code 655) with fewer than twenty employees as one firm equivalent. Firms with more than twenty employees counted as three firm equivalents. If the area had a real estate industry (two-digit SIC code 65) but no separate listing for developer/subdivider firms, I assigned one developer firm equivalent. If the area had no real estate industry listing (a Bureau of the Census convention indicating the entire industry had fewer than fifty total employees), I assigned no developer firm equivalents.

19. Sources for these variables are as follows. For population size: U.S. Bureau of the Census, *1988 City and County Data Book*, app. E. For metropolitan age, U.S. Bureau of the Census, *Census of Population* (Washington, D.C.: U.S. Government Printing Office, various editions, 1910–1980); and U.S. Bureau of the Census, *1988 City and County Data Book*, app. E. For functional breadth: U.S. Bureau of the Census, *1982 Census of Governments*, vol. 1, no. 1, app. A.

20. See, for example, Roland J. Liebert, *Disintegration and Political Action* (New York: Academic Press, 1976); Terry Nichols Clark, Lorna C. Ferguson, and Robert Y. Shapiro, "Functional Performance Analysis: A New Approach to the Study of Municipal Expenditures and Debt," *Political Methodology* 8, no. 2 (1982): 87–123; and Thomas R. Dye and John A. Garcia, "Structure, Function and Policy in American Cities," *Urban Affairs Quarterly* 14, no. 1 (1978): 103–22.

21. Data for this index are from the state profiles on government organization in U.S. Bureau of the Census, *1987 Census of Governments*, vol. 1, no. 1, app. A. The index is a tally of the different functional types of districts authorized by general enabling legislation. Each distinct functional type enabled counts as one function. If state law places moderate restrictions on formation of districts of a particular function (for example, by specifying a minimum population threshold for formation of a sewer district), I count one-half of a function. If state law places severe restrictions on formation of districts of a particular function (for example, by specifying a narrow population band or specific location for an airport authority), I count one-quarter of a function. Where separate laws enable districts of substantially the same function (for example, a water district and a waterworks district, both empowered to provide similar services), I count a single function for both. I exclude from the tally any functional types of districts formed by special enabling legislation only. The index tallies district functions as consistently as possible across states, despite interstate variation in legal frameworks.

22. The STATA statistical software used in this analysis permits a maximum of thirty-eight explanatory variables in regression models. As a consequence, testing the ANOVA model required creating thirty-eight "states" out of the total forty-nine states in the sample (fifty states minus Alaska and Hawaii, plus the District of Columbia). The following state combinations enabled this calculation: Arizona and New Mexico; Delaware, D.C., and Maryland; Idaho, Montana, and Wyoming; North Dakota, South Dakota, and Nebraska; New Hampshire, Vermont, and Maine; Rhode Island and Connecticut; Nevada and Utah; and Kentucky and West Virginia. All other states entered the ANOVA model individually.

**23.** On homeowners' associations, see Evan McKenzie, *Privatopia: Homeowner Associations and the Rise of Residential Private Government* (New Haven: Yale University Press, 1994).

**24.** ACIR, *State and Local Roles*, pp. 254–56; and, generally, J. Bollens, *Special District Governments*.

**25.** See Flickinger and Murphy, "Special Districts"; Keating, *Building Chicago*; and Hoffman, *Municipal Authorities in Pennsylvania*.

**26.** Such efforts, for example, are becoming more prevalent in New Jersey, a state with broad municipal home-rule powers. See New Jersey Department of Community Affairs, Regionalization and Special Services Unit, *Interlocal Services: Working Together* (Trenton: New Jersey Department of Community Affairs, 1991); and Eugene J. Schneider, *The Challenge of Local Partnerships* (Trenton, N.J.: Governor's Task Force on Local Partnerships, 1992).

**27.** See Leutwiler, "Playing Taps for Urban Growth Control"; and Biggs, "No Drip, No Flush, No Growth."

**28.** Cox and Nartowicz, "Jurisdictional Fragmentation."

**29.** Charles Hoch, "City Limits: Municipal Boundary Formation and Class Segregation," in *Marxism and the Metropolis*, 2nd ed., ed. William K. Tabb and Larry Sawers (New York: Oxford University Press, 1984), pp. 101–19; Logan and Molotch, *Urban Fortunes*, pp. 185–87; and, generally, Peterson, *City Limits*.

**30.** See McKenzie, *Privatopia*; and Mark A. Weiss and J. W. Watts, "Community Builders and Community Associations: The Role of Real Estate Developers in Private Residential Governance," in *Residential Community Associations: Private Governments in the Intergovernmental System?* ed. Advisory Commission on Intergovernmental Relations (Washington, D.C.: U.S. Government Printing Office, 1989), pp. 95–104.

**31.** See note 22 above.

**32.** W. E. Lyons, David Lowery, and Ruth Hoogland DeHoog, *The Politics of Dissatisfaction: Citizens, Services, and Urban Institutions* (Armonk, N.Y.: M. E. Sharpe, 1992).

**33.** Peiser, "The Economics of Municipal Utility Districts."

# 6

# Does Specialized Governance Cost More?

A familiar assertion of the political economy literature is that institutions matter. By extension, then, institutional choices matter. The analysis in the previous chapter revealed that multiple factors affect institutional choices, specifically the choice to rely on special-purpose as opposed to general-purpose governments for service delivery. In this and the next chapter I focus on the consequences of that choice. Chapter 7 will investigate the policy implications of specialized governance, particularly how it may affect the allocation of resources in metropolitan areas. This chapter examines the cost effects of specialized governance. The central question is whether metropolitan areas that rely on special-purpose governments pay more for services than do areas that rely on general-purpose governments.

## THEORETICAL HYPOTHESES

A remarkable point of agreement across the four theoretical perspectives reviewed in chapter 2 is that specialized service provision will lead to higher per capita spending than will general-purpose provision. Not so remarkably, the perspectives offer different reasons for that effect, which I call upward spending bias.

The public choice perspective holds the most favorable view of upward spending bias, observing that special-purpose governments are *intended* to enable more spending on a service. The strength of specialized governments, public choice proponents argue, is that they provide a means for satisfying service demands at the levels consumers prefer, even or especially when that level entails higher spending.[1] Joining public choice theorists in at least one respect are metropolitan ecologists who note that upward spending bias is a predictable outcome when entities are created to circumvent limitations on general-purpose government taxing and borrowing. Public officials, who typically seek reelection, take advantage of the purchasing power of special-purpose governments to maintain service levels while holding down municipal expenditures and avoiding politically risky tax increases. The outcome is higher spending by specialized governments than would occur under a general-purpose government. Some ecologists acknowledge that spending under such conditions may be a good thing: special districts can fund socially desirable projects that politically sensitive and spending-shy general-purpose governments are unable or unwilling to support.[2]

Other metropolitan ecologists, joined by institutional reformers and structuralist scholars, take a far less benign view of upward spending bias. For several reasons, these theorists contend that district attributes fuel unnecessary spending. As a functional fiefdom with an independent source of financing, districts may channel all their energies—and resources—into district programs, regardless of alternative needs and without competition from rival departments at budget time.[3] Like departments of general-purpose governments that enjoy earmarked funding, special-purpose governments have the means to spend more than they would if in a more competitive budgetary environment.[4] Districts' spatial monopolies are another culprit for upward spending bias. To the extent that districts have few or no competitors in an area, they have substantial economic freedom to spend (and price their goods) with relative impunity.[5] Because threats to relocate out of districts lack credibility—residents rarely incur the costs of a move on account of a single service—inflationary effects may be more severe and insoluble than in general-purpose governments.

A related catalyst for upward spending bias is districts' political isolation and limited access, which limit opportunities for citizen participation. This impairs the ability of citizens and the media to act as budgetary watchdogs, stay informed of district activity, or protest development projects, all of which might hold the reins on spending.[6] The practical difficulty of monitoring spending for upward of a dozen specialized governments results in more project approvals and higher expenditures than would likely occur in a more public and centralized decision-making environment.[7]

Last, institutional reformers allege that upward spending bias results also from the combination of functional specialization and special-district multiplicity, which inflate costs of administration and coordination.[8] Each specialized government bears independently the expense of accountants, attorneys, personnel directors, and other administrators whose talents and costs general-purpose governments can spread across numerous departments. In addition, argue reformers, compartmentalizing water, sewer, roads, housing, hospitals, natural resources, and other services into separate entities that have neither a mandate to cooperate nor an umbrella organization to provide oversight, leads to disorderly, duplicative, and costly service provision.[9]

The four theoretical perspectives are thus consistent in their forecast of higher costs associated with special-purpose versus general-purpose government, albeit for different reasons. The critical question is whether upward spending bias in fact pertains. If so, why? If not, why not?

## ASSESSING UPWARD SPENDING BIAS

### Methods

In methodological terms, the question is whether per capita spending is significantly higher in metropolitan areas that rely on special-purpose governments (hereafter district-reliant areas) than metropolitan areas that do not (hereafter nonreliant areas). This question is appropriately investigated separately for individual functions, as diagrammed schematically in figure 6–1. To determine the cost impact of *the fact*, as opposed to *the degree*, of special-purpose governance, a metropolitan area that relies at least to some degree on special districts for a function under investigation is considered district-reliant.

The existence of upward spending bias can be determined using difference of means tests, which in this instance would reveal whether there is a significant difference in mean per capita spending in district-reliant versus nonreliant metropolitan areas. This analysis requires two variables, one measuring per capita spending and another measuring degree of district reliance within a metropolitan area.

For fifteen different functions in each of the 311 metropolitan areas in the study, I calculated per capita spending as:

Per Capita Spending = Total Local-Government Expenditures/
Metropolitan Area Population.

The fifteen functions analyzed are airports, ports, transit, highways, fire protection, water, sewer, sanitation, natural resources (primarily flood control and drainage), parks and recreation, housing and community development, health and hospitals, parking, libraries, and utilities (gas and electric).

To overcome the shortcomings of tally-based measures of district reliance, as discussed in chapter 3, I measured district reliance for each of the fifteen functions in each metropolitan area as a ratio of district expenditures to total local-government expenditures on a function, as follows:

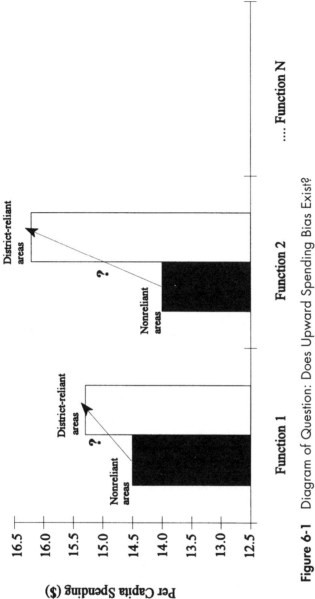

**Figure 6-1**  Diagram of Question: Does Upward Spending Bias Exist?

District Reliance = Spending by Special Districts/
                   Spending by Total Local Governments.[10]

For both measures, total local governments includes counties, municipalities, townships, and special districts and excludes school districts.[11] Throughout the analyses, only metropolitan areas with any local-government spending on a function are included in tests related to that function. For example, only the 114 of 311 metropolitan areas in which any local governments made expenditures on ports were included in analyses related to port services.

Data for calculating per capita spending and district reliance levels for metropolitan areas are available from the U.S. Bureau of the Census in the governments data file of the *1987 Census of Governments*. From this source, I collected information on the attributes and finances of the 12,565 special districts and 12,877 general-purpose governments in U.S. metropolitan areas in 1987. I aggregated this information into a smaller data set with 311 metropolitan area observations, each containing variables measuring local-government structure and finances.[12]

### Patterns of District Reliance

Before investigating the existence and extent of upward spending bias, it is important to understand the underlying patterns of district reliance, as reported in table 6–1. District reliance levels vary widely by function, from a low of 1.3 percent for highways to 47.1 percent for housing and community development. In the latter case, the relatively high reliance levels reflect the presence of federally funded, independent housing authorities in most metropolitan areas. With the exception of highways, development-oriented functions, namely airports, ports, water, sewer, transit, and utilities, rely to relatively high degrees on special-purpose governments for service. Reliance levels are lower for housekeeping services, namely fire protection, parks and recreation, libraries, and parking, which are commonly staples of municipal service provision. A social welfare function, health and hospitals, has an average level of district reliance.

The large standard deviations and the large number of 0 reliance values for most functions signal the need for caution in interpreting reliance levels. The 39 percent reliance level for transit, for example, implies that an average of about two-fifths of total local government spending on transit services in metropolitan areas is made by special-purpose governments. Although accurate, the figure is misleading in that sharing transit service responsibility between special-purpose and general-purpose governments is not typical. More precise and useful

**TABLE 6-1** District Reliance, by Function, 1987

| Function | $N^a$ | District Reliance Mean | District Reliance Standard Deviation | Range |
|---|---|---|---|---|
| Housing and Community Development | 311 | .471 | .312 | .000 (56 metropolitan areas) to 1.000 (Bismarck, N.Dak.; Decatur, Ala.; Victoria, Tex.) |
| Ports | 114 | .436 | .478 | .000 (56 metropolitan areas) to 1.000 (37 metropolitan areas) |
| Transit | 249 | .390 | .469 | .000 (139 metropolitan areas) to 1.000 (55 metropolitan areas) |
| Natural Resources | 307 | .300 | .338 | .000 (55 metropolitan areas) to 1.000 (8 metropolitan areas) |
| Airports | 292 | .202 | .278 | .000 (206 metropolitan areas) to 1.000 (20 metropolitan areas) |
| Sewer | 305 | .178 | .271 | .000 (128 metropolitan areas) to 1.000 (Greensboro, N.C.; Asheville, N.C.; Burlington, N.C.) |
| Water | 311 | .167 | .254 | .000 (112 metropolitan areas) to 1.000 (Portland, Maine) |
| Health and Hospitals | 311 | .167 | .303 | .000 (174 metropolitan areas) to .995 (Williamsport, Pa.; Sarasota, Fla.) |
| Libraries | 309 | .137 | .308 | .000 (227 metropolitan areas) to 1.000 (13 metropolitan areas) |
| Utilities (Gas and Electric) | 228 | .120 | .295 | .000 (177 metropolitan areas) to 1.000 (6 metropolitan areas) |
| Parks and Recreation | 311 | .077 | .187 | .000 (206 metropolitan areas) to .967 (Peoria, Ill.) |
| Fire Protection | 311 | .073 | .145 | .000 (173 metropolitan areas) to .744 (Naples, Fla.) |
| Parking | 266 | .050 | .193 | .000 (244 metropolitan areas) to 1.000 (Albany, Ga.) |
| Highways | 311 | .013 | .075 | .000 (250 metropolitan areas) to .975 (Boise, Idaho) |
| All Functions | 311 | .150 | .155 | .000 (Shreveport, La.; Monroe, La.) to .886 (Richland, Wash.) |

**Source:** Compiled from U.S. Bureau of the Census, *1987 Governments File.*

**Note:** District reliance is defined as special-district expenditures/total local-government expenditures.

a. $N$ = number of metropolitan areas (of 311 total) with any local-government spending on function.

153

is knowing that of the 249 metropolitan areas that provide transit at all, 194 of them, or 78 percent, have either complete reliance on special districts or no reliance at all.

Table 6–2 reports the number and mean reliance levels by function for metropolitan areas with reliance levels of .01 or higher, that is, areas in which districts account for at least 1 percent of total local-government spending on a function. The data indicate the pervasiveness and degree of district service provision. Services most widely provided by special-purpose governments are housing and community development (253 of 311 metropolitan areas, or over 80 percent, rely to least some degree on districts for these services) and natural resources (234 of 311, or 76 percent). The functions least widely provided by districts are highways, parking, and sanitation, each of which relies on districts to any degree in fewer than forty metropolitan areas.

The data in table 6–2 also indicate that for certain functions, namely transit, ports, and airports, metropolitan areas with at least some district

TABLE 6-2   District Reliance for Metropolitan Areas with Reliance Levels >.01, by Function

| | | District Reliance | |
| Function | $N^a$ | Mean | Standard Deviation |
| --- | --- | --- | --- |
| Transit | 109 | .891 | .235 |
| Ports | 57 | .871 | .272 |
| Airports | 80 | .736 | .358 |
| Parking | 20 | .665 | .300 |
| Utilities (Gas and Electric) | 44 | .620 | .378 |
| Housing and Community Development | 253 | .579 | .240 |
| Libraries | 79 | .534 | .399 |
| Health and Hospitals | 120 | .432 | .352 |
| Natural Resources | 234 | .393 | .337 |
| Sewer | 157 | .345 | .292 |
| Water | 182 | .284 | .278 |
| Sanitation | 36 | .281 | .289 |
| Parks and Recreation | 91 | .264 | .266 |
| Fire Protection | 115 | .197 | .180 |
| Highways | 23 | .170 | .225 |

Source:   Compiled from U.S. Bureau of the Census, *1987 Governments File.*
Note:   District reliance is defined as special-district expenditures/total local-government expenditures.
a. $N$ = number of metropolitan areas (out of total shown in table 6-1) with district reliance level greater than .01 for function.

reliance tend to rely on districts to a large degree—89.1 percent, 87.1 percent, and 73.6 percent, respectively. In other words, at the metropolitan scale, transit, ports, and airports are typically provided *either* by special districts *or* by general-purpose governments, but not ordinarily shared between the two. By contrast, low or medium district reliance levels at the metropolitan scale for highways, parks and recreation, and fire protection imply that even in metropolitan areas that have at least some district reliance, reliance on special districts is relatively mild.[13]

More precise depictions of the distribution of district reliance levels by function are illustrated by the histograms in figure 6–2. Functions can be divided into five general categories based on their patterns of reliance. Transit, airports, and ports have *bimodal, high-magnitude* patterns. As noted, these functions tend to be provided wholly by special districts or wholly by general-purpose governments, but rarely shared within a metropolitan area by both local-government types. A similar, but less extreme, pattern of district reliance holds for utilities and library functions, which have *bimodal, low-magnitude* distributions. These functions tend to be the responsibility of either special- or general-purpose governments, but the number of metropolitan areas in which districts take the lead is smaller than for functions with bimodal, high-magnitude distributions. By contrast, housing and community development and natural resources functions have *dispersed, high-magnitude* patterns of reliance. A relatively large number of metropolitan areas rely to varying degrees on special-purpose governments for these functions. Reliance patterns are also dispersed but across far fewer metropolitan areas in the *dispersed, low-magnitude* category. This group comprises water, health and hospitals, sewer, parks and recreation, and fire protection functions. The *minimal* reliance category contains highways, sanitation, and parking functions, for which a small number of metropolitan areas rely to any degree on special-purpose governments. Because low *n* values compromise the reliability of statistical tests, I exclude the highways, sanitation, and parking functions from subsequent analyses of district consequences.

## FINDINGS

The results of difference of means tests, shown in table 6–3, provide ample evidence of upward spending bias in district-reliant metropolitan areas. For all twelve functions tested, district-reliant metropolitan areas have significantly higher spending per capita than do nonreliant metropolitan areas.[14] In other words, for each function, metropolitan areas that forgo specialized governance spend significantly less per capita than do metropolitan areas that embrace specialized governance at least to some degree.[15]

*Bimodal Reliance, High Magnitude*

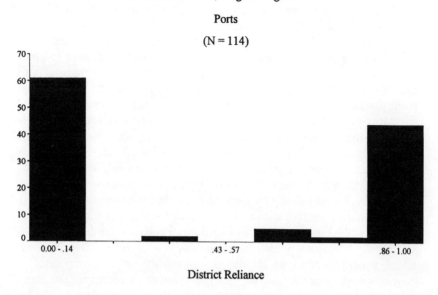

Ports

(N = 114)

District Reliance

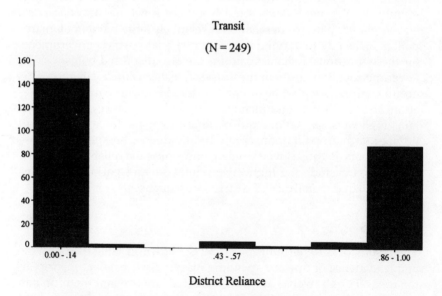

Transit

(N = 249)

District Reliance

**Figure 6-2** Patterns of District Reliance, by Function

*Bimodal Reliance, High Magnitude (con't.)*

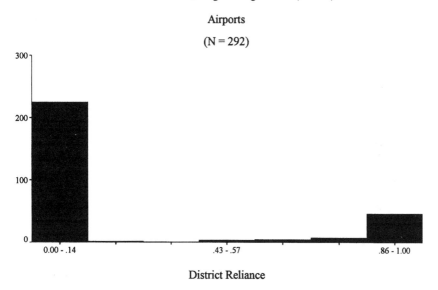

Airports

(N = 292)

District Reliance

*Bimodal Reliance, Low Magnitude*

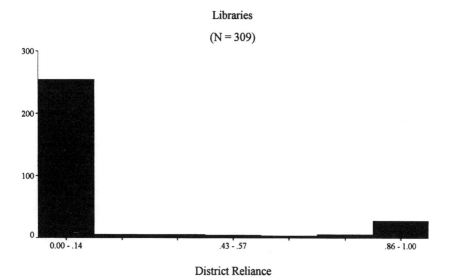

Libraries

(N = 309)

District Reliance

**Figure 6-2**   *continued*

*Bimodal Reliance, Low Magnitude (con't.)*

Utilities

(Gas and Electric)

(N = 228)

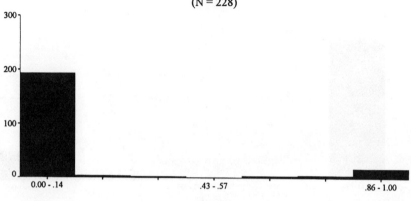

District Reliance

*Dispersed Reliance, High Magnitude*

Housing and Community Development

(N = 311)

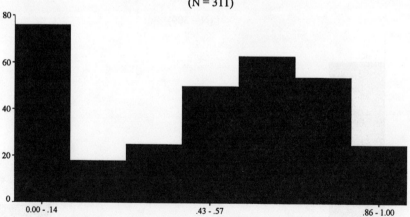

District Reliance

**Figure 6-2**   *continued*

*Dispersed Reliance, High Magnitude (con't.)*

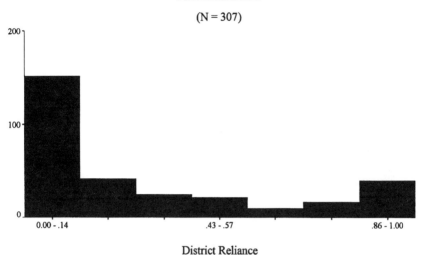

**Natural Resources**

(N = 307)

*Dispersed Reliance, Low Magnitude*

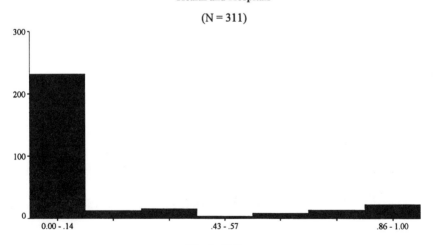

**Health and Hospitals**

(N = 311)

**Figure 6-2** *continued*

*Dispersed Reliance, Low Magnitude (con't.)*

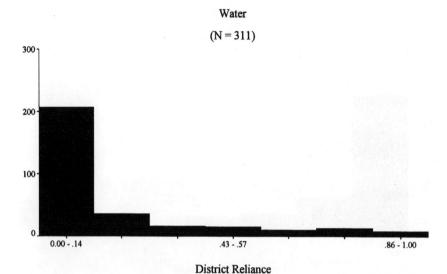

Water

(N = 311)

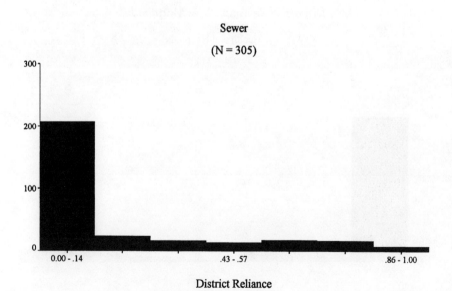

Sewer

(N = 305)

**Figure 6-2**   *continued*

*Dispersed Reliance, Low Magnitude (con't.)*

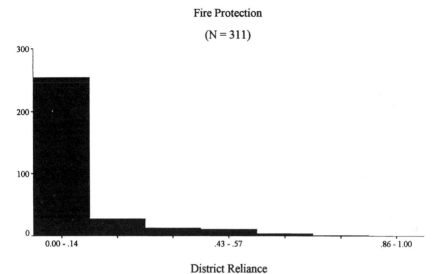

Fire Protection

(N = 311)

District Reliance

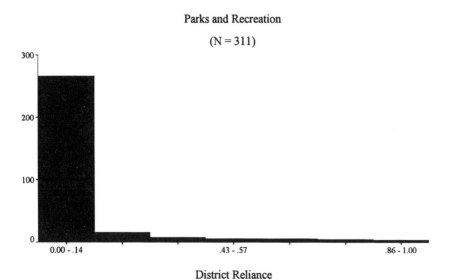

Parks and Recreation

(N = 311)

District Reliance

**Figure 6-2** *continued*

*Minimal Reliance*

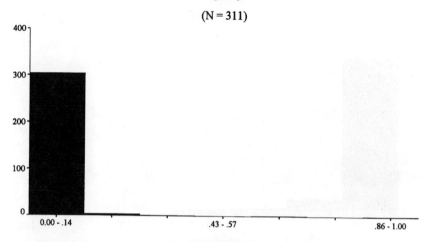

Highways

(N = 311)

District Reliance

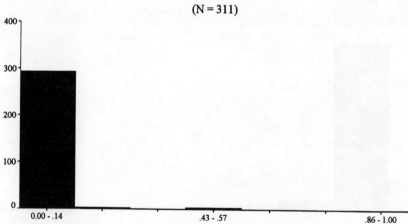

Sanitation

(N = 311)

District Reliance

**Figure 6-2**   *continued*

*Minimal Reliance (con't.)*

Parking

(N = 266)

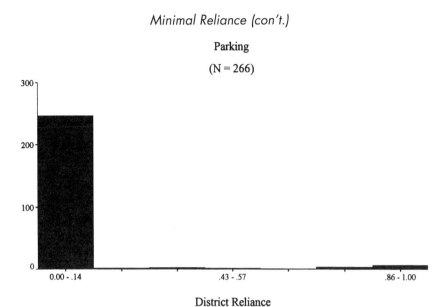

District Reliance

**Figure 6-2**   *continued*

The district-reliant versus nonreliant analysis is most appropriate for functions with bimodal distributions, for which district-reliant signifies a high degree of reliance. For services with dispersed patterns of reliance, of additional interest is the strength of the relationship between per capita spending and district reliance. That is, does per capita spending increase in lockstep with district reliance levels? The value of simple correlation coefficients (*Pearson's r*) between spending and reliance levels for the six functions with dispersed distributions reveals limited support. Water, fire protection, housing and community development, natural resources, and parks and recreation functions have positive but weak to mild relationships between per capita spending and district reliance. The only function with at least a moderate correlation (*r* = .53) is health and hospitals.[16] The results thus suggest an important dimension of upward spending bias. Higher spending associated with district reliance is not strongly correlated with actual levels of reliance. The factors driving upward spending bias appear to kick in even at low reliance levels. This implies that institutional attributes of specialized governments themselves, rather than aspects of special-purpose service provision, underlie upward spending bias.

The analysis of upward spending bias yields two clear findings: first, that district-reliant metropolitan areas spend more per capita than

**TABLE 6-3**  Per Capita Spending in District-Reliant versus Nonreliant Metropolitan Areas, by Function.

| | | Per Capita Spending ($) | | | |
| | | | | | |
| Function and Area Type | N | Mean | Standard Deviation | Difference of Means | $t^a$ |
| --- | --- | --- | --- | --- | --- |
| Airports | | | | | |
| District-reliant: | 80 | 20.30 | 26.14 | 6.58 | 2.02* |
| Nonreliant: | 206 | 13.72 | 20.59 | | |
| Ports | | | | | |
| District-reliant: | 57 | 21.36 | 29.83 | 15.59 | 3.38** |
| Nonreliant: | 56 | 6.17 | 15.96 | | |
| Transit | | | | | |
| District-reliant: | 109 | 39.86 | 55.96 | 27.79 | 5.65* |
| Nonreliant: | 139 | 12.06 | 13.64 | | |
| Utilities (Gas and Electric)[b] | | | | | |
| District-reliant: | 36 | 390.63 | 418.10 | 263.57 | 3.64** |
| Nonreliant: | 177 | 127.06 | 257.37 | | |
| Sewer | | | | | |
| District-reliant: | 157 | 69.41 | 43.06 | 20.56 | 4.74** |
| Nonreliant: | 128 | 48.85 | 29.95 | | |
| Water | | | | | |
| District-reliant: | 182 | 91.30 | 76.38 | 21.35 | 2.43* |
| Nonreliant: | 112 | 69.94 | 71.03 | | |
| Fire Protection | | | | | |
| District-reliant: | 115 | 44.44 | 15.92 | 7.80 | 4.12** |
| Nonreliant: | 173 | 36.64 | 15.47 | | |
| Parks and Recreation | | | | | |
| District-reliant: | 91 | 43.42 | 33.31 | 13.66 | 3.70** |
| Nonreliant: | 206 | 29.76 | 17.37 | | |
| Natural Resources | | | | | |
| District-reliant: | 234 | 11.06 | 26.45 | 7.12 | 3.77** |
| Nonreliant: | 55 | 3.94 | 5.68 | | |
| Libraries | | | | | |
| District-reliant: | 79 | 15.76 | 8.71 | 5.68 | 5.39** |
| Nonreliant: | 227 | 10.08 | 5.88 | | |
| Housing and Community Development | | | | | |
| District-reliant: | 253 | 39.69 | 34.43 | 14.07 | 3.40** |
| Nonreliant: | 56 | 25.63 | 26.44 | | |
| Health and Hospitals | | | | | |
| District-reliant: | 120 | 172.64 | 166.74 | 85.86 | 4.95** |
| Nonreliant: | 174 | 86.77 | 109.88 | | |

**Note:**  District-reliant areas are defined as metropolitan areas with district reliance level greater than .01. Nonreliant areas are defined as metropolitan areas with district reliance level less than or equal to .01.

**a.** $t$-statistic and two-tailed significance against the null hypothesis that difference of means is equal to 0.

**b.** Data exclude eight metropolitan areas that serve as headquarters for suprametropolitan utilities agencies (see note 14).

*$p < .05$      **$p < .01$

do nonreliant metropolitan areas; and second, that the magnitude of upward spending bias is only mildly correlated with levels of district reliance.

What accounts for these findings? Does upward spending bias stem, as public choice theorists contend, from demand for more or higher levels of service, which districts readily provide? Alternatively, does upward spending bias originate in cost-inflating political, administrative, and financial attributes of districts, as institutional reformers, metropolitan ecologists, and structuralist scholars argue? Or might some other factor account for the higher spending found in district-reliant as opposed to nonreliant metropolitan areas?

Aggregate-level data cannot pinpoint the reasons for upward spending bias. Only case study analysis can untangle the complex web of consumer demand, service-delivery patterns, and political contexts that influence spending and institutional choices within individual special districts and metropolitan areas. Aggregate analysis can, however, shed light on the validity of certain hypothesized reasons for upward spending bias. Three of these reasons with relevance to theoretical claims are (1) districts' orientation toward capital spending, (2) the inflationary effects of district multiplicity, and (3) factors associated with metropolitan demand.

## Capital-Spending Orientation

A common observation about special-purpose governments is that they are more inclined than are general-purpose governments to undertake major capital investment projects.[17] Driving this tendency are financial imperatives that prompt district boards to select large, revenue-generating projects with the greatest potential for repayment of revenue-bond debt. "The preference for profitable projects that is born of revenue bond financing, business boards, and internal yearnings for organizational autonomy," one observer noted,

> favors highways over rail transportation, water supply and power production over pollution abatement and recreational use of water resources, school building over expansion of student counseling, sports arenas over open space, industrial parks over small business assistance, and middle-income and luxury housing mortgage finance over rehabilitation and low-income housing construction.[18]

The inclination toward large-scale capital projects is reinforced by districts' focus on long-term strategic, rather than on short-term political or financial, considerations. Reliance on long-range demand results in more sewer systems, dormitories, mass transit lines, and industrial parks, for example, than would likely occur were capital investment decisions more closely tied to actual, rather than anticipated, needs.[19] Moreover, districts' low political visibility, exclusion from the need for voter approval of bond issues, and relative freedom from administrative controls make them an ideal institutional choice for capital projects. Readily available funding for projects, relatively speedy development approvals, and limited political visibility thwart public opposition that might slow, downsize, or obstruct capital development projects.[20]

To the extent that capital projects cost more than operations and maintenance activities, districts' orientation toward capital investments might well account for upward spending bias. To test this possibility requires two steps. The first is to verify that special-purpose governments devote proportionally more resources to capital projects than do general-purpose governments. The second is to determine whether significant spending differences between district-reliant and nonreliant metropolitan areas persist for operations and maintenance services only.

The spending data in table 6–4 confirm districts' orientation relative to general-purpose governments toward capital spending. For ten of the twelve functions analyzed, special districts allocate proportionally more resources to capital expenditures than do general-purpose governments. The only two exceptions are libraries, on which districts and general-purpose governments devote similar shares to capital expenditures, and housing and community development, on which general-purpose governments allocate proportionally more to capital expenditures than do districts.[21] Districts quite evidently provide a qualitatively different brand of service delivery, one more focused on capital projects. Given this, perhaps upward spending bias can be accounted for by districts' orientation toward the relatively expensive capital projects. If there exists evidence of no significant difference between district-reliant and nonreliant areas in per capita spending on operations and maintenance activities only, it would constitute support for public choice claims that upward spending bias results from responsiveness to citizen demands for development facilities, rather than from the political or administrative factors distinctive to special-purpose governments.

To test this possibility, I recalculated mean per capita spending levels for district-reliant and nonreliant metropolitan areas using operations and maintenance expenditures only. The results, shown in table 6–5, indicate that capital investment by districts contributes to, but by no means accounts for, upward spending bias. Although omitting capital and debt expenditures narrows the magnitude of per capita

**TABLE 6-4**  Spending Shares by Expenditure Category, General-Purpose versus Special-Purpose Governments (percentage of total spending)

| Function and Government Type | $N^a$ | Operations and Maintenance | Capital | Debt |
|---|---|---|---|---|
| | | Expenditure Category | | |
| Airports | | | | |
| General-purpose | 614 | 68 | 32 | 0 |
| Special-purpose | 103 | 54 | 40 | 6 |
| Ports | | | | |
| General-purpose | 147 | 75 | 24 | 1 |
| Special-purpose | 84 | 62 | 30 | 8 |
| Transit | | | | |
| General-purpose | 477 | 88 | 10 | 2 |
| Special-purpose | 167 | 85 | 13 | 2 |
| Utilities (Gas and Electric) | | | | |
| General-purpose | 752 | 89 | 6 | 5 |
| Special-purpose | 75 | 76 | 10 | 14 |
| Sewer | | | | |
| General-purpose | 5,576 | 81 | 19 | 0 |
| Special-purpose | 1,495 | 70 | 22 | 9 |
| Water | | | | |
| General-purpose | 5,663 | 76 | 14 | 10 |
| Special-purpose | 1,989 | 66 | 22 | 12 |
| Fire Protection | | | | |
| General-purpose | 9,403 | 91 | 9 | na |
| Special-purpose | 1,967 | 82 | 19 | na |
| Parks and Recreation | | | | |
| General-purpose | 7,823 | 87 | 13 | 0 |
| Special-purpose | 519 | 73 | 18 | 8 |
| Natural Resources | | | | |
| General-purpose | 1,559 | 92 | 8 | na |
| Special-purpose | 1,299 | 87 | 13 | na |
| Libraries | | | | |
| General-purpose | 4,269 | 94 | 6 | na |
| Special-purpose | 313 | 92 | 8 | na |
| Housing and Community Development | | | | |
| General-purpose | 2,130 | 73 | 27 | 0 |
| Special-purpose | 1,180 | 77 | 15 | 8 |
| Health and Hospitals | | | | |
| General-purpose | 4,370 | 97 | 3 | 0 |
| Special-purpose | 388 | 76 | 8 | 16 |

**Source**:   Calculated from U.S. Bureau of the Census, *1987 Governments File*.
**Note**:   na = not available. The *1987 Governments File* contains no separate line item for these debt categories.
**a.** Number of local governments with spending on the designated function. For special-purpose governments, N includes all entities making expenditures on the function regardless of type of district. Expenditures for multifunction districts are allotted across functions as appropriate.

**TABLE 6-5**  Per Capita Spending in District-Reliant versus Nonreliant Metropolitan Areas, Operations and Maintenance Expenditures Only, by Function.

| Function and Area Type | N | Mean | Standard Deviation | Difference of Means | $t^a$ |
|---|---|---|---|---|---|
| | | *Per Capita Spending ($)* | | | |
| Airports | | | | | |
| District-reliant: | 80 | 8.49 | 9.45 | 2.14 | 1.80 |
| Nonreliant: | 206 | 6.35 | 7.91 | | |
| Ports | | | | | |
| District-reliant: | 57 | 9.78 | 13.94 | 7.45 | 3.81** |
| Nonreliant: | 56 | 2.33 | 4.82 | | |
| Transit | | | | | |
| District-reliant: | 109 | 30.77 | 43.08 | 20.49 | 4.85** |
| Nonreliant: | 139 | 10.27 | 10.64 | | |
| Utilities (Gas and Electric)[b] | | | | | |
| District-reliant: | 36 | 250.72 | 256.33 | 165.76 | 3.76** |
| Nonreliant: | 177 | 84.96 | 143.71 | | |
| Sewer | | | | | |
| District-reliant: | 157 | 35.42 | 19.87 | 8.70 | 4.25** |
| Nonreliant: | 128 | 26.72 | 14.67 | | |
| Water | | | | | |
| District-reliant: | 182 | 41.42 | 23.85 | 8.10 | 3.40* |
| Nonreliant: | 112 | 33.33 | 16.91 | | |
| Fire Protection | | | | | |
| District-reliant: | 115 | 41.17 | 15.23 | 6.55 | 3.61** |
| Nonreliant: | 173 | 34.62 | 14.85 | | |
| Parks and Recreation | | | | | |
| District-reliant: | 91 | 30.69 | 19.58 | 7.34 | 3.31** |
| Nonreliant: | 206 | 23.34 | 12.09 | | |
| Natural Resources | | | | | |
| District-reliant: | 234 | 7.71 | 18.03 | 4.48 | 3.48** |
| Nonreliant: | 55 | 3.23 | 3.85 | | |
| Libraries | | | | | |
| District-reliant: | 79 | 13.64 | 7.56 | 4.73 | 5.14** |
| Nonreliant: | 227 | 8.91 | 5.32 | | |
| Housing and Community Development | | | | | |
| District-reliant: | 253 | 25.22 | 15.25 | 7.73 | 2.98** |
| Nonreliant: | 56 | 17.49 | 18.04 | | |
| Health and Hospitals | | | | | |
| District-reliant: | 120 | 140.07 | 129.43 | 58.68 | 4.18** |
| Nonreliant: | 174 | 81.39 | 100.26 | | |

Note: District-reliant areas are defined as metropolitan areas with district reliance level greater than .01. Nonreliant areas are defined as metropolitan areas with district reliance level less than or equal to .01.

a. $t$-statistic and two-tailed significance against the null hypothesis that difference of means is equal to 0.

b. Data exclude eight metropolitan areas that serve as headquarters for suprametropolitan utilities agencies (see note 14).

*$p < .05$      **$p < .01$

spending differences, district-reliant metropolitan areas spend significantly more per capita for a range of services than do nonreliant metropolitan areas on operations and maintenance expenditures. Only in the case of airport services are the differences in per capita spending statistically insignificant, indicating that capital-spending orientation accounts for upward spending bias for this function.

These findings counter the claim that upward spending bias can be explained by the capital-intensive nature of district service delivery. Special-purpose governments are clearly more oriented to capital spending than are general-purpose governments. This tendency does not, however, account for the persistence of upward spending bias for operations and maintenance expenditures. Other factors are at work.

## District Multiplicity

If institutional reformers are correct, one factor that may help account for upward spending bias is district multiplicity. In general-purpose governments, legal, financial, personnel, and administrative overhead can be apportioned across all departments. By contrast, in special-purpose governments overhead costs fall wholly on a single entity. The more numerous specialized governments are in an area, the higher the cumulative costs due to duplication of overhead expenditures. In addition, as the number of specialized governments increases, so too do transaction and coordination costs. Although the separate effects of different types of administrative costs are impossible to discern from aggregate analysis, it is possible to determine the overall spending impact of institutional multiplicity.

In methodological terms, the question is the extent to which upward spending bias is a function of the number of special-purpose governments in an area. To determine the possible influence of district multiplicity, I compare per capita spending in nonreliant metropolitan areas with spending in district-reliant areas that provide services with fewer than three special districts.[22] A finding that per capita spending levels are statistically indistinguishable between nonreliant metropolitan areas and areas that rely on just one or two districts for service constitutes support for the hypothesis that administrative costs associated with district multiplicity promote upward spending bias.

The data in table 6–6 provide evidence for the inflationary role of district multiplicity and associated administrative costs in upward spending bias. The data, which compare per capita spending (operations and maintenance expenditures) in nonreliant metropolitan areas with per capita spending in metropolitan areas that achieve reliance levels with fewer than three special districts, indicate that district multi-

**TABLE 6-6** Per Capita Spending in District-Reliant (with Fewer than Three District Providers) versus Nonreliant Metropolitan Areas, by Selected Function

| Function and Area Type | N | Per Capita Spending ($) | | Difference of Means | $t^b$ |
|---|---|---|---|---|---|
| | | Mean | Standard Deviation | | |
| Sewer | | | | | |
| District-reliant: | 65 | 33.19 | 20.40 | 6.47 | 2.28* |
| Nonreliant: | 128 | 26.72 | 14.67 | | |
| Water | | | | | |
| District-reliant: | 54 | 39.82 | 21.53 | 6.49 | 1.95 |
| Nonreliant: | 112 | 33.33 | 16.91 | | |
| Fire Protection | | | | | |
| District-reliant: | 16 | 45.51 | 19.18 | 10.89 | 2.21* |
| Nonreliant: | 173 | 34.62 | 14.85 | | |
| Parks and Recreation | | | | | |
| District-reliant: | 45 | 26.50 | 19.13 | 3.16 | 1.06 |
| Nonreliant: | 206 | 23.34 | 12.09 | | |
| Natural Resources | | | | | |
| District-reliant: | 98 | 2.92 | 5.47 | −0.31 | 0.41 |
| Nonreliant: | 55 | 3.23 | 3.85 | | |
| Libraries | | | | | |
| District-reliant: | 43 | 14.33 | 9.40 | 5.42 | 3.67** |
| Nonreliant: | 227 | 8.91 | 5.32 | | |
| Housing and Community Development | | | | | |
| District-reliant: | 105 | 22.26 | 14.79 | 4.77 | 1.70 |
| Nonreliant: | 56 | 17.49 | 18.04 | | |
| Health and Hospitals | | | | | |
| District-reliant: | 75 | 133.85 | 140.60 | 52.45 | 2.93** |
| Nonreliant: | 174 | 81.39 | 100.26 | | |

Notes: District-reliant areas are defined as metropolitan areas with district reliance level greater than .01. Nonreliant areas are defined as metropolitan areas with district reliance level less than or equal to .01. Analysis not conducted for four functions with an average of fewer than two districts per metropolitan area: airports, transit, ports, and utilities.

a. N for district-reliant areas includes only metropolitan areas with fewer than three special districts providing function (also see note 23).

b. t-statistic and two-tailed significance against the null hypothesis that difference of means is equal to 0.

*$p < .05$    **$p < .01$

plicity does in some cases account for spending differences between the two types of metropolitan areas.[23] For natural resources, parks and recreation, and, to a lesser extent, housing and community development, and water functions, institutional parsimony offsets the per capita spending differences between district-reliant and nonreliant metropolitan areas. For these functions, service arrangements characterized by multiple (three or more) districts providing a function account for upward spending bias. When fewer than three special districts provide these functions, there is no statistically significant difference in per capita spending between district-reliant and nonreliant metropolitan areas. At least for natural resources, parks and recreation, housing and community development, and water services, institutional reformers are correct that district multiplicity, perhaps because of its attendant duplication of overhead, transaction, and coordination costs, has an inflationary effect.

The effect of district multiplicity does not account for upward spending bias for fire protection, sewer, library, and health and hospitals services. Even when only a few districts provide services, district-reliant metropolitan areas have significantly higher per capita spending than nonreliant metropolitan areas. For these services, the higher spending associated with districts cannot be attributed to the administrative costs of institutional duplication, as reformers argue.

Two exceptions to the general pattern illuminate another dimension of upward spending bias. Contrary to institutional-reform hypotheses, for both library and health and hospital services, metropolitan areas with only one or two districts actually have higher per capita spending levels than do metropolitan areas with three or more districts, although spending differences for libraries fail to achieve statistical significance at the .10 level. To the extent fewer districts implies larger districts, this finding suggests that upward spending bias may originate in larger, region-serving districts, which commonly offer a broader— and, hence, more expensive—package of services than smaller districts. A regional hospital, for example, may offer specialized treatment facilities, a trauma center, and a neonatal unit, facilities not typically found in smaller, local hospitals. A regional library district similarly may offer a full range of audiovisual, computerized cataloging, or government documents services not found at local libraries.[24] In these cases, the higher service costs associated with regional facilities evidently outweigh the higher administrative costs associated with multiple districts.[25]

On balance, the effects of district multiplicity are mixed. For water, parks and recreation, housing and community development, and natural resources functions, district multiplicity accounts for upward spending bias. For sewer, libraries, health and hospitals, and fire protection, district multiplicity does not explain the higher per capita spending levels associated with special-purpose governance. Thus there is partial confirmation of institutional-reformers' claims of the inflationary effects of institutional multiplicity. Multiplicity is not the whole story, however; still other factors operate.

## Metropolitan Demand Factors

A third set of possible contributors to upward spending bias originates in the service demands of metropolitan residents. Of particular interest are three often-cited determinants of spending levels: metropolitan population size, metropolitan area age, and per capita income. In particular, larger metropolitan areas are associated with higher per capita spending because the number and range of programs and facilities provided tend to increase with metropolitan size.[26] If larger metropolitan areas are also those that rely most on special districts, then spending differences attributed to institutional choices may actually be due to the positive association between spending and metropolitan population size.

Observers offer two major reasons for a positive relationship between metropolitan area age and spending levels. First, older centers incur higher expenses to operate and maintain aging facilities. Second, older centers tend to be responsible for a wider breadth of urban functions.[27] If older metropolitan areas are also those with higher levels of district reliance, then higher per capita spending levels may actually be a function of metropolitan area age.

Last, a sizeable body of research concludes that for most functions there is a positive association between per capita income and the demand for, and hence spending on, public services.[28] If higher- as opposed to lower-income metropolitan areas have higher district reliance levels, then perhaps income levels, rather than institutional choices, are responsible for upward spending bias.

Multiple regression analysis offers a useful technique for testing the influence of these demand factors on upward spending bias. In methodological terms, the question of interest is whether district reliance has a positive and significant effect on per capita spending levels, after controlling for metropolitan population size, metropolitan area age, and per capita income. If so, then demand factors cannot account for upward spending bias, implying that other factors, perhaps inherent to special-purpose governments themselves, are at work.

In conducting these tests I measure district reliance in two ways. For functions with dispersed reliance distributions (see figure 6–2), district reliance is the actual level of reliance. For functions with bi-modal distributions, reliance is measured as a binary variable, which takes the value 0 for no district reliance and 1 for any reliance level greater than .01. Except for the minor differences indicated below, both definitions of reliance lead to the same conclusions.

Of preliminary interest in the regression results, shown in table 6–7, are three findings related to the control variables. First, the data confirm that larger, older, more affluent metropolitan areas tend to have higher per capita spending levels. The only exceptions relate to metropolitan area age: younger metropolitan areas have significantly higher per capita spending on natural resources and health and hospitals services than do older metropolitan areas, after controlling for other factors.[29] Second, per capita income tends to have a stronger relationship with per capita spending than do metropolitan age and

TABLE 6-7  Summary of Regression Results, Determinants of Per Capita Spending, By Function (statistical significance at < .05 level)

| | Explanatory Variables | | | |
| Function | Population Size | Metropolitan Area Age | Per Capita Income | District Reliance[a] |
|---|---|---|---|---|
| Airports | + | ns | + | ns |
| Transit | + | ns | + | ns |
| Ports | ns | ns | ns | + |
| Utilities[b] | ns | ns | ns | + |
| Sewer | ns | + | + | + |
| Water | + | ns | + | ns |
| Fire Protection | ns | ns | + | ns |
| Natural Resources | ns | − | + | + |
| Library | ns | ns | + | + |
| Parks and Recreation | ns | ns | + | + |
| Housing and Community Development | + | + | ns | + |
| Health and Hospitals | + | − | ns | + |

Notes:   Dependent variables are per capita operations and maintenance expenditures for indicated function. Entries signify significance (at .05 level) of explanatory variable: "+" = positive and significant; "−" = negative and significant; "ns" = not significant.
a. Measured as actual reliance level except for functions with bimodal distributions (airports, ports, transit, utilities, library), for which reliance is measured as a binary variable using 1 for reliance level greater than .01.
b. Data exclude eight metropolitan areas that serve as headquarters for suprametropolitan utilities agencies (see note 14).

population size. Third, for all but four functions—utilities, ports, health and hospitals, and housing and community development—per capita spending is positive and significantly related to metropolitan income levels.[30]

The findings are mixed with respect to the central variable of interest, district reliance. For four services—airports, transit, fire protection, and water—there is no significant difference in per capita spending between district-reliant and nonreliant metropolitan areas, after controlling for demand factors. In particular, the demands of higher income and larger metropolitan areas are more influential than is district reliance in accounting for higher per capita spending on these services.

For the remaining services—utilities, ports, library, natural resources, sewer, housing and community development, health and hospitals, and parks and recreation—district reliance has a positive and significant association with per capita spending, even after controlling for the inflationary effects of population size, metropolitan age, and affluence. Demand attributes cannot explain why district-reliant metropolitan areas spend higher amounts per capita than do nonreliant areas. For any given metropolitan area population size, age, or income level, the institutional choice to use special-purpose governments leads to higher per capita spending than does the choice to use general-purpose governments.

## Summary

What are the lessons of upward spending bias? The primary message is that specialized service delivery is associated with higher per capita spending. The reasons for this outcome vary, as summarized in table 6–8. Districts' orientation toward capital projects contributes to upward spending bias, however it cannot account for the persistence of higher per capita spending on operations and maintenance in district-reliant versus nonreliant metropolitan areas. For a few services, district multiplicity, metropolitan population size, metropolitan area age, and per capita income levels underlie upward spending bias, which lends support to institutional-reform contentions about the costs of administrative duplication and public choice contentions about consumer demand. Of considerable interest is that upward spending bias persists for sewer, library, health and hospitals, ports, and utilities services. This persistence supports assertions of reformers, structuralists, and metropolitan ecologists that upward spending bias stems from distinctive attributes of special-purpose governments themselves. Although aggregate analysis cannot isolate their independent effects, the inflationary influence of political isolation, functional specialization, and

**TABLE 6-8** Summary of Findings on Upward Spending Bias (answer to question, "Is there statistical evidence (.05 significance level) of upward spending bias?")

| Function | Total Expenditures | Does Upward Spending Bias Exist? | | After Controlling for Demand Factors[c] |
| --- | --- | --- | --- | --- |
| | | After Controlling for Capital Expenditures[a] | After Controlling for District Multiplicity[b] | |
| Airports | yes | no | —[d] | no |
| Transit | yes | yes | — | no |
| Ports | yes | yes | — | yes |
| Utilities | yes | yes | — | yes |
| Sewer | yes | yes | yes | yes |
| Water | yes | yes | no | no |
| Fire Protection | yes | yes | yes | no |
| Natural Resources | yes | yes | no | yes |
| Library | yes | yes | yes | yes |
| Parks and Recreation | yes | yes | no | yes |
| Housing and Community Development | yes | yes | no | yes |
| Health and Hospitals | yes | yes | yes | yes |

a. Operations and maintenance expenditures only; "no" signifies upward spending bias accounted for by district capital-expenditure orientation (see table 6-5).

b. Operations and maintenance expenditures only; "no" signifies upward spending bias for operations and maintenance functions accounted for by district multiplicity (see table 6-6).

c. Operations and maintenance expenditures only; "no" signifies upward spending bias for operations and maintenance accounted for by demand factors: metropolitan population size, metropolitan area age, or per capita income (see table 6-7).

d. "—" signifies test not applicable to this function.

administrative and financial flexibility cannot be ruled out as likely sources of upward spending bias.

Although the reasons for upward spending bias vary, as a phenomenon it shows remarkable stability and persistence. The principal lesson is that the institutional choice to rely on special districts, as opposed to general-purpose governments, engenders higher costs.

## A DYNAMIC VIEW

The cross-sectional analysis peels several layers from the complex issue of the cost implications of district service delivery. Factoring in additional control variables or information on the production processes of specific services would perhaps shed additional light. Yet even with more detailed specifications, cross-metropolitan differences not accounted for by statistical models would remain.

Rather than pursue the cross-sectional path, I shift focus to the dynamic effect of switching over time from general-purpose to special-purpose governments for service delivery. Dynamic analysis takes advantage of the internal controls provided by comparing the same metropolitan area at two points in time. Factors such as regional location, legal and institutional framework, historical culture, and, to a certain extent, demographic attributes remain relatively fixed, permitting comparison of the cost effects of institutional choices over time.

### Measuring Upward Spending Bias over Time

The central concern of the dynamic analysis is the impact on per capita spending levels when a metropolitan area switches from general-purpose governments to special districts for service delivery. Does upward spending bias operate over time? That is, do per capita spending levels increase more following a switch from general- to special-purpose governments than they would if the metropolitan area continued to provide services using general-purpose governments? To investigate this issue, I examine how metropolitan area per capita spending levels for a function changed between 1962 and 1987 depending on institutional choices made in that twenty-five-year period. Comparing per capita spending at two distant time points minimizes the potential to capture short-term spending spikes associated with institutional start-up costs. The analysis instead captures the long-term cost implications that are of greatest policy interest.

The first dynamic analysis examines metropolitan areas that did not rely on special districts in 1962. For each function, I identify three possible paths for nonreliant metropolitan areas based on the institutional outcome in 1987. To be specific, for any function, metropolitan areas that were nonreliant in 1962 had three institutional choices by 1987: (1) to continue providing the function using general-purpose governments, that is, to be nonreliant areas in 1987; (2) to become district-reliant at a low reliance level, which I define as a reliance level below the mean reliance level for all metropolitan areas for the function; or (3) to become district-reliant at a high reliance level, defined as a reliance level at or above the mean reliance level for all metropolitan areas for the function. Metropolitan areas could, of course, follow different institutional-choice paths for different functions.

Diagrammatically, for each function, nonreliant metropolitan areas in 1962 made one of three institutional choices by 1987:

| *Metropolitan Area in 1962:* | *Metropolitan Area in 1987:* |
|---|---|
| Nonreliant | 1) Nonreliant; or |
| | 2) District-reliant, low level; or |
| | 3) District-reliant, high level |

where low level and high level signify district reliance levels below or above, respectively, the mean reliance level for all metropolitan areas for a function.

Associated with each institutional-choice path are changes in per capita spending levels. To determine these changes over time, I derive an index that measures how a metropolitan area's spending on a selected function compares to mean per capita spending on that function for all metropolitan areas. This spending index is calculated as:

Per capita spending index = Per capita expenditures in a metropolitan area/mean per capita expenditures in all metropolitan areas.

Index values below 1 indicate that the metropolitan area spends less per capita than the aggregate metropolitan average on a service. Index values above 1 indicate that the metropolitan area spends higher than the aggregate average. An index value equal to 1 indicates that the metropolitan area spends exactly the mean per capita level for all metropolitan areas.

If the choice to use special-purpose governments does lead to higher per capita spending, then index values should increase over the twenty-five-year period in metropolitan areas that switch from no reliance to either low or high district reliance by 1987. Index levels should remain relatively stable (or may decrease if switching to special-purpose governments is widespread) for metropolitan areas that remain nonreliant.[31]

The *1962 Census of Governments* provides data on local government expenditures by function and by type of local government for all counties designated metropolitan as of 1962.[32] From this source I collected spending data by function for special districts and total aggregate local governments. Because the 1962 census used a more expansive definition for utilities services and did not report financial statistics for either nonmetropolitan counties or New England county equivalents, it was necessary to modify 1987 spending data to achieve comparability across time. This entailed four adjustments: (1) combining transit, and gas and electric utilities for 1987 into a single utilities category; (2) excluding New England metropolitan areas from the analysis; (3) excluding metropolitan areas so designated after 1962; and (4) modifying 1987 data to exclude spending by any counties added to a metropolitan area after 1962. These adjustments yielded a data set comprising 190 metropolitan area observations with boundaries equivalent to those delimited in 1962.[33] From this data set, which has comparable financial data for eleven functions, I calculated per capita spending indices for each function in each metropolitan area for 1962 and 1987.

## Upward Spending Bias over Time

Before assessing upward spending bias over time, of preliminary interest is how district reliance levels changed between 1962 and 1987 by function. The data in table 6–9 reveal that for all but one function, reliance levels increased over the twenty-five-year period. The largest absolute increases in district reliance levels occurred for airports, ports, library, and sewer services. Smaller, though often proportionally significant, increases occurred for water, natural resources, health and hospitals, utilities, parks and recreation, and fire protection. The only service bucking the trend toward greater district reliance is housing and community development. Although still quite reliant on special-purpose governments in absolute terms, housing and community development authorities were in 1987 relatively less dominant with respect to providing these functions than they were in the early 1960s when federally funded urban renewal activity was especially vigorous.

The results of the dynamic analysis are reported in table 6–10. Due to the unreliability of figures based on low *n* values, I analyze only those functions for which at least seven metropolitan areas follow each choice path. This criterion eliminates three functions (ports, natural resources, and housing and community development) that in 1962 had relatively few nonreliant metropolitan areas. It also eliminates one function (fire protection) that had numerous nonreliant metropolitan areas in 1962 (140 of 189), but only 19 of these shifted from nonreliant

**TABLE 6-9**  Change in District Reliance, 1962–1987, by Function

| Function | N (1962/1987)[a] | 1962 | 1987 | Change, 1962–1987[b] |
|---|---|---|---|---|
| | | District Reliance Level | | |
| Airports | 171/176 | .085 | .250 | .165 |
| Ports | 61/69 | .329 | .461 | .132 |
| Libraries | 185/187 | .061 | .144 | .083 |
| Sewer | 190/189 | .138 | .198 | .060 |
| Water | 190/190 | .116 | .168 | .052 |
| Natural Resources | 186/189 | .236 | .282 | .046 |
| Health and Hospitals | 190/190 | .095 | .139 | .044 |
| Utilities (gas, electric, transit) | 127/128 | .084 | .116 | .032 |
| Parks and Recreation | 190/190 | .071 | .096 | .025 |
| Fire Protection | 190/190 | .034 | .057 | .023 |
| Housing and Community Development | 168/190 | .567 | .445 | −.122 |

**Sources:**  Compiled from data in U.S. Bureau of the Census, *1962 Census of Governments*, vol. 5, pp. 282–460, table 13; and U.S. Bureau of the Census, *1987 Governments File*.
**Note:**  District reliance is defined as special-district expenditures/total local-government expenditures for function.
**a.** N = number of metropolitan areas (of 190 total, constant 1962 boundaries) with any local-government spending on the function in 1962 and 1987, respectively.
**b.** Figures denote absolute, not percentage, change in district-reliance level.

to low or high district reliance by 1987 (and, of these, only two switched to high reliance). Drawing inferences from choice path data with fewer than fifteen or so cases warrants caution.

Of preliminary note is that most nonreliant metropolitan areas in 1962 remained nonreliant in 1987. The per capita spending index for these areas in 1962 was generally at or below 1, confirming that nonreliant metropolitan areas spent less per capita than did district-reliant metropolitan areas at that time. Likewise, nonreliant metropolitan areas in 1987 had lower-than-average levels of per capita spending, consistent with the hypothesis of upward spending bias over time.

The findings of greatest interest are those shown in the third line under each service. This line indicates the effect on relative per capita spending of shifting between 1962 and 1987 from no reliance on special-purpose governments to high reliance. For all functions analyzed, the per capita spending indices increase along with the shift from nonreliance to high district reliance. For four services—airports, water, health

**TABLE 6-10** Dynamic Analysis of Upward Spending Bias, 1962–1987

| Function | Number of Metropolitan Areas | | | | Index of Per Capita Expenditures | |
|---|---|---|---|---|---|---|
| | No reliance 1962 | No reliance 1987 | Low reliance 1987 | High reliance 1987 | 1962 | 1987 |
| Airports | 146 → | 113 | 7 | 26 | 1.04 | 0.87 |
| | | | | | 1.01 | 0.69 |
| | | | | | 0.96 | 1.42 |
| Sewer | 113 → | 79 | 20 | 14 | 1.02 | 0.84 |
| | | | | | 0.94 | 1.05 |
| | | | | | 0.76 | 0.84 |
| Water | 107 → | 70 | 26 | 11 | 0.82 | 0.85 |
| | | | | | 1.09 | 1.01 |
| | | | | | 0.88 | 1.10 |

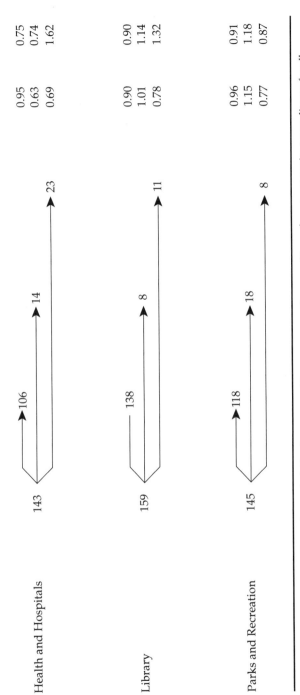

Health and Hospitals

Library

Parks and Recreation

**Notes:** *****Index of Per Capita Expenditures is defined as metropolitan area per capita expenditures/mean per capita expenditures for all metropolitan areas (of 190) providing function. *N* indicates number of metropolitan areas switching from no district reliance in 1962 to no, low, or high reliance by 1987.

and hospitals, and libraries—the change in index value is appreciable, typically increasing from well below to well above 1. Although aggregate analysis cannot discern the reasons for this phenomenon, the outcome is clear: metropolitan areas that had lower per capita spending than average on these functions in 1962 had, after switching to special districts by 1987, considerably higher than average per capita spending for these functions.

The persistence and strength of upward spending bias over time are reinforced somewhat, although not wholly, by the experience of metropolitan areas that switched from high district reliance in 1962 to no or low district reliance by 1987. It is not surprising that far fewer metropolitan areas made this choice, which prevents analysis of several functions. Still, at least ten metropolitan areas switched from high district reliance in 1962 to either no or low reliance by 1987 for five functions: sewer, water, natural resources, health and hospitals, and housing and community development.

The results, shown in table 6–11, provide mixed support for upward spending bias. For three of the five functions, spending index levels fall over the twenty-five-year period, in the case of natural resources quite considerably. There are two exceptions. Per capita spending on housing and community development functions in the metropolitan areas that switched from district reliance to nonreliance or low reliance by 1987 starts and remains well below average. This may be an artifact of the uncommon case of housing services, for which district provision is the norm in both years. The second exception is the health and hospitals function for which increases in the spending index accom-

---

**TABLE 6-11**  Dynamic Analysis of Upward Spending Bias, High Reliance to No or Low Reliance, by Selected Function

| Function | N | Index of Per Capita Expenditures | |
| --- | --- | --- | --- |
| | | *1962* | *1987* |
| Sewer | 10 | 1.13 | 1.00 |
| Water | 14 | 1.24 | 1.18 |
| Housing and Community Development | 19 | .59 | .69 |
| Natural Resources | 17 | 1.46 | 1.00 |
| Health and Hospitals | 15 | 1.05 | 1.29 |

Note:  Index of per capita expenditures is defined as metropolitan area per capita expenditures/mean per capita expenditures for all metropolitan areas (of 190) providing function. *N* indicates number of metropolitan areas switching from high district reliance in 1962 to no or low reliance by 1987. Metropolitan areas with extreme high per capita spending (determined separately for each function) omitted from analysis.

pany the switch from special-purpose to general-purpose governance. The high- to low-reliance analysis overall provides mixed confirmation of the dynamic dimension of upward spending bias. Only for selected functions do metropolitan areas that switch *from* special-purpose *to* general-purpose governments reduce their relative per capita spending levels.

On balance, the dynamic analyses demonstrate that upward spending bias operates over time. Switching from general-purpose to special-purpose governance leads to significant increases in relative spending levels. The consistency of this dynamic effect across a range of functions implies that factors inherent to special districts, rather than to some aspect of service demand, drive upward spending bias over time. Whether metropolitan interest groups intend it, the institutional choice to rely on specialized governments induces higher costs.

## CONCLUSION

Analysis of the fiscal consequences of special-purpose governance yields three major findings. First, per capita public spending is positively related to the institutional choice to use special-purpose, as opposed to general-purpose, governments for service delivery. For a wide range of functions, district-reliant metropolitan areas spend more per capita than do nonreliant metropolitan areas. A relatively insignificant amount of this upward spending bias can be attributed to districts' greater orientation toward expensive capital projects relative to less costly operations and maintenance activities. For some functions the inflationary effects of district multiplicity or demand-related factors of large metropolitan populations, older metropolitan age, or relatively high per capita income levels account in part for the higher levels of spending in district-reliant metropolitan areas. For several other functions, namely sewer, health and hospitals, ports, utilities, and libraries, the institutional choice to rely on special districts is itself associated with higher costs, even after controlling for other factors. The analysis thus points to institutional attributes of specialized governments as the likely sources of higher spending.

The second finding is verification of the conceptual framework's contention that special districts cannot be understood as an undifferentiated local-government category. Different functional subtypes of districts are indeed associated with different fiscal outcomes. Although upward spending bias applies to all functions, the reasons for this bias vary by function. Higher per capita spending is driven sometimes by districts' capital spending orientation, sometimes by the costs of district multiplicity, sometimes by factors related to service demand, and sometimes by attributes distinctive to special-purpose governments themselves. Once again, to assume that special-purpose governments comprise an undifferentiated class of local governments is to make a faulty assumption.

The third finding is that upward spending bias operates over time. For many functions, the institutional choice to switch from general-purpose to special-purpose service delivery increases relative spending from below-average to above-average levels. Metropolitan interest groups—residents, local government officials, and developers—should be made aware that, at least in the aggregate, the choice to rely on special districts for service delivery means spending more per capita than does the choice to deliver services using general-purpose governments.

Support for upward spending bias is thus quite robust over time and place. It is important, however, to clarify what upward spending bias does not imply. Service cost is not equivalent to service efficiency. Efficiency refers to a measure of service value, specifically the value of outcomes (in both consumer preferences and production terms) per unit of input, which is sometimes referred to colloquially as "bang for the buck." To measure efficiency requires information on consumer service preferences (or, ex post facto, consumer service satisfaction) and production factors (service costs, quality, and quantities). Because such data are not readily available and difficult to collect, gauging efficiency is often impossible as a practical matter. Although researchers sometimes make the expedient assumption that service expenditure is a proxy for output quality, this adjustment is misleading.[34] Findings based on public expenditures, in this chapter and elsewhere, are appropriately interpreted as insights into the cost, not the efficiency, of service provision. That is, public expenditure data measures the "buck" part of "bang for the buck." The analysis of upward spending bias indicates that district-reliant metropolitan areas spend more per capita than do nonreliant metropolitan areas. Whether metropolitan residents get more value for their higher costs—that is, whether service provision is more efficient—has not been determined by these tests.

## CHAPTER NOTES

**1.** Bish, *The Public Economy*, pp. 67–68; and Hawkins, *Self-Government by District*, pp. 55–61.

**2.** Danielson and Doig, *The Politics of Urban Regional Development*, pp. 160–61, 184.

**3.** See Theodore J. Lowi, "Machine Politics—Old and New," *The Public Interest* 9 (Fall 1967): 83–92; John J. Harrigan, *Political Change in the Metropolis*,

4th ed. (Glenview, Ill.: Scott, Foresman, 1989), pp. 196–99; Barney Warf, "The Port Authority of New York–New Jersey," *Professional Geographer* 40, no. 3 (1988), p. 295; Jones, "Local Government Organization," p. 580; Minge, "Special Districts," p. 705; and Danielson, Hershey, and Bayne, *One Nation, So Many Governments*, p. 79.

**4.** Earmarking guarantees to a department or program a fixed revenue stream that cannot be reallocated to another cause. Economists argue that earmarking distorts decisionmaking in favor of the earmarked service, regardless of demand, thus promoting inefficiency. See James M. Buchanan, "The Economics of Earmarked Taxes," *Journal of Political Economy* 71, no. 5 (1963): 457–69. For an application to special districts, see Danielson and Doig, *The Politics of Urban Regional Development*, pp. 159, 162.

**5.** Walsh, *The Public's Business*, p. 5; also see Fisher, *State and Local Public Finance*, pp. 259–65; and Hanson, "Land Development and Metropolitan Reform," p. 30.

**6.** Hamilton and Wells, *Federalism, Power, and Political Economy*, pp. 134–35; and Jeffrey S. Zax, "The Effects of Jurisdiction Types and Numbers on Local Public Finance," in *Fiscal Federalism: Quantitative Studies*, ed. Harvey S. Rosen (Chicago: University of Chicago Press, 1988), p. 81.

**7.** Committee for Economic Development, *Modernizing Local Government*. Studies conducted at the national level find a positive relationship between the number of special interest groups and total government spending. See Dennis C. Mueller and Peter Murrell, "Interest Groups and the Size of Government," *Public Choice* 48 (1986): 125–45. For a state-level example relevant to special-purpose governments, see Heiman, *The Quiet Evolution*, pp. 143–52.

**8.** See, for example, Anderson, *American City Government*, pp. 82–83; J. Bollens, *Special District Governments*, pp. 252–56; and Don L. Bowen, "Reshaping Special Districts Government in Arizona: Issues and Approaches," *Arizona Review* 32, no. 1 (1984): 12–25.

**9.** Robert G. Smith, *Public Authorities, Special Districts, and Local Government* (Washington, D.C.: National Association of Counties Research Foundation, 1964), pp. 175–80. For an example, see Zaleski, "A New Authority for Massachusetts," p. 537.

**10.** An alternative method is to measure reliance on districts that have specific geographic or financial, rather than functional, attributes. Because of widely different levels of spending across functions, however, such a method is problematic. For any geographic or financial subtype, expenditures by districts providing high-cost services, such as utilities, would obscure the expenditures of districts providing lower-cost functions, such as libraries. Analysis of spending effects by district function eliminates this problem.

**11.** Because education is not one of the functions analyzed and because the U.S. Bureau of the Census attributes all school district spending to the education function, excluding school districts from "all local governments" has no effect on per capita spending or district-reliance measures.

**12.** As in analyses of district distribution in chapter 5, because of peculiarities in the data file of the *1987 Census of Governments*, Alexandria (La.) Metropolitan Area is not considered in analyses of district cost and policy effects.

13. The phrase "at the metropolitan scale" is important. Although district reliance levels are measured for metropolitan units of analysis, within the metropolitan area a particular household either is or is not reliant on districts for a function. Two more precise interpretations of high reliance are first, that one or more districts provide the function throughout the metropolitan area, or second, that the function is provided within selected parts of the metropolitan area only and that districts provide services in these parts. Low and medium reliance levels apply when districts provide a function in some places within a metropolitan area and general-purpose governments provide it in others.

14. In the case of gas and electric utilities figures reflect the omission of eight metropolitan areas with misleadingly high expenditures on utilities. These areas are Salt Lake City, Utah; Austin, Tex.; Raleigh, N.C.; Phoenix, Ariz.; Springfield, Mass.; Richland, Wash.; Omaha, Nebr.; and Tallahassee, Fla. Expenditures reflect total spending by suprametropolitan utilities districts that are headquartered for purposes of financial reporting in the central counties of these metropolitan areas. The agencies and the total number of counties or states they serve are: Intermountain Power Agency (thirteen counties, headquartered in Salt Lake County, Utah); Lower Colorado River Authority (six counties, headquartered in Travis County, Tex.); North Carolina Municipal Power Agency (fourteen counties, headquartered in Wake County, N.C.); Salt River Project Agricultural Improvement and Power District (three counties, headquartered in Maricopa County, Ariz.); Massachusetts Municipal Wholesale Electric Company (eight counties, headquartered in Hampden County, Mass.); Washington Public Power and Supply System (three states, headquartered in Benton County, Wash.); Omaha Public Power District (fourteen counties, headquartered in Douglas County, Nebr.); and Florida Municipal Power Agency (one state, headquartered in Leon County, Fla.).

15. I ran additional tests to examine whether significant differences held after eliminating from the analysis any metropolitan area with total per capita spending below a certain minimum threshold (determined separately for each service). The concern was that in metropolitan areas with minimal need for a particular service, say natural resources, there would be little reason to form a special district. As a consequence, the lowest per capita totals would cluster in nonreliant metropolitan areas, thereby depressing these areas' mean per capita spending values. The test results indicated that, with the exception of ports, the significant spending differences remained even after eliminating metropolitan areas with minimal spending on a function. It is interesting that for several functions metropolitan areas with low per capita spending sometimes had high district reliance levels. Thus, the concern that prompted these tests was itself not borne out. Metropolitan areas apparently do not use special districts solely when high spending levels are desired.

16. The simple correlation coefficient decreased to .43 after omitting eight metropolitan areas with extremely high levels of spending (greater than $500 per capita) on health and hospitals in the study year. Six of these metropolitan areas—Sarasota, Fla.; Panama City, Fla.; Tuscaloosa, Ala.; Athens, Ga.; Anniston, Ala.; and Midland, Tex.—relied on special-purpose governments to high degrees for health and hospital services. The other two metropolitan areas—

Owensboro, Ky., and Columbia, Mo.—had no reliance on special districts for these services.

17. See, for example, Walsh and Leigland, "The Only Planning Game in Town," pp. 6–7; Doig, "Expertise, Politics, and Technological Change," pp. 37–40; Hanson, "Land Development and Metropolitan Reform," pp. 30–32; and Walsh, *The Public's Business*, pp. 6–7.

18. Walsh, *The Public's Business*, p. 338.

19. Ibid., pp. 163, 339.

20. Danielson and Doig, *The Politics of Urban Regional Development*, pp. 158, 162; and Heiman, *The Quiet Evolution*, pp. 128–29.

21. This latter result is unexpected. Because housing and community development in general-purpose governments often includes neighborhood services and planning operations, I expected a greater orientation toward operations and maintenance expenditures relative to housing authorities, which are traditionally more focused on housing production and capital projects. The contrary finding may stem from federal cutbacks in aid for housing production, which in the 1980s relegated housing authorities to a largely administrative role. Consequent declines in authority housing production may have been offset by municipal and county housing development programs, resulting in a greater orientation toward capital spending in general-purpose government housing budgets than commonly expected.

22. Only functions with an average of at least two districts per metropolitan area (as indicated in table 5–8) logically have potential for district multiplicity. This criterion eliminates airports, ports, transit, and utilities services, which rarely have more than one district service provider per metropolitan area, from consideration in this analysis.

23. In the cases of sewer and water functions, which are provided by both single-function and multifunction districts, a metropolitan area had to have fewer than three each of single-function (sewer or water) districts and multifunction sewer-water districts to be included in the analysis.

24. For more, see Larry DeBoer, "Economies of Scale and Input Substitution in Public Libraries," *Journal of Urban Economics* 32 (1992): 257–68.

25. I also tested whether the results on multiplicity hold when examining only those metropolitan areas with high levels of district reliance, defined as levels greater than .70. The concern was that high reliance, not multiplicity, underlies upward spending bias. In fact, this is not the case. Even for metropolitan areas highly reliant on special districts there is an insignificant difference between nonreliant areas and those with just a few district providers for water, natural resources, and housing and community development services. As reported, spending differences for libraries and health and hospitals services remain. This analysis can not be conducted for parks and recreation and fire protection services due to the low number of cases with reliance levels greater than .70. These results reinforce that district multiplicity, not the combined effect of higher reliance with district multiplicity, underlies the findings in table 6–6.

26. Economic theory reaches this conclusion by linking larger populations to heterogeneity of demand for public services. As a result, the range and

variety of services demanded in large centers is larger than in small centers. See, for example, Chicoine and Walzer, *Governmental Structure*, p. 36. Geographic theory, which emphasizes minimum threshold populations for facilities of particular types, links larger populations to their ability to support more types of services, which translates into higher costs. See, for example, Brian J. L. Berry and Frank E. Horton, *Geographical Perspectives on Urban Systems* (Englewood Cliffs, N.J.: Prentice Hall, 1970), pp. 173–75.

27. Stein, *Urban Alternatives*, pp. 31–34.

28. For a review of studies, see Fisher, *State and Local Public Finance*, pp. 292–95. Empirical research reveals that the positive relationship between income and spending levels holds for social services, despite the alleged lower demand for these services by higher-income residents. See Peterson, *City Limits*, pp. 53–56.

29. Younger centers, which are apt to be less-developed and faster-growing than older centers, may plausibly demand greater investment in drainage, flood control, and other natural resource services than do older, more fully urbanized metropolitan areas. Younger centers are also popular havens for older persons and retirees whose demand for health and hospital services is particularly high. On this latter point, see Daniel R. Mullins and Mark S. Rosentraub, "Fiscal Pressure? The Impact of Elder Recruitment on Local Expenditures," *Urban Affairs Quarterly* 28, no. 2 (1992), pp. 345–48.

30. There are plausible explanations for the exceptions. Ports and utilities expenditures relate more to geographic and climatic factors than to consumer income levels. Public sector provision of health and hospitals and housing and community development services is typically oriented to needy, rather than affluent, clients. These services are also more likely to receive state and federal aid, which is passed through to local expenditures.

31. The absolute value of the spending index is ambiguous, as it depends on the magnitude of district use for a service.

32. U.S. Bureau of the Census, *1962 Census of Governments*, vol. 5. *Local Government in Metropolitan Areas* (Washington, D.C.: U.S. Government Printing Office, 1964), pp. 282–460, table 13.

33. Making inferences from this smaller sample to the universe of 1987 metropolitan areas requires moderate caution. The 107 metropolitan areas excluded by virtue of being designated after 1962 were not only younger (mean age of nineteen years compared with sixty years) than the 190 metropolitan areas remaining in the sample, they were also smaller in population (mean of 184,000 compared with 810,000) and less affluent (mean per capita income in 1979 of $7,950 compared with $8,776). On average, the excluded metropolitan areas also had fewer special districts (although more districts per capita) than the 190 metropolitan areas in the sample.

34. Chicoine and Walzer, *Governmental Structure*, pp. 232–33.

# 7

# Does Specialized Governance
# Shape Policy Outcomes?

If government institutions were interchangeable, institutional choices would be trivial. Metropolitan areas would vary according to fiscal, social, political, and other conditions, but their choices of local-government arrangements would attract little attention. Theory and practice suggest that institutional choices do matter, however. At least for the choice to rely on special-purpose versus general-purpose entities, government types are not interchangeable.

The analysis in chapter 6 suggests that one implication of the institutional choice to rely on special districts rather than general-purpose governments is an increase in the size of the spending pie in metropolitan areas. I consider now the related but distinct question of how specialized governance may influence the *relative size* of functional slices in the pie. If the proportional amount of spending devoted to specific functions reflects a society's priorities, then resource allocation outcomes are important expressions of collective preferences and policy. These expressions are particularly revealing in a zero sum game environment, in which proportional increases in spending for one function must be offset by decreases in others.

The institutional choice to rely on special-purpose governments raises numerous policy questions. For example, how does specialized governance affect the relative proportion of local-government resources devoted to particular functions? Does special-purpose governance systematically favor some services over others? Alternatively, does specialized governance reproduce general-purpose government resource allocations under different institutional cloth? The answers to these and similar questions go to the heart of the policy consequences of specialized governance.

The empirical analysis in this chapter focuses specifically on three related issues: first, how the functional allocation of resources in nonreliant metropolitan areas compares with that of district-reliant metropolitan areas; second, whether district service delivery systematically favors or penalizes particular functions; and third, how switching over time from general-purpose to special-purpose service delivery alters the distribution of resources across functions within a metropolitan area.

## THEORETICAL HYPOTHESES

The theoretical perspectives reviewed in chapter 2 show remarkable agreement about the policy implications of specialized governance. Analysts concur that special-purpose governance will result in a different allocation of resources than would result if services were provided by general-purpose governments. Like their nominal agreement about fiscal effects, however, the theoretical perspectives differ about the direction and desirability of predicted policy implications.

With the exception of public choice proponents—who accept resource allocation outcomes, regardless of institutional provider, as the expression of preferences of rational individuals—observers are generally critical of districts' influence on resource allocations. The primary objection is that functional specialization prevents districts from brokering the tradeoffs and compromises central to policy prioritization in a democratic society.[1] By their nature, districts do not "weigh and balance" the multiple factors affecting policy decisions, but focus "on one issue only, to the exclusion of all else."[2]

Theorists allege that high district reliance results in higher proportional investment on district-provided services than would occur if services were provided by general-purpose governments,[3] an outcome I call resource allocation bias. Special districts are seen as a legal but underhanded means to achieve greater spending on a service than would occur in a more competitive setting for resource allocation.

The literature cites two main reasons for resource allocation bias. The first is that clients with intense preferences about a district's services—recreation enthusiasts in the case of recreation districts, health practitioners in the case of hospital districts, and so forth—are more likely to participate in district affairs, either as board members, lobbyists, or involved citizens.[4] Because the resulting public input encourages district activities, citizen responsiveness leads to higher investment in district functions than would occur if the board heard from the more diverse public that typically addresses general-purpose governments.[5] In effect, the role of a watchful, diverse citizenry is replaced in the case of special districts by targeted interest groups predisposed to sanction a district's investment choices. Not only might input from special interest groups result in higher spending, as the analysis in chapter 6 suggests, it might also distort the composition of that spending, specifically to favor the preferences of interest groups over those of the general public.[6] In this way, allocation decisions of special-purpose governments stand in sharp contrast to those made by general-purpose governments, which operate under more open and functionally competitive conditions.

Proponents of the institutional reform, metropolitan ecology, and structuralist perspectives cite districts' low political visibility and accountability as a second source of resource allocation bias.[7] Scant media coverage, little-publicized elections, and infrequent board meetings thwart meaningful citizen involvement in districts' resource allocation choices.[8] "Non-representative governments," noted one observer,

> have an advantage in that they enable functions to be distanced from the political arena and performed in a manner that meets technical requirements. However, democracy is weakened and accountability is reduced. This may not be a problem for services such as sewerage and water supply, where technical requirements usually have priority, but it can easily be a problem for services such as police protection and libraries; and certainly it is a problem if a significant proportion of local government functions are performed by such authorities.[9]

The logical outcome of low political visibility and accountability, critics argue, is greater proportional investment in a service than would occur if that service were one of numerous functions to which a citizenry allocates scarce public resources.

Resource allocation bias is especially troublesome to some because shifts in spending priorities seem to systematically favor certain services at the expense of others. Structuralist scholars argue that resource allocation bias favors development-oriented functions.[10] They contend that prodevelopment interest groups collaborate with progrowth public officials to place control over critical development services in the hands of independent, limited-access special-purpose governments. Progrowth interests find special districts particularly appealing in light of their track record in making speedy approvals, implementing development projects, and supporting development even when proposals face strong popular opposition.[11]

Others argue that resource allocation bias systematically harms social welfare services to the benefit of development-oriented and development-responsive functions, such as public safety, libraries, recreation, and sanitation. The alleged source of this bias is a district's inability to practice full-line forcing. Under full-line forcing, public services are bundled as a service package rather than offered as individual items. Some analysts fault full-line forcing because it decreases individual utility.[12] Most tolerate it, however, because service bundling facilitates the provision of socially necessary, if unpopular, services that might go unfunded if subjected to a vote. Social welfare services, with their typically small and politically weak constituencies are particularly vulnerable in an environment of unbundled funding.[13] Because specialized governance frustrates full-line forcing, it favors popular services like libraries, fire protection, and recreation at the expense of targeted services like low-income housing and welfare assistance.

Still others note that social services are in particular funding jeopardy when special-purpose governments skim development-oriented services from general-purpose government portfolios. In this instance, politically vulnerable social services must compete head-to-head against widely beneficial and politically secure services like police and fire protection.[14] Because there is "little doubt as to which [type of service] suffer[s] from the least political clout," the likely budgetary outcome is proportionally lower spending on social welfare functions and proportionally more on housekeeping services than would occur if all services were provided by general-purpose governments.[15]

In short, the theoretical literature predicts two principal outcomes of specialized governance. The first is that specialized governance leads to resource allocation bias, which means proportionally more spending on district-provided services in district-reliant metropolitan areas than in nonreliant areas. The second is that specialized service delivery promotes development-oriented and housekeeping functions at the expense of social welfare functions, albeit for different political and fiscal reasons. Does empirical analysis bear out these predictions?

## ASSESSING RESOURCE ALLOCATION BIAS

Investigation of the policy implications of specialized governance focuses on three issues: (1) whether there is a significant difference in the allocation of resources across functions in district-reliant and nonreliant metropolitan areas; (2) whether this difference, if any, is systematically biased toward or against particular functions; and (3) how resource allocations change over time when metropolitan areas switch from general-purpose to special-purpose service delivery.

### Methods

The empirical analysis of district policy effects mirrors that of district cost effects in chapter 6. The cross-sectional analysis of resource allocation bias examines 311 metropolitan areas using data from the *1987 Census of Governments*. The dynamic analysis examines the 190 metropolitan areas for which comparable spending and geographic data are available for 1962 and 1987. For each of twelve functions analyzed, the fundamental comparison is between district-reliant metropolitan areas—those that rely on special districts to at least some degree—and nonreliant areas, which turn instead to general-purpose governments for service delivery.

I measure the resource allocation share for each function in each metropolitan area as the percentage of total (noneducation) local-government expenditures devoted to the function, as follows:

Resource Allocation Share = Total Local-Government Expenditures on Function/Total Local-Government Expenditures on all Noneducation Functions

Resource allocation shares, which I also refer to as spending shares, vary from 0, for a function to which metropolitan area local governments allocate no resources, to 1, for a function that captures 100 percent of all noneducation local-government spending in the area.

The central question of the cross-sectional analysis, diagrammed in figure 7–1, is whether specialized governance leads to resource allocation bias. Difference of means tests can determine the statistical significance of the difference between the mean spending shares in district-reliant and nonreliant metropolitan areas. Mean spending shares that are significantly larger in district-reliant areas constitute empirical support for resource allocation bias.

## FINDINGS

Results of difference of means tests, shown in table 7–1, confirm the presence of resource allocation bias. For most functions, metropolitan areas with at least some special district provision of a function devote a significantly higher proportion of total local government spending to that function than do nonreliant metropolitan areas. With the exception of parks and recreation services, the greater spending shares associated with specialized service delivery do not stem from districts' greater orientation toward capital expenditures (see table 6–4). When present, resource allocation bias holds not only for total expenditures, but also for operations and maintenance expenditures.[16]

The exceptions are worth noting. For airports and fire protection functions, the type of service provider has an insignificant effect on spending share. For airports, it may be that federal regulations narrow institutional differences that might otherwise distinguish between types of operators. For fire protection, it may be that differences in type of employment—full-time or volunteer—has more influence on spending share than does the type of institution providing the service.

The findings imply that specialized service delivery is not a policy-neutral substitute for general-purpose service delivery. To the contrary,

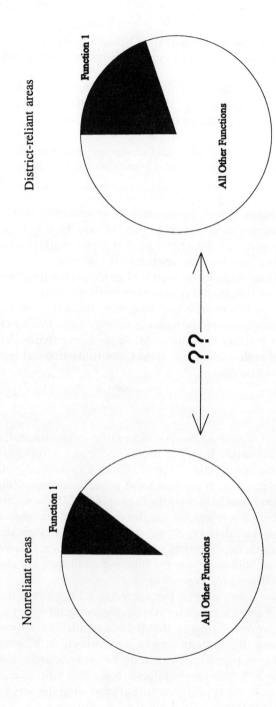

**Figure 7-1** Diagram of Question: Does Resource Allocation Bias Exist?

special-purpose governance skews spending in favor of district-provided services more so than would occur under a general-purpose
government environment. The institutional choice to use special districts clearly has policy ramifications.

What accounts for resource allocation bias? The data in table 7–1
indicate that with the exception of parks and recreation services, resource allocation bias cannot be explained by districts' tendency toward
capital projects. Perhaps noninstitutional factors, such as intermetropol-
itan differences in resource endowment, demographics, metropolitan
age, and political culture, influence the size of spending shares. If
district reliance levels correlate with these noninstitutional factors, then
spending shares attributed to institutional choices may actually be
spurious relationships.

## Interregional Factors

Theory suggests three noninstitutional variables, metropolitan population size, metropolitan area age, and regional location, as potential
sources of resource allocation bias. Population size determines whether
there is a sufficient minimum threshold population to support provision of particular services.[17] Services with large minimum population
requirements, such as transit, would logically capture larger shares
of spending in large metropolitan areas than they would in small
metropolitan areas.

Metropolitan age influences the portfolio of public sector functions.
Local governments in older areas are more apt to provide uncommon
functions, such as welfare, hospitals, and public housing than are newer
areas.[18] As a consequence, the share of spending on uncommon functions is typically greater in older metropolitan areas, regardless of the
role played by special-purpose governments in service provision.

A number of studies conclude that interregional variation in natural
resource endowments, service demand and costs, and political culture
influence patterns of resource allocation.[19] Metropolitan areas in the
northeast, for example, tend to provide a wider range of services than
those in the west or, to a lesser extent, south or midwest.[20] As a more
specific example, spending shares for water service are likely to be
smaller in metropolitan areas in the northeast, where water supplies
are abundant and accessible to densely settled customers, than in the
west or southwest where water is scarce and geographically distant
from dispersed customers.

To test these potential effects, I use multiple regression analysis
to determine the independent effect of district reliance on resource
allocation shares, after controlling for metropolitan population, age,

**TABLE 7-1**   Spending Shares by Expenditure Category in District-Reliant versus Nonreliant Metropolitan Areas, by Function

| Function and Area Type | N | Total Expenditures | | Operations and Maintenance Expenditures Only | |
|---|---|---|---|---|---|
| | | Spending Share | Difference of Means[a] | Spending Share | Difference of Means[a] |
| | | (%) | | (%) | |
| Airports | | | | | |
| District-reliant: | 80 | 1.66 | 0.41 | 1.13 | 0.20 |
| Nonreliant: | 206 | 1.25 | | 0.93 | |
| Ports | | | | | |
| District-reliant: | 57 | 1.90 | 1.39** | 1.29 | 1.01** |
| Nonreliant: | 56 | 0.51 | | 0.28 | |
| Transit | | | | | |
| District-reliant: | 109 | 3.13 | 1.89** | 3.58 | 2.05** |
| Nonreliant: | 139 | 1.24 | | 1.53 | |
| Utilities (Gas and Electric)[b] | | | | | |
| District-reliant: | 37 | 24.90 | 15.80** | 24.4 | 14.8** |
| Nonreliant: | 175 | 9.10 | | 9.6 | |
| Sewer | | | | | |
| District-reliant: | 157 | 6.95 | 1.66** | 5.24 | 1.16** |
| Nonreliant: | 128 | 5.29 | | 4.08 | |
| Water | | | | | |
| District-reliant: | 182 | 8.48 | 1.46* | 5.93 | 0.87* |
| Nonreliant: | 112 | 7.02 | | 5.06 | |
| Fire Protection | | | | | |
| District-reliant: | 115 | 4.22 | 0.20 | 5.65 | 0.21 |
| Nonreliant: | 173 | 4.02 | | 5.44 | |

and region. District reliance in a metropolitan area is measured in one of two ways, depending on a function's underlying reliance distribution (see figure 6–2). For functions with bimodal distributions (airports, ports, transit, utilities, and libraries), district reliance is a binary variable that takes the value 0 for no reliance and 1 for any reliance level greater than .01. For functions with dispersed distributions (water, sewer, natural resources, parks and recreation, health and hospitals, and housing and community development), district reliance is the actual level of reliance.

Metropolitan population is measured at October 1986 population levels. Metropolitan area age is the number of years prior to 1995 that an area was designated "metropolitan." Region is determined

TABLE 7-1 *continued*

| Function and Area Type | N | Total Expenditures | | Operations and Maintenance Expenditures Only | |
|---|---|---|---|---|---|
| | | *Spending Share* | *Difference of Means*[a] | *Spending Share* | *Difference of Means*[a] |
| Parks and Recreation | | | | | |
| District-reliant: | 91 | 3.70 | 0.73** | 3.98 | 0.48 |
| Nonreliant: | 206 | 3.01 | | 3.50 | |
| Natural Resources | | | | | |
| District-reliant: | 234 | 0.85 | 0.48** | 0.90 | 0.44** |
| Nonreliant: | 55 | 0.37 | | 0.45 | |
| Libraries | | | | | |
| District-reliant: | 79 | 1.73 | 0.73** | 2.02 | 0.72** |
| Nonreliant: | 227 | 1.00 | | 1.30 | |
| Housing and Community Development | | | | | |
| District-reliant: | 253 | 4.12 | 1.72** | 3.82 | 1.49** |
| Nonreliant: | 56 | 2.40 | | 2.33 | |
| Health and Hospitals | | | | | |
| District-reliant: | 120 | 13.64 | 5.12** | 15.61 | 4.72** |
| Nonreliant: | 174 | 8.52 | | 10.89 | |

**Note:** District-reliant areas are defined as metropolitan areas with district reliance level greater than .01. Nonreliant areas are defined as metropolitan areas with district reliance level less than or equal to .01.
**a.** Significance based on two-tailed t-tests, assuming unequal variances.
**b.** Data exclude eight metropolitan areas that serve as headquarters for suprametropolitan utilities agencies (see chapter 6, note 14).
*$p < .05$     **$p < .01$

according to the nine-region classification of the U.S. Bureau of the Census.[21] Regional variables enter the regression as a series of binary variables. All functions except fire protection, libraries, and housing and community development use the Mid-Atlantic region as base case. Because metropolitan areas in the Mid-Atlantic region on average have the highest spending shares for fire protection, libraries, and housing and community development, I use the West Mountain region as base case for these functions. This modification permits a more accurate view of regional influence than would retaining Mid-Atlantic as the base case.

Results of the regression analysis are summarized in table 7–2. Of preliminary, though secondary, interest is that the findings provide

**TABLE 7-2** Determinants of Spending Shares, by Function (standardized regression coefficients)

| Explanatory Variables | Airports | Ports | Transit | Utilities | Sewer | Water |
|---|---|---|---|---|---|---|
| | | | | *Dependent Variables:* | | |
| District Reliance[a] | .09 | .19 | .17** | .27** | .17** | .11 |
| Metropolitan Population | .06 | −.19 | .54** | −.05 | −.20** | −.04 |
| Metropolitan Age | .12 | .15 | .09 | −.09 | .12* | −.01 |
| North Central East | −.08 | −.05 | .06 | .01 | .22* | .19 |
| North Central West | .17 | −.01 | .06 | .01 | −.05 | .13 |
| New England | −.14 | −.04 | .01 | −.06 | .18* | .01 |
| Mid-Atlantic[b] | — | — | — | — | — | — |
| South Atlantic | .06 | .12 | −.01 | .19 | −.11 | .39** |
| South Central East | −.06 | .04 | −.05 | .35** | −.18* | .04 |
| South Central West | .10 | .37** | .02 | .07 | −.00 | .47** |
| West Mountain[b] | .20* | −.03 | .03 | .08 | −.05 | .14 |
| West Pacific | −.07 | .26 | .03 | −.05 | −.11 | .10 |
| N | 292 | 114 | 249 | 218 | 305 | 311 |
| Adjusted $R^2$ | .10 | .21 | .43 | .20 | .22 | .15 |

Note:   Regressions include only those metropolitan areas in which any local government spent money on the designated function.
**a.** Measured as actual level of reliance except for functions with bimodal distributions (airports, ports, transit, utilities, libraries), for which reliance is measured as a binary variable using 1 for reliance level greater than .01.
**b.** The Mid-Atlantic region is used as the base case, except for fire protection, library, and housing and community development functions, on which the Mid-Atlantic region has extreme values. The base case for these functions is the West Mountain region.
*$p < .05$    **$p < .01$

mixed support for the influence of metropolitan population,[22] metropolitan area age,[23] and regional location[24] on spending shares by function. Of primary interest are the data in the top row of results, which reveal for each function the nature of the relationship between district reliance and spending share. The findings indicate that specialized governance has a consistently significant and positive influence on resource allocation shares. Even after controlling for metropolitan population, age, and region, metropolitan areas that rely on special districts to provide transit, utilities, sewers, parks and recreation, fire protection, natural resources, libraries, housing and community development, and health and hospitals devote proportionately more of total local government expenditures to these services than do metropolitan areas that rely on general-purpose governments. Only for airports, ports, and water

TABLE 7-2 *continued*

*Operations and Maintenance Expenditures for:*

| Fire Protection[b] | Parks and Recreation | Natural Resources | Library[b] | Housing and Community Development[b] | Health and Hospitals |
|---|---|---|---|---|---|
| .14* | .27** | .33** | .32** | .21** | .34** |
| −.12* | −.01 | .01 | −.06 | −.05 | .06 |
| .26** | .17** | −.15* | .08 | .31** | −.11 |
| .00 | .11 | .09 | .12 | .04 | .23* |
| −.01 | .30** | .09 | .05 | .06 | .16* |
| −.22** | −.04 | .10 | −.06 | .03 | .07 |
| .29** | — | — | .18** | .28** | — |
| −.07 | .22* | .12 | .01 | .16 | .27** |
| −.10 | .01 | −.03 | −.15* | −.03 | .33** |
| .10 | .25** | .14 | −.05 | .02 | .28** |
| — | .37** | .10 | — | — | .12 |
| −.06 | .06 | .41** | .01 | .02 | .15 |
| 311 | 311 | 307 | 309 | 311 | 311 |
| .20 | .24 | .26 | .22 | .22 | .21 |

functions are institutional choices not a significant factor in resource allocation shares.

The magnitude of the coefficients indicates that resource allocation bias is strong for certain functions. For example, district reliance accounts for most of the metropolitan variation in spending shares for libraries. In general, district reliance is typically one of the top two strongest explanatory variables accounting for variation in resource allocation shares.

The results imply that although age, population, and region sometimes influence relative spending levels, the institutional choice to rely on special-purpose governments has a consistently positive effect on resource allocations. District-reliant metropolitan areas devote significantly more resources to a service than do nonreliant metropolitan areas for the same service, after controlling for metropolitan attributes. There is ample support for theoretical claims that specialized service delivery engenders resource allocation bias.[25]

## EVIDENCE OF SYSTEMATIC BIAS

The evidence supporting the presence of resource allocation bias leaves unanswered whether specialized governance is *systematically* biased in favor of or against particular functions. This concern raises two specific questions: (1) does specialized service delivery favor development-oriented services over development-responsive services? and (2) does district provision of development services jeopardize social welfare services by pitting them against popular housekeeping services in competition for general-purpose government funds?

To answer these questions requires categorizing services into groups on the basis of their orientation toward development. I classify functions as either development-oriented or development-responsive, as follows:

Development-oriented functions     = airports, utilities, transit, ports, water, sewer, highways, and housing and community development; and

Development-responsive functions = fire protection, health and hospitals, natural resources, libraries, parks and recreation, sanitation, and parking.

To test specific hypotheses about systematic bias, I categorize functions into social welfare, housekeeping, or development functions, as follows:

Social welfare functions  = health and hospitals, housing and community development, and welfare assistance;

Housekeeping functions = fire protection, natural resources, libraries, parks and recreation, sanitation, parking, and police protection; and

Development functions  = airports, ports, transit, water, sewer, and highways.

Analyses using this three-way classification also include an "other" category to round out total local-government spending. Other functions comprise general government (financial administration, judicial, legislative, central staff, general support, and general public buildings) and miscellaneous (miscellaneous commercial activities, interest payments, and unallocable functions). Because the absolute magnitude of spending on utilities (gas and electric) is much higher than spending on other development functions, analyses using functional categorizations exclude utilities expenditures.

Categorizing housing and community development services is problematic. The "housing" component of this service includes both development-oriented activities, such as housing construction and mortgage financing, and social welfare activities, such as housing subsidies for low-income households. The "community development" component likewise includes development activities like urban redevelopment and central city renewal oriented toward downtown property owners and developers, and also social welfare activities like neighborhood programs that provide social services to disadvantaged populations. Given these considerations, when an analysis calls for the two-way classification I categorize housing and community development a development-oriented function. When an analysis requires the more specific three-way classification I categorize housing and community development a social welfare function.

## Does Specialized Governance Favor Development-Oriented Functions?

The data in tables 6–2 and 7–1 offer a preliminary answer to whether special district service delivery favors development-oriented services over development-responsive ones. At first glance, metropolitan areas do apparently rely on districts to relatively greater degrees for development-oriented services than for development-responsive ones (table 6–2). The top six of fifteen services ranked by district reliance are development-oriented. Three of the top four services with the most widespread district involvement, measured by the number of metropolitan areas that rely on districts to some degree, are development-oriented.

Examination of the data in table 7–1, however, reveals that resource allocation bias is by no means limited to development-oriented functions. Resource allocation bias affects all five development-responsive functions but only four of seven development-oriented ones. Despite the tendency in the literature and practice to link special districts to development services, it appears that services not commonly associated with districts—health, fire protection, and parks and recreation, for example—also experience resource allocation bias.

## Does Specialized Governance Jeopardize Social Welfare Functions?

The second question is whether district provision of development-oriented services indirectly diminishes the spending share allocated to social welfare services by leaving the latter to compete for scarce resources against popular housekeeping services. Assessing this hypothesis requires calculating district reliance and spending shares for each of the three functional categories, development, housekeeping, and social welfare.

I determine district reliance by functional category by dividing total district spending on all services in a category by total local-government spending on these services. I then classify reliance levels as either low or high, depending on whether the level is below (low) or above (high) the aggregate metropolitan mean reliance level for the functional category.[26] Based on 1987 data for the 311 metropolitan areas in the sample, the mean reliance levels used to determine low or high reliance are 16.5 percent for development functions (not including utilities), 7.2 percent for housekeeping functions, and 25.8 percent for social welfare functions.[27]

A metropolitan area falls into one of eight groups based on its status as having either high or low district reliance for each of the three functional categories, as follows:

|  | District Reliance Level | | |
| Group | Development Functions | Housekeeping Functions | Social Welfare Functions |
| --- | --- | --- | --- |
| 1 | low | low | low |
| 2 | low | low | high |
| 3 | low | high | low |
| 4 | high | low | low |
| 5 | low | high | high |
| 6 | high | low | high |
| 7 | high | high | low |
| 8 | high | high | high |

Metropolitan areas in group 1, in which all three functional categories have low district reliance have the most functionally integrated, or *generalized*, service arrangements. In these areas, general-purpose governments dominate the delivery of development, housekeeping, and social welfare functions. At the other pole, metropolitan areas in group 8, which have high district reliance for all three functional categories, have the most functionally fragmented, or *specialized*, service arrangements. In these areas, special-purpose governments are relatively dominant players for a wide range of functions.

Between these extremes are metropolitan area groups that tend toward generalized or specialized service arrangements. Groups 2–4 include metropolitan areas with mostly generalized service delivery (two of three categories have low district reliance). These groups are distinguished by which one functional category—development, house-keeping, or social welfare—has high district reliance. Metropolitan areas in groups 5–7 have mostly specialized service delivery (two of three functional categories have high district reliance). These groups are distinguished from one another by which one functional category has low district reliance.

Comparing resource allocation shares across the eight metropolitan groups permits analysis of the level and direction of systematic bias in specialized service delivery, should it exist. The data in table 7–3 report the mean spending shares by functional category for the eight metropolitan area groups. Immediately noticeable is the overall stability of spending shares by functional category. With remarkably little variation, metropolitan areas devote just shy of 30 percent of total local-government spending to development services, about 22 percent each to housekeeping and social welfare services, and about 26 percent to other services. The overall stability reflects both spending mandates from higher level governments and the penchant of metropolitan regions to copycat one anothers' budgetary choices.[28] A statistical consequence of this stability, however, is that seemingly small swings of three or four percentage points represent significantly different policy choices about how to allocate discretionary funds.

The data cannot support the hypothesis that district provision of development services jeopardizes social welfare functions. The relevant comparison is between metropolitan areas in group 1, in which district reliance is low for all three functional categories, and group 4, in which district reliance is high for development functions and low for house-keeping and social welfare functions. Analysis of spending shares for the two groups indicates that differences are statistically insignificant. Social welfare services are not sacrificed to housekeeping functions when district reliance is high for development functions. Further contradicting the hypothesis is the finding that housekeeping functions do not increase their relative spending share in metropolitan areas in which there is high district reliance for development functions.[29]

## A Closer Look

Although the data cannot confirm specific hypotheses of systematic resource allocation bias they do reveal intriguing and significant resource allocation differences between metropolitan areas that make different institutional choices for service delivery. Certain government arrangements are clearly superior for capturing shares of total government spending at the metropolitan level. Analysis of "best case" and "worst case" arrangements sheds light on the resource allocation consequences of specialized service delivery.

**TABLE 7–3** Spending Shares for Functional Categories, by Metropolitan Areas Grouped by District Reliance Status

| Metropolitan Area Group | N | District Reliance Status[a] | Spending Share (%) | | | |
|---|---|---|---|---|---|---|
| | | | | Functional Categories | | |
| | | | Develop- ment | House- keeping | Social Welfare | Other |
| 1 | 92 | Dev. Low Hskp. Low Soc. Low | 28.6 | 21.8 | 21.9 | 27.7 |
| 2 | 55 | Dev. Low Hskp. Low Soc. High | 30.8 | 22.9 | 21.1 | 25.2 |
| 3 | 33 | Dev. Low Hskp. High Soc. Low | 27.2 | 22.1 | 23.4 | 27.2 |
| 4 | 33 | Dev. High Hskp. Low Soc. Low | 30.2 | 21.5 | 21.8 | 26.6 |
| 5 | 19 | Dev. Low Hskp. High Soc. High | 27.6 | 23.4 | 21.4 | 27.6 |
| 6 | 24 | Dev. High Hskp. Low Soc. High | 29.2 | 19.0 | 25.3 | 26.5 |
| 7 | 33 | Dev. High Hskp. High Soc. Low | 29.3 | 22.2 | 23.5 | 25.1 |
| 8 | 22 | Dev. High Hskp. High Soc. High | 33.8 | 25.1 | 15.8 | 25.3 |

**a.** Dev. = Development; Hskp. = Housekeeping; Soc. = Social Welfare. Development functions: airports, ports, transit, water, sewer, and highways. Housekeeping functions: fire protection, natural resources, libraries, parks and recreation, sanitation, parking, and police protection. Social Welfare functions: health and hospitals, housing and community development, and welfare assistance. Low and High are defined as district reliance level below or above, respectively, the mean reliance level for that category.

The most fundamental comparison is between metropolitan areas with the most generalized service-delivery arrangements (group 1) and those with the most specialized arrangements (group 8). Relative to metropolitan areas with low district reliance for all three functional categories, metropolitan areas with high district reliance for all three devote significantly more budget share to development functions (33.8

percent to 28.6 percent) and housekeeping functions (25.1 percent to 21.8 percent) and significantly less to social welfare functions (15.8 percent to 21.9 percent). It is quite clear that metropolitan areas that compartmentalize service delivery using special districts favor development and housekeeping services and disfavor social welfare functions relative to metropolitan areas with the most generalized service arrangements. At the extremes, the data validate the hypothesis that specialized governance is less friendly to social welfare spending than is generalized governance. This implies that the service bundling and high political accountability that characterize general-purpose governments help secure for social welfare services a larger slice of the budgetary pie than they receive under other types of institutional arrangements.

Similar patterns are evident in table 7–4, which indicates the service-delivery arrangements associated with the highest and lowest spending shares for development, housekeeping, and social welfare functions. Not only do development and housekeeping functions compare favorably to social welfare functions in the group 1 versus group 8 comparison, they actually capture their greatest shares of resources under the most specialized metropolitan arrangements. In other words, specialized service arrangements are not merely advantageous to development and housekeeping functions, they are the *most* advantageous of all possible arrangements for capturing resources. Supporters of development and housekeeping functions do well to promote local-government arrangements with high reliance on special-purpose governments. At the same time, sponsors of social welfare services are well-advised to curtail specialized service delivery. Social welfare functions capture their smallest shares of resources under the most specialized arrangements. In a competitive budgetary environment, the benefits of specialization for development and housekeeping services seem to come at the expense of social services.

Although social welfare services fare worst under the most specialized service-delivery arrangements, they do not necessarily fare best under the most generalized arrangements. Social welfare functions capture their highest share of total local-government resources in metropolitan areas in group 6, those in which district reliance is high for social welfare and development functions, and low for housekeeping functions. Social welfare functions are more likely to capture resource allocation share when they do not compete directly against housekeeping functions for a share of total spending. This finding is consistent with the hypothesis that social welfare functions face tough odds when competing against the traditionally popular housekeeping functions for a slice of local-government spending.

As a general rule, social welfare services secure a greater share of

**TABLE 7-4** District Reliance Status for Highest and Lowest Spending Shares, by Functional Category

| Functional Category | Lowest Spending Share (%) | District Reliance Status[a] | Highest Spending Share (%) | District Reliance Status[a] | Difference Highest-Lowest[b] |
|---|---|---|---|---|---|
| Development | 27.2 | Group 3:<br>Dev. Low<br>Hskp. High<br>Soc. Low | 33.8 | Group 8:<br>Dev. High<br>Hskp. High<br>Soc. High | 6.6** |
| Housekeeping | 19.0 | Group 6:<br>Dev. High<br>Hskp. Low<br>Soc. High | 25.1 | Group 8:<br>Dev. High<br>Hskp. High<br>Soc. High | 6.0** |
| Social Welfare | 15.8 | Group 8:<br>Dev. High<br>Hskp. High<br>Soc. High | 25.3 | Group 6:<br>Dev. High<br>Hskp. Low<br>Soc. High | 9.5** |

a. Dev. = Development; Hskp. = Housekeeping; Soc. = Social Welfare. Development functions: airports, ports, transit, water, sewer, and highways. Housekeeping functions: fire protection, natural resources, libraries, parks and recreation, sanitation, parking, and police protection. Social Welfare functions: health and hospitals, housing and community development, and welfare assistance. Low and High are defined as district reliance level below or above, respectively, the mean reliance level for that category.
b. Significance of two-tailed t-test that difference of highest and lowest spending shares equals 0.
**p < .01

206

total spending when they are included in the bundled service package of general-purpose governments. If housekeeping functions also have low district reliance, however, then social welfare functions can secure larger shares if provided by special-purpose governments. In all three instances when social welfare services capture greater than 23 percent of total local government spending (groups 3, 6, and 7), social welfare and housekeeping services have opposing levels (low or high) of district reliance. To hold their own, social welfare functions evidently need either the budgetary protection offered by special-purpose governments (group 6) or an uncompetitive general-purpose environment where housekeeping and, optionally, development functions (groups 3 and 7) have high district reliance.

The interplay between service-delivery arrangements and resource allocation outcomes is further illuminated by the metropolitan areas in group 6, for which housekeeping functions have their smallest spending shares. Housekeeping functions capture their lowest share of resources when district reliance is low and development and social welfare functions have high district reliance. This arrangement coincides with characteristics of minimalist government, in which general-purpose governments retain control over basic housekeeping functions and farm out nonhousekeeping (development and social welfare) functions to special-purpose governments. In this way, municipal governments attempt to hold down costs by focusing on a relatively narrow range of services. Institutional choices are once again shown to influence spending outcomes and reflect policy preferences.

Together the resource allocation analyses yield several important findings. In broadest terms, specialized governance is not policy neutral. Across metropolitan areas, there are clear and significant differences in spending priorities between specialized and generalized service arrangements. In particular, development and housekeeping functions capture their largest shares of government resources under the most specialized service-delivery arrangements. By contrast, social welfare functions capture their lowest shares under the most specialized arrangements and generally fare better in a general-purpose government environment. Social welfare functions fare especially well if shielded from competition against housekeeping and development functions for a share of total government resources.

## DYNAMIC ANALYSIS

The final question is whether resource allocation bias persists over time. What are the resource implications of the institutional choice to continue relying on general-purpose governance for services or,

alternatively, to switch to special-purpose governments? The methodology for this analysis mirrors that of the dynamic analysis of spending
effects in chapter 6. I focus on metropolitan areas that in 1962 did not
rely on special districts. For each function, nonreliant metropolitan
areas make one of three service delivery choices by 1987: (1) to continue
providing the function using general-purpose governments; (2) to
switch to low reliance on special districts; or (3) to switch to high
reliance on special districts. The dynamic analysis excludes newer metropolitan areas and those in the New England states for which comparable data for 1962 and 1987 are not available. The resulting sample
comprises 190 metropolitan areas with boundaries delimited in 1962.
Examining the same metropolitan area at two points in time permits
controlling for many regional, political, demographic, and cultural factors that may influence resource allocation outcomes across metropolitan areas.

The central question is how resource allocation shares change over
the period as a result of institutional choices. To compare spending
shares over time, I calculate an index that relates a metropolitan area's
share of total spending on a function to the mean percent spending
share for all metropolitan areas on that function, as follows:

Spending Share Index = Spending Share for Function in Metropolitan
Area/Mean Spending Share for Function for All Metropolitan Areas.

Spending share indexes were calculated for 1962 and 1987 for each
function in each of the 190 metropolitan area in the sample. Index
values below 1 denote metropolitan areas with smaller than average
spending shares on a function, while values above 1 signify larger than
average spending shares. If resource allocation bias occurs over time,
then index values for metropolitan areas that switch from nonreliance to
low or high district reliance should increase. Conversely, metropolitan
areas that continue to provide services using general-purpose governments (nonreliance to nonreliance) should have relatively stable spending share index values.

Before examining the results of the dynamic analysis, it is useful
to compare spending shares by function for 1962 and 1987. These data,
shown in table 7–5, indicate the remarkable stability over the twenty-
five-year period in spending shares. Despite changes in technology,
society, and public sector responsibilities, most functions had approximately the same spending share in 1987 that they had in 1962.[30] The
largest absolute increases in spending shares occur for two increasingly
important public sector services, utilities (gas, electric, and transit), and
health and hospitals. Increases in spending shares for these services

**TABLE 7-5**   Change in Spending Share, 1962–1987, by Function

| Function | N (1962/87)[a] | Spending Share 1962 | Spending Share 1987 | Change, 1962–87[b] |
|---|---|---|---|---|
| Utilities (gas, electric, transit) | 127/128 | .096 | .137 | .041 |
| Health and Hospitals | 190/190 | .072 | .092 | .020 |
| Housing and Community Development | 168/190 | .043 | .043 | .000 |
| Airports | 171/176 | .018 | .018 | .000 |
| Parks and Recreation | 190/190 | .036 | .036 | .000 |
| Sewer | 190/189 | .063 | .063 | .000 |
| Libraries | 185/187 | .012 | .012 | .000 |
| Natural Resources | 186/189 | .014 | .006 | −.008 |
| Fire Protection | 190/190 | .052 | .043 | −.009 |
| Ports | 61/69 | .026 | .012 | −.014 |
| Water | 190/190 | .099 | .081 | −.018 |

**a.** N = number of metropolitan areas (of 190 total) with any local-government expenditures on function in 1962 and 1987, respectively.
**b.** Figures denote absolute, not percentage, change in spending share.

come at the expense of spending on four traditional functions, water, ports, fire protection, and natural resources. In the case of water services, the decrease in relative spending is sufficiently great to drop water from highest in absolute magnitude in 1962 to third highest (behind utilities and health and hospitals) in 1987.

## Resource Allocation Bias Over Time

The results of the dynamic analysis are shown in table 7–6. Consistent with the analysis in chapter 6, the data compare spending share index values over time for metropolitan areas that start with no reliance on districts in 1962, then follow one of the three institutional choice paths by 1987. I report data for only those functions for which at least seven metropolitan areas follow each possible institutional choice path.

The results confirm that resource allocation bias operates over time. Spending share index values for 1962 are generally at or below 1, signifying that metropolitan areas that did not rely on special districts in 1962 devoted relatively smaller shares of spending to a function than did district-reliant metropolitan areas. For all functions analyzed,

**TABLE 7-6** Dynamic Analysis of Resource Allocation Bias, No Reliance to Low or High Reliance, 1962—1987

| Function | Number of Metropolitan Areas | | | | Index of Spending Share | |
|---|---|---|---|---|---|---|
| | No reliance 1962 | No reliance 1987 | Low reliance 1987 | High reliance 1987 | 1962 | 1987 |
| Airports | 144 | 112 | 7 | 25 | 1.06 | 0.95 |
| | | | | | 0.99 | 0.58 |
| | | | | | 0.82 | 1.24 |
| Sewer | 113 | 79 | 20 | 14 | 1.05 | 0.90 |
| | | | | | 1.01 | 1.05 |
| | | | | | 0.49 | 0.81 |
| Water | 108 | 71 | 26 | 11 | 0.85 | 0.93 |
| | | | | | 1.14 | 1.03 |
| | | | | | 0.99 | 1.26 |

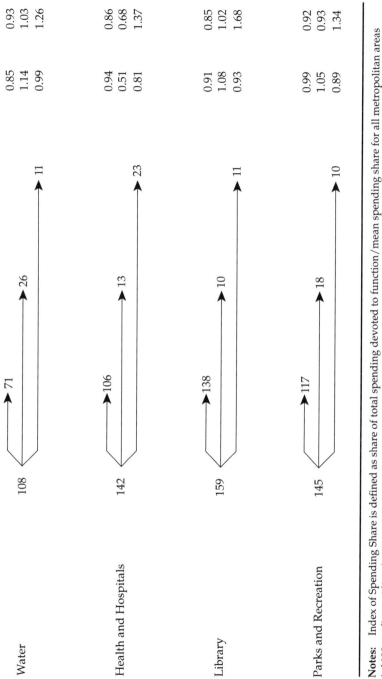

Water 108 → 71 → 26 → 11

0.85 0.93
1.14 1.03
0.99 1.26

Health and Hospitals 142 → 106 → 13 → 23

0.94 0.86
0.51 0.68
0.81 1.37

Library 159 → 138 → 10 → 11

0.91 0.85
1.08 1.02
0.93 1.68

Parks and Recreation 145 → 117 → 18 → 10

0.99 0.92
1.05 0.93
0.89 1.34

**Notes:** Index of Spending Share is defined as share of total spending devoted to function/mean spending share for all metropolitan areas (of 190 total) providing function. *N* indicates number of metropolitan areas switching from no district reliance in 1962 to no, low, or high district reliance by 1987.

211

the choice to remain nonreliant on districts by 1987 yields spending share index levels less than 1.

Of central interest are the resource allocation implications of switching from nonreliance to high district reliance, shown in the third row under each function. The results indicate strong support for resource allocation bias: all functions experience sharp increases in spending share index levels when metropolitan areas switch from no to high reliance between 1962 and 1987. The 1987 spending share index values are significantly greater than 1 for all functions except sewer. The share of total local government expenditures devoted to libraries is a substantial 68 percent larger than the mean spending share for library services for all 190 metropolitan areas in the sample.

The exceptional case of sewer services deserves comment. Although the spending share index increases appreciably from .49 to .81 in the fourteen metropolitan areas that switched from no to high district reliance, the index remains significantly less than 1 in 1987. The explanation may be that post-1962 shifts to district-operated sewer systems signified use of new and presumably more efficient sewage collection and treatment facilities, which in turn led to decreased relative spending on sewer services. By contrast, sewer systems that already existed in 1962 might by 1987 have required high operations and maintenance expenditures to sustain the aging system. This reasoning is consistent with the finding of somewhat higher spending share index values for metropolitan areas that relied on general-purpose governments for sewer services in both 1962 and 1987 (.90 and 1.05, respectively).

Analysis of the relatively few cases in which metropolitan areas switch from high district reliance in 1962 to no or low reliance by 1987 strengthens the case for the existence of resource allocation bias over time. Table 7–7 reports the spending share index values for 1962 and 1987 for the five services for which at least ten metropolitan areas made the institutional choice to switch from high to no or low district reliance over the twenty-five-year period. For four of the five services (the only exception is housing and community development) spending share index values decrease, usually from above one to near or below one. Metropolitan areas that made the institutional choice to switch from high to no or low reliance experience a drop in spending share for the function.

The central message of the dynamic analysis is that resource allocation bias operates not only cross-sectionally, but also over time. Metropolitan areas that at an earlier period allocated below-average resource shares to a function are the same metropolitan areas that have above-average spending shares after switching to special-purpose governments for service delivery.

TABLE 7-7 Dynamic Analysis of Resource Allocation Bias, High Reliance to No or Low Reliance, 1962–1987

| Function | $N^a$ | Index of Spending Share | |
| --- | --- | --- | --- |
| | | 1962 | 1987 |
| Sewer | 10 | 1.01 | .91 |
| Water | 15 | 1.25 | 1.01 |
| Housing and Community Development | 20 | .82 | 1.02 |
| Natural Resources | 17 | 1.67 | 1.34 |
| Health and Hospitals | 16 | 1.11 | 1.00 |

Notes: Index of Spending Share is defined as share of total spending devoted to function/mean spending share for all metropolitan areas (of 190 total) providing function. $N$ indicates number of metropolitan areas switching from high district reliance in 1962 to no or low reliance by 1987.

## CONCLUSION

Empirical analysis of the policy implications of specialized governance yields three important findings. First, the results confirm theoretical predictions that metropolitan areas that rely on special districts for service delivery allocate proportionally more of total local-government resources to a service than do metropolitan areas that rely on general-purpose governments for service delivery. This resource allocation bias pertains to a wide range of functions and applies to both total expenditures (capital, debt service, and operations and maintenance) and operations and maintenance expenditures. Resource allocation bias persists after controlling for metropolitan population size, age, and regional location. The only functions apparently not subject to resource allocation bias are airports, fire protection, and, for operations and maintenance expenditures, parks and recreation services.

Second, resource allocation bias operates over time. Metropolitan areas that in 1962 did not rely on special districts for delivery of airports, water, sewer, libraries, parks and recreation, and health and hospitals (the only services tested) had below-average to average spending shares for those services. The subset of these metropolitan areas that by 1987 had switched from general-purpose to special-purpose governments experienced large increases in relative spending shares, typically to levels well above the metropolitan average. The institutional choice to use special districts resulted in a significantly higher proportion of total metropolitan spending devoted to district-provided functions than did the choice to continue using general-purpose governments for service delivery.

Third, and perhaps most critical, the analysis provides ample evidence that specialized service delivery arrangements—classified by the degree to which a metropolitan area relies on special districts for development, housekeeping, and social welfare functions—foster systematic bias for and against certain functional categories of services. Development and housekeeping functions capture their largest spending in a functionally compartmentalized, district-reliant service world. These functions generally fare worst in resource allocation terms when they are the sole functional category that remains under general-purpose control. Social welfare functions, by contrast, generally capture their highest shares of spending when they are provided through general-purpose governments. Social welfare functions fare best if sheltered from direct competition against housekeeping functions for shares of scarce resources. Social welfare functions fare worst in metropolitan areas with the most highly specialized service arrangements. The full-line forcing and high political visibility of general-purpose governments apparently are important safeguards for social welfare functions in the competitive world of resource allocation.

## CHAPTER NOTES

   **1.** Dilys M. Hill, *Democratic Theory and Local Government* (London: George Allen & Unwin, 1974), pp. 30, 36–40; and Stewart, *The Responsive Local Authority*, p. 136.
   **2.** Michael A. Pane, *Functional Fragmentation and the Traditional Forms of Municipal Government in New Jersey* (Trenton: New Jersey County and Municipal Government Study Commission, 1985), chap. 5, p. 4.
   **3.** See, for example, Walsh, *The Public's Business*, pp. 6–7; and Jones, "Local Government in Metropolitan Areas," p. 580.
   **4.** Jones, "Local Government in Metropolitan Areas," pp. 574, 581; Hill, *Democratic Theory*, pp. 31–32, 150; and, generally, Institute for Local Self Government, *Special Districts or Special Dynasties?* For an example, see Walsh, *The Public's Business*, chap. 7, esp. pp. 175, 184–208.
   **5.** Minge, "Special Districts," p. 704; Zax, "The Effects of Jurisdiction Types," pp. 82–83; and J. Bollens, *Special District Governments*, pp. 10–11.
   **6.** Dwight R. Lee, "Special Interest Inefficiency: A Case For or Against Government Spending Limits?" *Social Science Quarterly* 70, no. 3 (1989): 765–66.
   **7.** See, for example, Walsh, *The Public's Business*, chap. 10; Henriques, *The Machinery of Greed*, chap. 6; Leigland, "External Controls on Public Authorities"; Jones, "Local Government in Metropolitan Areas," pp. 579–82; Axelrod, *Shadow Government*, pp. 92–117; and Heiman, *The Quiet Evolution*, pp. 148–52.
   **8.** Hamilton and Wells, *Federalism, Power and Political Economy*, pp. 134–35; and Scott and Corzine, "Special Districts in the San Francisco Bay Area," pp. 201–14.

**9.** Barlow, *Metropolitan Government*, p. 7.

**10.** See, for example, Logan and Molotch, *Urban Fortunes*, pp. 73–74.

**11.** See Cox and Nartowicz, "Jurisdictional Fragmentation," pp. 203–4; Piven and Friedland, "Public Choice and Private Power," pp. 411–12; Olin, "Intraclass Conflict," p. 237; Jonas, "Urban Growth Coalitions," p. 217; Sanders, "Building the Convention City," pp. 137–39, 153–55; Vogel and Swanson, "The Growth Machine," p. 74; and Walsh, *The Public's Business*, p. 337–41.

**12.** See, for example, Hall, *Great Planning Disasters*, p. 226. As Hall colorfully puts it, full line forcing "is rather as if, in the market economy, the buyer was forced to choose between a bundle consisting of a Mercedes car, a ton of bananas and a spin dryer, and another consisting of a bicycle, a ton of potatoes and a holiday in Spain, without any consideration of his preferences for any one item."

**13.** See Peterson, *City Limits*, pp. 48–50; Oates, "Decentralization of the Public Sector," pp. 44–45; and Hill, *Democratic Theory*, pp. 40, 43–44.

**14.** Colman, "A Quiet Revolution," p. 14.

**15.** Ibid.

**16.** Further analysis indicates weak to mild evidence of continuous effects in resource allocation bias. Metropolitan areas with higher levels of district reliance are only slightly more likely to have higher relative spending shares, a finding consistent with results for upward spending bias. The only exception is natural resources services for which the few metropolitan areas that devote high proportions of local-government spending to natural resources invariably have high district reliance levels.

**17.** Robert M. Stein, "Tiebout's Sorting Hypothesis," *Urban Affairs Quarterly* 23, no. 2 (1987): 144.

**18.** See Adrian, *A History of American City Government*, chap. 7; Eric H. Monkkonen, *America Becomes Urban: The Development of U.S. Cities and Towns, 1780–1980* (Berkeley: University of California Press, 1988), pp. 218–23, 240, 243; Dye and Garcia, "Structure, Function and Policy," pp. 110–11, 120; and Roland J. Liebert, "Municipal Functions, Structure, and Expenditures," *Social Science Quarterly* 54, no. 1 (1974): 765–83.

**19.** See Stein, "Tiebout's Sorting Hypothesis," pp. 142–43; Roy W. Bahl, "Effects of Regional Shifts in Population and Economic Activity on the Finances of State and Local Governments: Implications for Public Policy," in *Alternatives to Confrontation*, ed. Victor L. Arnold (Lexington, Mass.: Lexington Books, 1980), pp. 165–69; George Palumbo, "City Government Expenditures and City Government Reality: A Comment on Sjoquist," *National Tax Journal* 36, no. 2 (1983): 249–51; and David Young Miller, "The Impact of Political Culture on Patterns of State and Local Government Expenditures," *Publius* 21 (Spring 1991): 83–100.

**20.** Dye and Garcia, "Structure, Function and Policy," pp. 108, 111.

**21.** Data sources vary. For population size: U.S. Bureau of the Census, *1988 City and County Data Book*, app. E. For metropolitan area age: U.S. Bureau of the Census, *Census of Population and Housing*, various editions, 1910–1980; and U.S. Bureau of the Census, *1986 State and Metropolitan Area Data Book* (Washington, D.C.: U.S. Government Printing Office, 1986). For region: U.S. Bureau of the Census, *1986 State and Metropolitan Area Data Book*, p. xvi. Regions and the states they include are: North Central East (Illinois, Indiana, Michigan,

Ohio, Wisconsin); North Central West (Iowa, Kansas, Minnesota, Missouri, North Dakota, Nebraska, South Dakota); New England (Connecticut, Massachusetts, Maine, New Hampshire, Rhode Island, Vermont); Middle Atlantic (New Jersey, New York, Pennsylvania); South Atlantic (Washington D.C., Delaware, Florida, Georgia, Maryland, North Carolina, South Carolina, Virginia, West Virginia); South Central East (Alabama, Kentucky, Mississippi, Tennessee); South Central West (Arkansas, Louisiana, Oklahoma, Texas); Western Mountain (Arizona, Colorado, Idaho, Montana, New Mexico, Nevada, Utah, Wyoming); and Western Pacific (California, Oregon, Washington).

**22.** Population is significant for only three services, transit, sewer, and fire protection. For transit the relationship is positive and strong, confirming that larger metropolitan areas devote significantly larger percentages of total spending to transit. By contrast, smaller metropolitan areas allocate proportionally more resources to sewer and fire protection services. This may reflect the relatively narrow functional portfolio of smaller metropolitan areas, which implies higher shares for each of the fewer services provided.

**23.** Age enters five of the twelve regressions with significance. Older areas devote larger spending shares to housing and community development, fire protection, parks and recreation, and sewers; younger areas devote proportionally more to natural resources. Higher shares for housing services likely reflect the typically more severe low-income housing needs in older metropolitan areas. The reasons for higher spending shares for parks and recreation, fire protection, and sewer services is less clear. Perhaps younger areas are more apt to farm out these services to nonpublic agencies. Or more established bureaucracies and greater likelihood of unionized public sectors in older areas may induce higher proportional expenditures on these services than in less bureaucratized and unionized younger areas. The negative association between metropolitan age and natural resource shares probably reflects the greater need for natural resource services in newer, less urbanized areas compared to more urbanized, older metropolitan areas.

**24.** Regional effects vary by function. With the exception of transit, all functions have at least one region in which spending shares are significantly different from those in the base case region. Positive and significant coefficients signal higher budget shares relative to Mid-Atlantic metropolitan areas (or West Mountain in the case of fire protection, libraries, and housing and community development). For some functions, the significance of region is largely due to a small set of often clustered metropolitan areas with extremely large spending shares. For example, significantly high spending shares for ports in the South Central West is due to high ports spending shares in Galveston, Beaumont-Port Arthur, Brownsville, and Corpus Christi metropolitan areas in Texas, and Lake Charles metropolitan area in Louisiana. High utilities spending in the South Atlantic region is similarly influenced by Knoxville, Nashville, Memphis, and Johnson City metropolitan areas in Tennessee, and Decatur, Huntsville, and Florence metropolitan areas in Alabama. Natural resources spending in the West is influenced by Bakersfield, Modesto, Fresno, Merced, Yuba City, and Visalia metropolitan areas in California, and Yakima Metropolitan Area in Washington. Airport spending in the West Mountain region is influenced by Las Vegas and Reno metropolitan areas in Nevada, and Billings, Montana; Boise, Idaho; and Denver, Colorado, metropolitan areas.

**25.** To the extent that other metropolitan factors such as physical attributes, demographics, or economic base characteristics influence resource allocations, the reliance variable may be picking up these effects. For an overview of other possible determinants of public spending, see Helen Ladd and John Yinger, *America's Ailing Cities* (Baltimore: Johns Hopkins University Press, 1989).

**26.** Because the distributions of reliance levels are skewed to the right, using the mean, rather than median, reliance level as the dividing line means that more metropolitan areas are classified as having low rather than high district reliance. I could ideally use district reliance levels for individual functions, rather than categories, to determine low and high reliance. A metropolitan area would be classified as having high district reliance for development functions, for example, if it had high district reliance for each individual development-oriented function. Unfortunately, this approach yields an insufficient number of high reliance metropolitan areas to enable reliable statistical testing.

**27.** The relatively high mean reliance value for social welfare services is at first glance surprising. The high mean makes sense, however, given that the social welfare category includes two services with relatively high district reliance, health and hospitals, and housing and community development.

**28.** For a discussion of copycatting behavior, see John Shannon, "Federalism's 'Invisible Regulator'—Interjurisdictional Competition," in *Competition Among States and Local Governments: Efficiency and Equity in American Federalism*, ed. Daphne A. Kenyon and John Kincaid (Washington, D.C.: Urban Institute, 1991), pp. 117–25; and Albert Breton, "The Existence and Stability of Interjurisdictional Competition," in *Competition Among States and Local Governments: Efficiency and Equity in American Federalism*, ed. Daphne A. Kenyon and John Kincaid (Washington, D.C.: Urban Institute, 1991), pp. 37–56.

**29.** The predicted effect also fails to materialize when using a narrower definition of social welfare functions that includes welfare assistance only. One possible explanation for the absence of significance is that the predicted effect operates at the municipal rather than metropolitan level. At the municipal level, district provision of sewer, water, airports, roads, and other development functions might lead to proportional gains for public safety, libraries, and other housekeeping services at the expense of health and hospitals, housing and community development, and welfare assistance services. The tendency for functions to be provided at different scales, however, precludes analysis of this hypothesis.

**30.** This is unexpected. I had anticipated that, for example, the share of spending devoted to airports would increase over the twenty-five-year period as air transportation became an increasingly common mode of travel and airports became requisite facilities for industrial development. The absence of this finding may be because nearly all of the metropolitan areas in the sample that provide airport services already did so in 1962. Were newer metropolitan areas included in the sample there might be increases in spending shares for airports. Including newer metropolitan areas might affect the stability of spending shares for other functions as well.

# 8*

# The Promise and Peril of Specialized Governance

Service-delivery decisions are matters of institutional choice. Why, given the array of public, private, and nonprofit options available, might a metropolitan society choose to use one service-delivery option over another? To be more specific, why would metropolitan interest groups choose special-purpose, as opposed to general-purpose, governments for service delivery? The findings of this research suggest that the answer is complex, involving an interplay between consumer goals, legal and political parameters shaping institutional choices, and the expected and actual consequences of particular service alternatives.

This study of special districts as increasingly prevalent institutional choices for metropolitan service delivery offers greater understanding and a useful way of thinking about specialized governance. In doing so the research sheds light on a number of important theoretical, empirical, and policy dimensions of institutional choice. Therein lie some lessons.

## RESEARCH LESSONS

The central messages of this research can be summarized in four lessons about the nature, causes, fiscal effects, and policy effects of specialized service delivery.

### Lesson One: "Special Districts" Is a Plural

The first lesson is the most fundamental. When analysts and policymakers speak of special districts, emphasis must be on the final "s." As the conceptual and empirical analyses have emphasized, districts are far from a uniform local government type motivated by a single factor and

*Parts of this chapter appeared in Kathryn A. Foster, "The Fish Stores of Government and Other Musings on Specialization," *Intersight* 3 (1995): 47–54. Reprinted by permission of the School of Architecture and Planning, State University of New York at Buffalo.

driven toward a single outcome. Rather, special-purpose governments comprise a number of subtypes distinguished by their reasons for formation and anticipated fiscal and policy implications. The attributes that most critically reveal districts' political-economic objectives and largely determine their consequences are geographic scope, mode of financing, and function. The motivations and implications of special districts as a class are not uniform: different geographic, financial, and functional subtypes of districts are associated with different causes and consequences.

The implication of this lesson for scholarship is its call to increase the sophistication of conceptual and empirical analyses of special-purpose governments. Proponents of an institutional-reform perspective, for example, contend that special districts are inefficient, inequitable, and unresponsive. Perhaps some are: certainly the capitalizing and privatizing districts described in chapter 4 neither intend nor likely achieve the economic efficiencies or redistributive outcomes that re-formers seek. But "special districts" is not an undifferentiated class of local government: regionalizing and collectivizing districts, for example, may well intend and achieve economic efficiency and social equity goals. In a similar vein, public choice, structuralist, and metropolitan ecology scholars obscure understanding of special-purpose governments when they draw conclusions about districts from theorizing about or examining one or two district subtypes. Lesson one counsels scholars to more explicitly differentiate districts by geographic and financial subtype to more finely determine their motivations and consequences.

In the policy realm practitioners tend instinctively to understand the lesson of districts with an "s." Local government officials, developers, and metropolitan residents propose specific and presumably appropriate district subtypes to achieve regionalizing, capitalizing, particularizing, collectivizing, and privatizing goals. A new subdivision's need for water service, for example, would hardly provoke a proposal for a countywide, tax-funded water district. At the state level, legislators' objectives for local service delivery and their awareness of the promise and perils of district subtypes are reflected in enabling laws that specify functions, geographic scopes, and revenue-raising powers for different brands of special-purpose governments.

Nonetheless, the lesson of districts with an "s" deserves greater attention from policy practitioners. Of vital importance is the need for improved collection and organization of data on special-purpose governments. Few states classify and analyze districts on the basis of financial, geographic, and functional attributes. Although the U.S. Bureau of the Census does distinguish districts by these (and other) attributes, it makes these data available in relatively inaccessible formats.[1] One improvement for research and policy making would be to classify every special-purpose government as one of the six geographic-financial subtypes outlined in chapter 4, thereby enabling analysis within and across district types. The current practice of grouping together special-purpose governments of widely different attributes impairs understanding of important trends and implications.

## Lesson Two: Legal Frameworks Matter

The second lesson stems from empirical analysis of the uneven distribution of special districts across metropolitan areas. The most consistently significant factor accounting for the number of special-purpose governments in an area is a legal parameter, the number of functional types of districts enabled by state law. Simply put, without legal permission to form special districts, special districts do not form. Factors related to local government structure and service demand certainly influence patterns of specialized service delivery. Moreover, merely because a legislature enables special-purpose governments does not guarantee that districts will form. Nonetheless, although a favorable legal environment is not a *sufficient* condition for district formation, it is clearly a *necessary* one.

Lending additional support to the importance of legal factors is the significant influence of municipal home-rule powers, boundary discretion, and revenue-raising powers on the cross-metropolitan distribution of districts. The centrality of legal factors to local government arrangements is not itself surprising, given that legal frameworks codify a society's values and preferences for its public and private institutions. Nonetheless, although straightforward and perhaps obvious, the relevance of legal parameters is too often overlooked by researchers and policy makers involved with special-purpose governments.

Lesson two bears on scholarly debates over metropolitan political organization and the determinants of special-purpose governments. Although each of the predominant theoretical perspectives on metropolitan political economies acknowledges the importance of legal provision, the metropolitan ecology perspective most forcefully underscores the centrality of legal factors to local government structure. The political, economic, and development factors highlighted by advocates of other perspectives matter, yet the influence of these nonlegal factors is conditioned by a legal framework that ultimately permits, prohibits, encourages, or discourages specific institutional choices.

The primary policy implication of lesson two is the key role for policy makers in institutional choices. Although officials can exercise little control over many technological, cultural, economic, and demographic forces, policy makers are largely in charge of legal levers that effect change. By manipulating these levers policy makers set the ground rules for how institutional choice games get played and what outcomes are possible and likely. Policy makers can control the permissiveness or restrictiveness of statutes related to local government formation, powers, and actions. Therefore, policy makers may predispose or strongly prevail upon institutional arrangements and outcomes.

## Lesson Three: Special Delivery Costs More

Lesson three imparts a message about the fiscal consequences of specialized service delivery. The analysis in chapter 6 revealed that for a wide range of functions the per capita costs of service delivery are significantly higher in district-reliant metropolitan areas than in nonreliant areas. This finding of upward spending bias is not unexpected. For nearly every function, special-purpose governments devote proportionally more than do general-purpose governments to relatively expensive capital projects. For this reason, specialized service delivery is qualitatively different from general-purpose service delivery and *ought* to cost more.

Less expected, however, is the finding that upward spending bias persists for operations and maintenance expenditures only. For many services, upward spending bias holds after controlling for service demand factors such as metropolitan population, age, and income level. For some other services, district multiplicity accounts for the higher costs of specialized governance, a finding that points toward administrative overhead as a source of higher per capita service costs. For still other functions, higher costs simply persist in district-reliant as opposed to nonreliant metropolitan areas. The constancy of effect suggests that institutional attributes inherent to special-purpose governments are the likely source of higher costs. The outcome is clear: specialized governance costs more than the general-purpose variety.

In the broadest sense, because each of the dominant theoretical perspectives predicts higher costs for special-purpose, as opposed to general-purpose, service delivery, lesson three merely confirms theoretical claims. But because theorists predict higher costs for different reasons, lesson three supports some theoretical arguments and conflicts with others. The finding of higher costs due to district multiplicity lends weight to institutional-reform claims about the fiscal costs of government fragmentation. The persistence of upward spending bias after controlling for metropolitan demand factors substantiates the claims of metropolitan ecology and structuralist scholars about institutional and political sources of higher costs in specialized governance. Although case studies are needed to pinpoint specific sources, aggregate results suggest factors such as institutional autonomy (associated with higher overhead, coordination costs, and dedicated revenue streams) and limited political visibility (associated with greater freedom to implement unpopular development projects and greater potential for financial mismanagement) as likely contributors to upward spending bias.

The policy implications of lesson three concern implementation and public relations. A common selling point for special districts is that they provide a cost-effective means to streamline government. This study finds that specialized governance is associated with higher service costs per capita. Although it is possible that higher costs merely reflect superior service quality—an issue of efficiency not easily established or resolved in this research—there is no reason to assume this situation. At the very least, policy makers should consider the likelihood of higher costs in specialized service delivery when making and implementing institutional choices.

The public relations task is to ensure that information on upward spending bias is disseminated to public officials, metropolitan residents, developers, and others engaged in and affected by institutional choices. Some might argue that officials and taxpayers make informed choices in favor of special districts because the benefits of specialized governance outweigh the higher costs that might result. The rhetoric of institutional choice rarely mentions the reality of upward spending bias, however. Good governance requires that policy makers be informed and inform others about the likelihood of higher costs associated with special-purpose government service delivery.

## Lesson Four: Specialized Governance Shapes Policy

The final lesson teaches that special districts are not substitutes for general-purpose governments. District-reliant metropolitan areas experience resource allocation bias; that is, they allocate greater shares of total resources to district-provided services than do nonreliant areas. In this way, specialized governance has nonneutral policy consequences. The most revealing and potentially foreboding of these is that social welfare functions capture their smallest shares of government spending in metropolitan areas with the most specialized service-delivery arrangements. By contrast, development and housekeeping functions capture their greatest shares of government spending under the most specialized service environments. Specialized governance systematically favors some functions, namely development and housekeeping ones, over others, namely social welfare services.

For scholars, lesson four dictates the need to clarify theoretical conceptions of special-purpose governments. Although increasingly out of favor, it is time to put to rest the notion that specialized governments are policy-neutral, technocratic public agencies. The institutional choice to rely on special-purpose governments is a policy-relevant choice. Districts' policy reach extends beyond the development functions scholars often cite as the focus of specialized governance. As the analysis in chapter 7 reveals, all types of districts, even those providing social welfare functions such as housing and health, can under the right conditions benefit from the institutional sanctuary provided by special-purpose governments.

More important, however, analysts must recognize that specialized service delivery favors development and housekeeping functions at the expense of social welfare functions. Most theoretical critiques of special-purpose governments rest on districts' political and economic impacts; equity-based critiques are rare. This study's verification of systematic bias in resource allocations points to the importance of further analysis on the policy biases of specialized governance.

The policy implications of lesson four are clear. The trend toward specialized governance threatens the ability of social welfare functions to hold their own in the competitive zero-sum game of resource allocation. Previous studies have documented that public support for social welfare functions is fragile.[2] Given an opportunity to make discrete, rather than bundled, choices in a public services marketplace, middle- and upper-income residents are apt to pass over social welfare services, from which they derive little direct benefit, in favor of development and housekeeping services, which offer more direct payoffs to individual utility. Lower-income residents, who are most apt to need and therefore choose welfare, health, and housing functions from the public services menu, are also most apt to lack the resources to pay for these functions without subsidies. As a consequence, social welfare functions are often provided by higher-level governments, which can cross-subsidize these without incurring severe political and economic penalties. When social services *are* provided at the local level, they are commonly part of a bundled service package that is funded collectively through taxes. Only by bundling services can the local government raise funds from its entire tax base for socially necessary, targeted programs. As lesson four dictates, specialized governance severs the protective bonds of service bundling and leaves social welfare functions to compete unsuccessfully against more popular public services. Given these equity implications of specialized governance, policy makers who choose special-purpose governments for service delivery do so to the potential peril of short- and long-term metropolitan welfare.

## SEEING THE FOREST FOR THE TREES

The four lessons provide a short course in the nature and implications of specialized governance. Special-purpose governments are the outcome of institutional choices shaped by legal rules for local government. Special-purpose governments come in a variety of noninterchangeable geographic, financial, and functional subtypes, each associated with different purposes and outcomes. District-reliant metropolitan areas spend more per capita than do nonreliant ones. Specialized service arrangements favor development and housekeeping functions to the detriment of social welfare functions.

These lessons are important in and of themselves and in the complex world of metropolitan service delivery. Yet these lessons, together with the phenomenal rise of special-purpose governments itself, are also important because they bear upon broader, unresolved issues of social science and policy. Three of these issues—institutional adaptability, privatization, and specialization—stand out because of their relevance to and potential to profit from lessons of special-purpose governance.

### Institutional Adaptability

One of the most profound and enduring tensions in modern society is how to secure order in an interdependent system without sacrificing the diversity of its component parts.[3] Societies seek order to protect themselves from the forces of anarchy, ensure that diverse factions have equal claim on collective resources regardless of political power, and capture the cost-saving efficiencies of standardization and mass production. Societies seek diversity to further individual or group expression, ensure that special interest groups can protect their interests, and derive the economic and political benefits of healthy competition in the marketplace for goods and ideas.

Although society widely acknowledges the benefits of order and diversity, it considers extreme levels of either of these values to be unhealthy. Too much order without diversity implies conformity, bureaucratization, and loss of individual freedom.[4] Too much diversity without order implies chaos, injustice, and self-interest.[5] As a result, most societies search for adaptive policies, programs, and institutions that will capture the rewards of order and diversity while eluding their harshest liabilities. It is in this light, staking the middle ground between order and diversity, that special-purpose governments may be viewed.

Special-purpose governments play an adaptive role by brokering the central challenge posed by the interdependent and diverse metropolis: How should a system of local governments be organized to ensure efficient, equitable, and responsive service delivery? Those who favor order over diversity advocate consolidated arrangements of government, arguing that the welfare of the regional whole is more important than the parochial interests of its individual communities. Those who favor diversity over order advocate polycentric government arrangements, arguing that the sovereignty of local jurisdictions is more important than the regionwide equity of unified government. There is no a priori resolution of which should take priority—the uniformity of an ordered system or the exercise of local prerogatives in a diverse system.[6]

Lesson one—"districts with an 's' "—challenges conventional wisdom about the adaptability of special districts in metropolitan political economies. The lesson clarifies that not all district subtypes execute their adaptive role in similar ways, nor, for that matter, do different subtypes necessarily play an adaptive role.

The key attribute determining the nature of district adaptability is geographic scope. In politically fragmented metropolitan areas, in which government multiplicity presents a challenge to order, regionalizing districts may standardize service delivery across a diverse and interdependent region. By contrast, in politically integrated metropolitan areas with relatively few general-purpose governments, particularizing districts may enable provision of nonuniform levels of service to accommodate the diverse and specialized service preferences of metropolitan residents. The critical implication of lesson one, however, is that not all districts serve as adaptive institutions. Capitalizing districts, for example, are not adaptive. Formed for political or fiscal reasons at the municipal scale, capitalizing districts reinforce, rather than reform, the geopolitical balance between order and diversity.

Lessons three and four on the fiscal and policy consequences of specialized service delivery shed additional light on the nature of institutional adaptability. Although adaptation implies moderation and balance, adaptive mechanisms are not by those grounds necessarily inconsequential. A zoning board's use of variances, for example, may accommodate special land use circumstances, but may also lead to arbitrary decisions and, if instituted widely, to frustration of local planning goals. The findings on special-purpose governments reinforce the consequentiality of institutional adaptation. Reliance on adaptive districts is neither fiscally nor politically neutral: metropolitan areas with specialized service arrangements spend significantly more per capita and allocate resources across functions in significantly different ways than do metropolitan areas with generalized service arrangements.

Institutional adaptation through special-purpose governments is thus neither automatic nor benign. Only the regionalizing and particularizing geographic subtypes of districts play adaptive roles. Still, adaptive districts do not replicate the status quo, they modify it. Whether these implications are selling points for special-purpose governments depends on the specific goals of metropolitan interest groups.

### Privatization

A second fundamental issue touched on by this study is the dividing line between public and private spheres. In recent decades one public-private issue of institutional choice, privatization, has generated enormous debate and a small industry's worth of articles, reports, books, and newspaper accounts.[7] As the public sector's "private" arm, special districts are often drawn into the privatization debate. The findings of this research suggest that special-purpose governments do impinge on questions of privatization, but in limited and specific ways only.

Determining the suitability of privatization is perplexing because there are few, if any, services that do not lend themselves to private provision. Market-oriented public services with definable outputs and relatively noncontroversial preference levels are frequent candidates for privatization.[8] Examples include solid waste disposal, wastewater treatment, infrastructure maintenance, and building security. But even social welfare functions increasingly find themselves on the privatization bandwagon: day-care services are routinely supplied by private providers; private health maintenance organizations and "managed competition" are the current watchwords of health services delivery; private educational consultants are making inroads into public school service delivery; and privatized prison management is increasingly common.[9] One account of the future of privatization predicts private control by 2015 of defense and redistribution, the twin mainstays of the public-sector portfolio.[10]

Proponents of privatization cite theoretical rationales and empirical evidence that privatization increases production efficiency, lowers service-delivery costs, and improves public responsiveness.[11] Even critics of privatization note that the case for privatization gains steam from recent international trends in which socialist, Eastern bloc, and Labour-controlled governments have enthusiastically joined the drive to privatize.[12]

Detractors of privatization stand behind theoretical arguments about equity and accountability, tales of corruption, and political-economic analyses noting that lower service-delivery costs may not mean greater efficiency and may signify exploitative labor practices.[13] Privatization has societal drawbacks, opponents caution, not the least of which is the blow it deals to public discussion of allocative and distributive issues.[14] In one of the more colorful, if not analytic, critiques of privatization, a large public sector union, the Civil Service Employees Association (CSEA), likens modern day privatization to the mercenary privateers who did government's bidding in days of yore. "Who do you want protecting your neighborhoods and your environment, maintaining your parks and roads, nurturing your children and your elderly, caring for your sick and your mentally ill," the text exhorts. "Privateers? Or public employees whose very motivation is the public good?"[15]

More careful treatments of privatization generally conclude that the two most critical elements of an effective privatization scheme are competition in contract bidding (or service delivery) and accountability to the public interest.[16] Where these elements both exist, analysts generally agree, private service delivery may provide more efficient and responsive service delivery than does the relatively bureaucratic, non-competitive public sector.

Given these considerations, where does specialized service delivery fit into the privatization debate? In a strict sense, because special-purpose governments are public entities they are ipso facto not agents of privatization. In a less restrictive sense, however, special-purpose governments may be likened to privatized agencies or contractors. To the extent districts share the motivations, intended outcomes, and service-delivery conditions of private enterprise, we would expect districts to share the blessings and burdens of privatization.

Lesson one on the need to distinguish special-purpose governments by subtypes clarifies that only certain districts have privatization as a service goal. The critical attribute is the form of financing. Taxing districts, which collectivize revenue raising, are clearly not instruments of privatization. By contrast, nontaxing districts, which raise revenues through user fees, tolls, rents, and other individual payments, do resemble private enterprises. Because privatizing districts are generally more permanent and insulated from municipal or county control than are private contractors, in fact, they may behave more like private corporations than do the agencies and contractors commonly associated with privatization.

Should we then expect specialized service-delivery outcomes to coincide with those of private enterprise? Only to a limited extent. Privatizing districts share with private enterprise similar disincentives for public accountability, but they do not share similar levels of competitiveness. With respect to accountability, the nonelected governing boards of nontaxing districts are perhaps more accountable to the underwriters and investors who finance district projects than they are to consumers of district services. Therefore, privatizing districts resemble private-sector corporations. With respect to competitiveness, special-purpose governments do not typically earn their franchise to provide public services by demonstrating expertise at competitive service-delivery tryouts. Nor do special districts compete for customers against rival service delivery agencies as a private business would. Rather, districts typically enjoy spatial monopolies within a region.

Privatizing districts and privatized contractors are thus similar on accountability grounds and different on competitiveness ones. Given this, districts and private firms should share similar policy implications, which are influenced by levels of accountability, and should differ in fiscal implications, which are driven by competitiveness. Lessons three and four bear out these predictions. Consistent with lesson three, specialized service delivery does not bring the lower costs allegedly associated with privatization, but rather the higher costs one would expect from a quasi-monopolistic service provider. Consistent with lesson four, metropolitan areas with highly specialized service-delivery arrangements devote fewer resources to social welfare functions than do metropolitan areas that rely more on public-interest-bound general-purpose governments. This outcome coincides with theoretical predictions for a privatized service-delivery world.

In short, specialized service delivery is like privatization in limited but revealing ways. Only the nontaxing district subtypes resemble the private enterprises of privatization schemes. Even this resemblance is limited, however. Although nontaxing districts and private entities have similar disincentives for accountability, they are less likely than private firms to operate under competitive conditions. Lessons three and four confirm what we would expect. In the absence of competition service costs are higher; where accountability is diminished policy bias pertains.

## Specialization

I turn finally to the issue of specialization itself. Functional specialization is a trait of special-purpose governments, regardless of their geographic scope or mode of financing. The steady increase in the number and importance of special-purpose governments over the past four decades signifies the rise of public-sector specialization.

The ascendance of special districts is by no means an isolated trend toward specialization, however. For all the recent fanfare about the interconnectedness of global environments, politics, economies, and cultures (we are "McWorld" in one formulation[17]), there are formidable apposite trends toward compartmentalization and functionalization. Specialized shopping malls catering to specialized consumer pools are infusing new energy into long-stagnant retail markets.[18] Scientific knowledge has become so specialized that technical versatility is an oxymoron.[19] Although cities and individual investors often strive for diversified economic portfolios, the less risk-averse know that specialized strategies can, with a dose of luck or clairvoyance in picking the right industry or right stock, bring even greater economic payoffs. The pendulum of education reform at the secondary level swings increasingly toward decentralized and thematized learning in junior and senior high schools.[20] At the university level, educational experts note that the once lustrous liberal arts degree has dulled considerably relative to more technically specialized degrees in the marketplace for graduates.[21]

What are the messages of this analysis for specialization in public services? Lesson two emphasizes that society, through its laws and regulatory practices, can control the number, use, and powers of special-purpose governments. Lesson three on upward spending bias and lesson four on systematic resource allocation bias reveal reasons why society might want to exercise these legal and regulatory controls over special-purpose governance.

Beyond these lessons, the study illuminates two corollary dimensions of specialization. The first is the notion that specialization is widely thought to breed expertise and expertise is widely associated with quality. Most would agree that technical expertise has obvious blessings, especially compared to inexpertise. Yet the dilemma of expertise in the public services realm is that too much faith in experts may delegitimize the claims of lay citizens to participate in policy discussions and decisions, a condition that may have profound and somber implications for democracy.[22]

The desire for specialized, and by that score allegedly expert, service delivery is a common rationale for special-purpose governments. Not surprisingly, a byproduct of specialized expertise is an aura of technocratic absolutism. Because special-purpose governments are isolated from political pressure and enjoy broad financial and administrative freedoms, proponents allege, districts can achieve efficient, technically optimal, and societally beneficial solutions to difficult and controversial service problems that politically responsive, less-specialized agencies find especially hard to solve.[23]

Lessons three and four teach that the implications of a system heavily reliant on technical experts costs more and yields a different blend of services from the outcomes generated in a less-specialized environment. Whether the downside of technical expertise is offset by other gains in efficiency or higher quality service outcomes is not evident. What is evident is that technical rationality in the public services realm appears to impede the provision of social welfare functions relative to development and housekeeping functions. At the very least, such a finding should give a liberal democracy pause.

A second dimension of specialization touched on by this study is the implications of specialization for coordinated, comprehensive approaches to decisionmaking. As society grows simultaneously more complex, specialized, and interdependent, so do the complexity and difficulty of economic, political, and cultural decisions about how to manage specialization and its consequent exchange relations.[24] How successfully a governance system coordinates service delivery is a common gauge of the responsiveness and efficiency of that system. Even to district loyalists, the Achilles' heel of specialized service delivery is its inability to coordinate the planning, budgeting, and delivery of services throughout a metropolitan area.

One aspect of lesson three is the finding of higher costs associated with institutional multiplicity. For a range of functions, metropolitan areas that rely on more, as opposed to fewer, special districts have higher per capita costs for service delivery. Coordination costs are not the only costs implicated by lesson three, of course, yet they are clearly one element of upward spending bias. Moreover, although it is impossible with aggregate data to gauge the coordination level of special-purpose versus general-purpose governments, it is possible to note the different nature of coordination problems that arise under each institutional choice. Governments of any type can experience a coordination disaster, for example, the road torn up one year to lay water pipes, demolished the next to lay sewer lines, ripped up again the following year to lay underground cable, and knocked out of service the year after that for routine road repair. When the problem of "the right hand not knowing what the left is doing" occurs on the watch of general-purpose government, it is a frustrating but tractable problem of poor management. When coordination problems occur in a specialized world with separate water, sewer, utility, and highway districts, however, these problems are predictable outcomes of institutional autonomy combined with functional specialization. Mandates for inter-district or district-nondistrict coordination are virtually nonexistent. Practical efforts to coordinate service delivery are often problematic and transitory.

At a minimum, specialization in institutions poses myriad challenges to metropolitan political economies. The empirical analysis finds that specialized service delivery costs more and alters the mix of services provided. Specialized arrangements generate more numerous and more difficult problems of service-delivery coordination. Although the aura of expertise surrounding district service delivery may enable districts to get the job done, it may also thwart citizen participation and drive a wedge between actual and demanded service outcomes.

## A FINAL WORD

As I complete this project the U.S. Bureau of the Census is simultaneously releasing detailed data from the *1992 Census of Governments* and completing its preparation for the *1997 Census of Governments*. All signs point to the likelihood that these censuses will echo their predecessors about the continued increase in special-purpose governments of various sizes, functions, and subtypes. As special-purpose governments widen their numerical lead over other local-government types, they will undoubtedly solidify their place as service providers of choice in many metropolitan regions. Together with growth in private homeowners' associations, business improvement districts, and privatized service alternatives, special-purpose governments are part of a more sweeping pendulum swing toward specialization, compartmentalization, and privatization of the public sphere.

In a society that reveres both individuality and unity, diversity and order, efficiency and equity, and liberty and justice, there is little reason to believe that society will cease to turn to accommodating and utilitarian specialized governments for services. Special districts satisfy many needs for many different interest groups. As the nation enters a new century of institutional choice it is important that scholars, policy makers, and metropolitan residents take notice and stock of specialized institutions and the ways they shape metropolitan political economies.

## CHAPTER NOTES

1. As a cost-cutting measure the U.S. Bureau of the Census stopped publishing data on government organization and finances by metropolitan area in 1977 and stopped publishing many data series at the individual county level in 1982. As a consequence, researchers must work with highly disaggregated data at the individual government unit level, much of which is available only in data files of censuses of governments.

2. See, for example, Joseph P. Viteritti, "Bureaucratic Environments, Efficiency, and Equity in Urban Service Delivery Systems," in *The Politics of Urban Public Services*, ed. Richard C. Rich (Lexington, Mass.: D.C. Heath, 1982), pp. 53–68; and, generally, Peterson, *City Limits*, esp. pp. 46–50.

3. The classic discussion of this tension in the American context is found in Alexis de Tocqueville, *Democracy in America* (New York: Random House, 1981), pp. 59–67. For an insightful contemporary discussion, see James A.

Stever, *Diversity and Order in State and Local Politics* (Columbia: University of South Carolina Press, 1980).

4. These themes find early expression in the papers of James Madison in Alexander Hamilton, James Madison, and John Jay, *The Federalist* (New York: Penguin Books, 1987), esp. nos. 10, 39. Later expressions include works advocating pluralist ideology and the public choice perspective, including Vincent Ostrom, *The Meaning of American Federalism* (San Francisco: Institute for Contemporary Studies, 1991); and Robert A. Dahl and Edward Tufte, *Size and Democracy* (Stanford: Stanford University Press, 1973). Critics of excessive order also include advocates of small-scale governance, including Milton Kotler, *Neighborhood Government: The Local Foundations of Political Life* (Indianapolis: Bobbs-Merrill, 1969); and Douglas T. Yates, Jr., *Neighborhood Democracy: The Politics and Impacts of Decentralization* (Lexington, Mass.: D.C. Heath, 1973).

5. These themes find early expression in the papers of Alexander Hamilton in Hamilton, Madison, and Jay, *The Federalist*, esp. nos. 17, 85. Later expressions include works in progressive and proplanning perspectives, including Robert C. Wood, *Metropolis Against Itself* (New York: Committee for Economic Development, 1959); Luther Gulick, *The Metropolitan Problem and American Ideas* (New York: Knopf, 1962); and Advisory Commission on Intergovernmental Relations (ACIR), *Metropolitan America: Challenge to Federalism* (Washington, D.C.: ACIR, 1966).

6. John C. Koritansky, "Decentralization and Civic Virtue in Tocqueville's 'New Science of Politics,'" *Publius* 5, no. 3 (1975): 63–81.

7. Among the offerings, several I draw upon for the following discussion are Donahue, *The Privatization Decision*; Werner Z. Hirsch, *Privatizing Government Services: An Economic Analysis of Contracting Out by Local Governments* (Los Angeles: Institute of Industrial Relations, University of California at Los Angeles, 1991); John B. Goodman and Gary W. Loveman, "Does Privatization Serve the Public Interest?" *Harvard Business Review* (November-December 1991): 26–38; and Ezra N. Suleiman and John Waterbury, eds., *The Political Economy of Public Sector Reform and Privatization* (Boulder, Colo.: Westview, 1990).

8. Donahue, *The Privatization Decision*, pp. 97–98.

9. Examples of these privatization efforts are found in David Osborne and Ted Gaebler, *Reinventing Government: How the Entrepreneurial Spirit is Transforming the Public Sector* (Chicago: Addison-Wesley, 1992). See also, on schools, Chubb and Moe, *Politics, Markets, and America's Schools*; and on prisons, Joan W. Allen, "Use of the Private Sector in Corrections Service Delivery," in *The Private Sector in State Delivery: Examples of Innovative Practices*, ed. Joan W. Allen et al. (Washington, D.C.: Urban Institute, 1989).

10. Norman Macrae, "A Future History of Privatisation, 1992–2022," *The Economist* (21 December–3 January 1992).

11. See, for example, E. S. Savas, *Privatization: The Key to Better Government* (Chatham, N.J.: Chatham House, 1987); and Marvin J. Levine, *Privatization of Government: The Delivery of Public Goods and Services by Private Means* (Alexandria, Va.: International Personnel Management Association, 1990).

12. Paul Starr, "The New Life of the Liberal State: Privatization and the Restructuring of State-Society Relations," in *The Political Economy of Public Sector*

*Reform and Privatization*, ed. Ezra N. Suleiman and John Waterbury (Boulder, Colo.: Westview, 1990), p. 26.

13. See, for example, American Federation of State, County, and Municipal Employees (AFSCME), *Passing the Bucks: The Contracting Out of Public Services* (Washington, D.C.: AFSCME, 1984); Starr, "New Life of the Liberal State"; and Dean Baquet with Martin Gottlieb, "Without Competing Bids, New York Pays the Price." *New York Times*, 19 February 1991, pp. A1, B4.

14. Paul Starr, "The Limits of Privatization," in *Prospects for Privatization*, ed. Steve H. Hanke (New York: Academy of Political Science, 1987).

15. Civil Service Employees Association, Advertisement in *New York Times* (19 April 1993), p. B2. The three-fifths-page advertisement was also signed by the American Federation of State, County, and Municipal Employees (AFSCME), another large public sector union.

16. Donahue, *The Privatization Business*, pp. 79–80, 92–93; Goodman and Loveman, "Does Privatization Serve the Public Interest?"; and Hirsch, *Privatizing Government Services*.

17. Benjamin R. Barber, "Jihad Vs. McWorld," *Atlantic Monthly* 269, no. 9 (1992): 53–65.

18. Margaret Crawford, "The World in a Shopping Mall," in *Variations on a Theme Park*, ed. Michael Sorkin (New York: Noonday Press, 1992), pp. 25–27.

19. The personal and disciplinary dilemmas of scientific specialization have inspired considerable reflection. See John Ziman, *Knowing Everything About Nothing* (Cambridge: Cambridge University Press, 1987).

20. Witness, for example, the effort in New York City schools, discussed in Sam Dillon, "New York City Readies 37 Specialized Schools," *New York Times* (5 April 1993), pp. A1, B6.

21. Edwin Harwood, "Viva the Liberal Arts! Viva Specialization!" in *Perspectives on Liberal Education*, ed. JoAnna M. Watson and Rex P. Stevens (Macon, Ga.: Mercer University Press, 1982), pp. 169–80.

22. See Fischer, *Technocracy and the Politics of Expertise*, pp. 18–20; and Etzioni and Halevy, *Bureaucracy and Democracy*, pp. 54–62. On dimensions of expertise more generally, see Brint, *In An Age of Experts*.

23. Danielson and Doig, *The Politics of Urban Regional Development*, p. 158; and Piven and Friedland, "Public Choice and Private Power," p. 414.

24. Elizabeth M. Brumfiel and Timothy K. Earle, "Specialization, Exchange and Complex Societies: An Introduction," in *Specialization, Exchange, and Complex Societies*, ed. Elizabeth M. Brumfiel and Timothy K. Earle (Cambridge: Cambridge University Press, 1987), pp. 1–9.

# Bibliography

Abbott, Carl. *Portland: Planning, Politics, and Growth in a Twentieth-Century City.* Lincoln: University of Nebraska Press, 1983.

Adams, Robert F. "On the Variation in the Consumption of Public Services." *Review of Economics and Statistics* 47, no. 4 (1965): 400–405.

Adrian, Charles R. "Suburbia and the Folklore of Metropology." In *Metropolitan Politics: A Reader,* edited by Michael N. Danielson, pp. 172–80. Boston: Little, Brown, 1966. First published in "Metropology: Folklore and Field Research," *Public Administration Review* 21, no. 2 (Summer 1961): 148–53.

———. *A History of American City Government: The Emergence of the Metropolis, 1920–1945.* Lanham, Md.: University Press of America, 1987.

Advisory Commission on Intergovernmental Relations (ACIR). *Impact of Federal Urban Development Programs on Local Government Organization and Planning.* Washington, D.C.: ACIR, 1964.

———. *The Problem of Special Districts in American Government.* Washington, D.C.: ACIR, 1964.

———. *Metropolitan America: Challenge to Federalism.* Washington, D.C.: ACIR, 1966.

———. *Regional Decision Making: New Strategies for Substate Districts.* Vol. 1 of *Substate Regionalism and the Federal System.* Washington, D.C.: ACIR, 1973.

———. *The Challenge of Local Government Reorganization.* Washington, D.C.: ACIR, 1974.

———. *State Limitations on Local Taxes and Expenditures.* Washington, D.C.: ACIR, 1977.

———. *The Federal Influence on State and Local Roles in the Federal System.* Washington, D.C.: ACIR, 1981.

———. *State and Local Roles in the Federal System.* Washington, D.C.: ACIR, 1982.

———. *The Organization of Local Public Economies.* Washington, D.C.: ACIR, 1987.

———. *Metropolitan Organization: The St. Louis Case.* Washington, D.C.: ACIR, 1988.

———. *Interjurisdictional Tax and Policy Competition: Good or Bad for the Federal System?* Washington, D.C.: ACIR, 1991.

———. *Metropolitan Organization: The Allegheny County Case.* Washington, D.C.: ACIR, 1992.

———. *Metropolitan Organization: Comparison of the Allegheny and St. Louis Case Studies.* Washington, D.C.: ACIR, 1993.

Aiken, Michael, and Robert R. Alford. 1970. "Comparative Urban Research and Community Decision-Making." *New Atlantis* 2 (Winter 1970): 85–110.

Allen, Joan W. "Use of the Private Sector in Corrections Service Delivery." In *The Private Sector in State Delivery: Examples of Innovative Practices*, edited by Joan W. Allen et al. Washington, D.C.: Urban Institute, 1989.

American Federation of State, County, and Municipal Employees (AFSCME). *Passing the Bucks: The Contracting Out of Public Services.* Washington, D.C.: AFSCME, 1984.

Anchondo, Jose Jorge. *Special Districts: A Growing Form of Government in Texas Metropolitan Areas.* Austin: Texas Advisory Commission on Intergovernmental Relations, 1985.

Anderson, William. *American City Government.* New York: Henry Holt and Company, 1925.

———. *The Units of Government in the United States: An Enumeration and Analysis.* Publication no. 42. Chicago: Public Administration Service, 1936.

———. *The Units of Government in the United States: An Enumeration and Analysis.* Rev. ed. Publication no. 83. Chicago: Public Administration Service, 1942.

Axelrod, Donald. *Shadow Government.* New York: John Wiley and Sons, 1992.

Bahl, Roy W. "Effects of Regional Shifts in Population and Economic Activity on the Finances of State and Local Governments: Implications for Public Policy." In *Alternatives to Confrontation*, edited by Victor L. Arnold, pp. 159–205. Lexington, Mass.: Lexington Books, 1980.

Baird, Robert N., and John H. Landon. "Political Fragmentation, Income Distribution, and the Demand for Government Services." *Nebraska Journal of Economics and Business* 11, no. 4 (1972): 171–84.

Banfield, Edward C., and Morton Grodzins. "Some Flaws in the Logic of Metropolitan Reorganization." In *Metropolitan Politics: A Reader*, edited by Michael N. Danielson, pp. 142–52. Boston: Little, Brown, 1966.

Barber, Benjamin R. "Jihad Vs. McWorld." *Atlantic Monthly* 269, no. 9 (1992): 53–65.

Barlow, I. M. *Metropolitan Government.* London: Routledge, 1991.

Barnes, William R., and Larry C. Ledebur. *City Distress, Metropolitan Disparities and Economic Growth.* Washington, D.C.: National League of Cities, 1992.

Barrett, William P. "Clear as Mud." *Forbes*, 15 June 1987, 96–98.

Beckley, Thomas M. "Leftist Critique of the Quiet Revolution in Land Use Control: Two Cases of Agency Formation." *Journal of Planning Education and Research* 12, no. 1 (1992): 55–66.

Beckman, Norman. "How Metropolitan are Federal and State Policies?" *Public Administration Review* 26, no. 2 (1966): 96–106.

Beer, Samuel H. "A Political Scientist's View of Fiscal Federalism." In *The Political Economy of Fiscal Federalism*, edited by Wallace E. Oates, pp. 21–46. Lexington, Mass.: Lexington Books, 1977.

Bennett, Robert J. *The Geography of Public Finance.* London: Methuen, 1980.

Berry, Brian J. L. *The Human Consequences of Urbanization.* New York: St. Martin's Press, 1973.

Berry, Brian J. L., and Frank E. Horton. *Geographical Perspectives on Urban Systems.* Englewood Cliffs, N.J.: Prentice Hall, 1970.

Berry, Brian J.L., and John Kasarda. *Contemporary Urban Ecology*. New York: Macmillan, 1977.

Biggs, Julie Hayward. "No Drip, No Flush, No Growth: How Cities Can Control Growth Beyond Their Boundaries by Refusing to Extend Utility Services." *Urban Lawyer* 22, no. 2 (1990): 285–305.

Bird, Frederick L. "The Contribution of Authorities to Efficient Municipal Management." *The Authority* (December 1949): 2–5.

Bird, Richard M., and Enid Slack. "Urban Finance and User Charges." In *State and Local Finance*, edited by George F. Break, pp. 211–37. Madison: University of Wisconsin Press, 1983.

Bish, Robert L. *The Public Economy of Metropolitan Areas*. Chicago: Markham, 1971.

Bish, Robert L., and Vincent Ostrom. *Understanding Urban Government*. Washington, D.C.: American Enterprise Institute, 1973.

Bollens, John C. *Special District Governments in the United States*. 2nd ed. Berkeley: University of California Press, 1961.

Bollens, John C., and Henry J. Schmandt. *The Metropolis: Its People, Politics, and Economic Life*. 2nd ed. New York: Harper and Row, 1970.

———. *The Metropolis: Its People, Politics, and Economic Life*. 3rd ed. New York: Harper and Row, 1975.

Bollens, Scott A. "Examining the Link between State Policy and the Creation of Local Special Districts." *State and Local Government Review* 18, no. 3 (1986): 117–24.

Bowen, Don L. "Reshaping Special Districts Government in Arizona: Issues and Approaches." *Arizona Review* 32, no. 1 (1984): 12–25.

Bowman, John H., Susan MacManus, and John L. Mikesell. "Mobilizing Resources for Public Services: Financing Urban Governments." *Journal of Urban Affairs* 14, nos. 3–4 (1992): 311–35.

Boyer, M. Christine. *Dreaming the Rational City*. Cambridge: MIT Press, 1983.

Boyne, George A. "Local Government Structure and Performance: Lessons from America?" *Public Administration* 70 (Autumn 1992): 333–57.

Bradley, Richard. "Downtown Renewal: The Role of Business Improvement Districts." *Public Management* (February 1995): 9–13.

Braun, Bradley M. "Measuring the Influence of Public Authorities Through Economic Impact Analysis: The Case of Port Canaveral." *Policy Studies Journal* 18, no. 4 (1990): 1032–44.

———. "Economic Benefits of Public Authorities: An Impact Analysis of Florida's Port Canaveral." In *Public Authorities and Public Policy*, edited by Jerry Mitchell, pp. 155–65. Westport, Conn.: Greenwood, 1992.

Break, George F. *Intergovernmental Fiscal Relations in the United States*. Washington, D.C.: Brookings Institution, 1967.

———. *State and Local Finance*. Madison: University of Wisconsin Press, 1983.

Brennan, Geoffrey, and James Buchanan. "Toward a Tax Constitution for Leviathan." *Journal of Public Economics* 8 (1977): 255–73.

———. *The Power to Tax: Analytical Foundations of a Fiscal Constitution*. Cambridge: Cambridge University Press, 1980.

Breton, Albert. "The Existence and Stability of Interjurisdictional Competition." In *Competition Among States and Local Governments*, edited by Daphne A.

Kenyon and John Kincaid, pp. 37–56. Washington, D.C.: Urban Institute, 1991.

Briffault, Richard. "Our Localism: The Structure of Local Government Law." Parts 1 and 2. *Columbia Law Review* 90, no. 1 (1990): 1–115 and no. 3 (1990): 346–454.

Brint, Steven. *In an Age of Experts: The Changing Role of Professionals in Politics and Public Life*. Princeton, N.J.: Princeton University Press, 1994.

Brumfiel, Elizabeth M., and Timothy K. Earle. "Specialization, Exchange and Complex Societies: An Introduction." In *Specialization, Exchange, and Complex Societies*, edited by Elizabeth M. Brumfiel and Timothy K. Earle, pp. 1–9. Cambridge: Cambridge University Press, 1987.

Brunn, Finn. "Dilemmas of Size: The Rise and Fall of the Greater Copenhagen Council." In *The Government of World Cities: The Future of the Metro Model*, edited by L. J. Sharpe, pp. 57–76. Chichester: John Wiley and Sons, 1995.

Buchanan, James M. "The Economics of Earmarked Taxes." *Journal of Political Economy* 71, no. 5 (1963): 457–69.

Burns, Nancy. *The Formation of American Local Governments*. New York: Oxford University Press, 1994.

Butler, Kent S., and Dowell Myers. "Boomtime in Austin, Texas." *Journal of the American Planning Association* 50 (Autumn 1984): 447–58.

Cameron, Juan. "Whose Authority?" *Atlantic Monthly* 204, no. 2 (1959): 38–42.

Carter, Luther J. *The Florida Experience: Land and Water Policy in a Growth State*. Baltimore: Johns Hopkins University Press, 1974.

Castells, Manuel. *The Urban Question*. London: Edward Arnold, 1977.

Chicoine, David L., and Norman Walzer. *Governmental Structure and Local Public Finance*. Boston: Oelgeschlager, Gunn & Hain, 1985.

Christenson, James A., and Carolyn E. Sachs. "The Impact of Government Size and Number of Administrative Units on the Quality of Public Services." *Administrative Science Quarterly* 25, no. 1 (1980): 89–101.

Chubb, John E., and Terry M. Moe. *Politics, Markets, and America's Schools*. Washington, D.C.: Brookings Institution, 1990.

Cion, Richard M. "Accommodation *Par Excellence*: The Lakewood Plan." In *Metropolitan Politics: A Reader*, edited by Michael N. Danielson, pp. 272–81. Boston: Little, Brown, 1966.

Clark, Gordon L. *Judges and the Cities: Interpreting Local Autonomy*. Chicago: University of Chicago Press, 1985.

Clark, Gordon L., and Michael Dear. *State Apparatus*. Boston: Allen and Unwin, 1984.

Clark, Terry N. "Community Structure, Decision-Making, Budget Expenditure and Urban Renewal in 51 American Communities." In *Community Politics: A Behaviorial Approach*, edited by Charles M. Bonjean, Terry N. Clark, and Robert L. Lineberry, pp. 293–314. New York: Free Press, 1971.

Clark, Terry Nichols, Lorna C. Ferguson, and Robert Y. Shapiro. "Functional Performance Analysis: A New Approach to the Study of Municipal Expenditures and Debt." *Political Methodology* 8, no. 2 (1982): 87–123.

Colman, William G. "A Quiet Revolution in Local Government Finance: Policy and Administrative Challenges in Expanding the Role of User Charges in

Financing State and Local Government." Paper prepared for the National Academy of Public Administration. Washington, D.C.: National Academy of Public Administration, 1983.

Colorado Division of Local Government. *Special District Service Plans*. Denver: Colorado Division of Local Government, n.d.

Committee for Economic Development. *Modernizing Local Government*. New York: Committee for Economic Development, 1966.

————. *Reshaping Government in Metropolitan Areas*. New York: Committee for Economic Development, 1970.

Connecticut Advisory Commission on Intergovernmental Relations (ACIR). *Independent Special Taxing Districts in Connecticut*. Hartford: Connecticut ACIR, 1988.

Cook, Gail C. A. "Toronto Metropolitan Finance: Selected Objectives and Results." In *Metropolitan Financing and Growth Management Policies*, edited by George F. Break, pp. 133–52. Madison: University of Wisconsin Press, 1978.

Coulter, Philip B., Lois MacGillivray, and William Edward Vickery. "Municipal Fire Protection Performance in Urban Areas: Environmental and Organizational Influences on Effectiveness and Productivity Measures." In *The Delivery of Urban Services: Outcomes of Change*, edited by Elinor Ostrom, pp. 231–60. Beverly Hills: Sage, 1976.

Cox, Kevin R., and Frank Z. Nartowicz. "Jurisdictional Fragmentation in the American Metropolis: Alternative Perspectives." *International Journal of Urban and Regional Research* 4, no. 2 (1980): 196–211.

Crawford, Margaret. "The World in a Shopping Mall." In *Variations on a Theme Park*, edited by Michael Sorkin, pp. 3–30. New York: Noonday Press, 1992.

Crouch, Winston W., and Beatrice Dinerman. *Southern California Metropolis*. Berkeley: University of California Press, 1963.

Cummings, Scott, ed. *Business Elites and Urban Development*. Albany: State University of New York Press, 1988.

Dahl, Robert A., and Edward Tufte. *Size and Democracy*. Stanford: Stanford University Press, 1973.

Danielson, Michael N. "The Adaptive Metropolis: The Politics of Accommodation." In *Metropolitan Politics: A Reader*, edited by Michael N. Danielson, pp. 231–37. Boston: Little, Brown, 1966.

————. "Differentiation, Segregation and Fragmentation in the American Metropolis." In *Governance and Population: The Governmental Implications of Population Change*, edited by A. E. Keir Nash, pp. 143–76. Washington, D.C.: U.S. Government Printing Office, 1972.

————. *The Politics of Exclusion*. New York: Columbia University Press, 1976.

Danielson, Michael N., and Jameson W. Doig. *New York: The Politics of Urban Regional Development*. Berkeley: University of California Press, 1982.

Danielson, Michael N., Alan M. Hershey, and John M. Bayne. *One Nation, So Many Governments*. Lexington, Mass.: Lexington Books, 1977.

Davis, Horace A. "Borrowing Machines." *National Municipal Review* 24, no. 6 (1935): 328–34.

Davis, Lance E., and Douglass C. North. *Institutional Change and American Economic Growth*. Cambridge: Cambridge University Press, 1971.

DeBoer, Larry. "Economies of Scale and Input Substitution in Public Libraries." *Journal of Urban Economics* 32 (1992): 257–68.

Deno, Kevin T., and Stephen L. Mehay. "Institutional Constraints on Local Jurisdiction Formation." *Public Finance Quarterly* 13, no. 4 (1985): 450–63.

De Torres, Juan. *Government Services in Major Metropolitan Areas: Functions, Costs, Efficiency.* New York: The Conference Board, 1972.

De Young, Tim. "Governing Special Districts: The Conflict Between Voting Rights and Property Privileges." *Arizona State Law Journal* 14 (1982): 419–52.

DiLorenzo, Thomas J. "The Expenditure Effects of Restricting Competition in Local Public Service Industries: The Case of Special Districts." *Public Choice* 37 (1981): 569–78.

———. "Economic Competition and Political Competition: An Empirical Note." *Public Choice* 40 (1983): 203–9.

Dixon, Robert G., Jr. "Rebuilding the Urban Political System: Some Heresies Concerning Citizen Participation, Community Action, Metros, and One Man-One Vote." *Georgetown Law Journal* 58, nos. 4–5 (1970): 955–86.

Doig, Jameson W. " 'If I See a Murderous Fellow Sharpening a Knife Cleverly. . .' The Wilsonian Dichotomy and the Public Authority Tradition." *Public Administration Review* 43, no. 4 (1983): 292–304.

———. "Expertise, Politics, and Technological Change: The Search for Mission at the Port of New York Authority." *Journal of the American Planning Association* 59, no. 1 (1993): 31–44.

Doig, Jameson W., and Jerry Mitchell. "Expertise, Democracy, and the Public Authority Model: Groping Toward Accommodation." In *Public Authorities and Public Policy*, edited by Jerry Mitchell, pp. 17–30. Westport, Conn.: Greenwood, 1992.

Dolan, Drew. "Fragmentation: Does it Drive Up the Costs of Government?" *Urban Affairs Quarterly* 26, no. 1 (1990): 28–45.

Donahue, John D. *The Privatization Decision: Public Ends, Private Means.* New York: Basic Books, 1989.

Douglas, Joel M. "The Influence of Labor Unions on Public Authorities in New York State: Problems and Prospects." In *Public Authorities and Public Policy*, edited by Jerry Mitchell, pp. 49–67. Westport, Conn.: Greenwood, 1992.

Downs, Anthony. *Opening Up the Suburbs: An Urban Strategy for America.* New Haven: Yale University Press, 1973.

———. *New Visions for Metropolitan America.* Washington, D.C.: Brookings Institution, 1994.

Dye, Thomas. R. *American Federalism: Competition Among Governments.* Lexington, Mass.: Lexington Books, 1990.

Dye, Thomas R., and John A. Garcia. "Structure, Function and Policy in American Cities." *Urban Affairs Quarterly* 14, no. 1 (1978): 103–22.

Eberts, Randal W., and Timothy J. Gronberg. "Can Competition Among Local Governments Constrain Government Spending?" *Economic Review* (Federal Reserve Bank of Cleveland) 24, no. 1 (1988): 2–9.

Eimicke, William B. "Housing New York: The Creation and Development of the Battery Park City Authority." In *Public Authorities and Public Policy*, edited by Jerry Mitchell, pp. 119–127. Westport, Conn.: Greenwood, 1992.

Einhorn, Robin L. *Property Rules: Political Economy in Chicago, 1833–1872.* Chicago: University of Chicago Press, 1991.

Elazar, Daniel J. *American Federalism: A View from the States.* New York: Thomas Y. Crowell, 1966.

Elkin, Steven L. *City and Regime in the American Republic.* Chicago: University of Chicago Press, 1987.

Erie, Steven P., John J. Kirlin, and Francine F. Rabinovitz. "Can Something Be Done? Propositions on the Performance of Metropolitan Institutions." In *Reform of Metropolitan Governments,* edited by Lowdon Wingo, pp. 7–42. Washington, D.C.: Resources for the Future, 1972.

Etzioni-Halevy, Eva. *Bureaucracy and Democracy.* London: Routledge and Kegan Paul, 1983.

Fainstein, Susan S., Norman I. Fainstein, Richard Child Hill, Dennis Judd, and Michael Peter Smith. *Restructuring the City.* New York: Longman, 1983.

Feagin, Joe R. *Free Enterprise City: Houston in Political-Economic Perspective.* New Brunswick, N.J.: Rutgers University Press, 1988.

Finn, Deborah Wathen. "Public Authorities and Social Problems: The Port Authority of New York and New Jersey Addresses the Homeless Problem in Its Facilities." In *Public Authorities and Public Policy,* edited by Jerry Mitchell, pp. 129–36. Westport, Conn.: Greenwood, 1992.

Fischer, Frank. *Technocracy and the Politics of Expertise.* Newbury Park, Calif.: Sage, 1990.

Fisher, Ronald C. *State and Local Public Finance.* Glenview, Ill.: Scott, Foresman, 1988.

Fitch, Lyle C. "Metropolitan Financial Problems." *Annals of the American Academy of Social and Political Science* 314 (November 1957): 66–73.

Flickinger, Ted, and Peter M. Murphy. "Special Districts." In *Illinois Local Government,* edited by James F. Keane and Gary Koch, pp. 151–81. Carbondale: Southern Illinois University Press, 1990.

Florida Advisory Commission on Intergovernmental Relations (ACIR). *Special District Accountability in Florida.* Tallahassee: Florida ACIR, 1987.

Forbes, Kevin F., and Ernest M. Zampelli. "Is Leviathan a Mythical Beast?" *American Economic Review* 79, no. 3 (1989): 568–77.

Foster, Kathryn A. "Exploring the Links Between Political Structure and Metropolitan Growth." *Political Geography* 12, no. 3 (1993): 523–47.

Fox, Kenneth. *Better City Government: Innovation in American Urban Politics, 1850–1937.* Philadelphia: Temple University Press, 1977.

Friesema, H. Paul. *Metropolitan Political Structure: Intergovernmental Relations and Political Integration in the Quad-Cities.* Iowa City: University of Iowa Press, 1971.

Frug, Gerald E. "The City as Legal Concept." *Harvard Law Review* 93, no. 6 (1980): 1058–154.

Fuchs, Esther. *Mayors and Money: Fiscal Policy for New York and Chicago.* Chicago: University of Chicago Press, 1992.

Garreau, Joel. *Edge City: Life on the New Frontier.* New York: Doubleday, 1991.

Gelfand, Mark I. *A Nation of Cities: The Federal Government and Urban America, 1933–1965.* New York: Oxford University Press, 1975.

Giddens, Anthony. *Central Problems in Social Theory.* Berkeley: University of California Press, 1979.

Glacel, Barbara Pate. *Regional Transit Authorities.* New York: Praeger, 1983.

Glendening, Parris N., and Mavis Mann Reeves. *Pragmatic Federalism: An Intergovernmental View of American Government.* 2nd ed. Pacific Palisades, Calif.: Palisades Publishers, 1984.

Goetz, Charles J. "Fiscal Illusion in State and Local Finance." In *Budgets and Bureaucrats: The Sources of Government Growth,* edited by Thomas E. Borcherding, pp. 176–87. Durham: Duke University Press, 1977.

Goodman, John B., and Gary W. Loveman. "Does Privatization Serve the Public Interest?" *Harvard Business Review* (November–December 1991): 26–38.

Gordon, David. "Capitalist Development and the History of American Cities." In *Marxism and the Metropolis,* edited by William K. Tabb and Larry Sawers, pp. 25–63. New York: Oxford University, 1978.

Gottdiener, Mark. "Understanding Metropolitan Deconcentration: A Clash of Paradigms." *Social Science Quarterly* 64, no. 2 (1983): 227–46.

———. *The Social Production of Urban Space.* Austin: University of Texas Press, 1985.

Gottlieb, Robert, and Margaret FitzSimmons. *Thirst for Growth: Water Agencies as Hidden Government in California.* Tucson: University of Arizona Press, 1991.

Greer, Scott. *Governing the Metropolis.* New York: John Wiley and Sons, 1962.

———. *Metropolitics: A Study of Political Culture.* New York: John Wiley and Sons, 1963.

Gulick, Luther. "Politics, Administration, and the 'New Deal.' " *Annals of the American Academy of Political and Social Science* 169 (September 1933): 55–66.

———. *The Metropolitan Problem and American Ideas.* New York: Knopf, 1962.

Gustely, Richard D. "The Allocational and Distributional Impacts of Governmental Consolidation: The Dade County Experience." *Urban Affairs Quarterly* 12, no. 3 (1977): 349–64.

Hagman, Donald G. "Regionalized-Decentralism: A Model for Rapprochement in Los Angeles." *Georgetown Law Journal* 58, nos. 4–5 (1970): 901–53.

Hall, Peter. *Great Planning Disasters.* Berkeley: University of California Press, 1980.

———. *Cities of Tomorrow.* Oxford: Basil Blackwell, 1988.

Halteman, James. "Private Water Supply Firms and Municipal Authorities: A Comparative Analysis in Pennsylvania." *State and Local Government Review* 11, no. 1 (1979): 29–34.

Hamilton, Alexander, James Madison, and John Jay. *The Federalist.* New York: Penguin Books, 1987.

Hamilton, Christopher, and Donald T. Wells. *Federalism, Power, and Political Economy.* Englewood Cliffs, N.J.: Prentice Hall, 1990.

Hamilton, Neil W., and Peter R. Hamilton. *Governance of Public Enterprise: A Case Study of Urban Mass Transit.* Lexington, Mass.: Lexington Books, 1981.

Hammack, David C. "Comprehensive Planning before the Comprehensive Plan: A New Look at the Nineteenth Century American City." In *Two Centuries of American City Planning,* edited by Daniel V. Schaffer, pp. 139–65. Baltimore: Johns Hopkins University Press, 1988.

Hanson, Royce. "Toward a New Urban Democracy: Metropolitan Consolidation and Decentralization." *Georgetown Law Journal* 58, nos. 4–5 (1970): 863–99.

———. "Land Development and Metropolitan Reform." In *Reform as Reorganization*, edited by Lowdon Wingo, pp. 9–40. Washington, D.C.: Resources for the Future, 1974.

Harrigan, John J. *Political Change in the Metropolis.* 4th ed. Glenview, Ill.: Scott, Foresman, 1989.

Harvey, David. *Social Justice and the City.* Baltimore: Johns Hopkins University Press, 1973.

Harwood, Edwin. "Viva the Liberal Arts! Viva Specialization!" In *Perspectives on Liberal Education*, edited by JoAnna M. Watson and Rex P. Stevens, pp. 169–80. Macon, Ga.: Mercer University Press, 1982.

Hawkins, Brett W., and Thomas R. Dye. "Metropolitan 'Fragmentation': A Research Note." In *Politics in the Metropolis.* 2nd ed., edited by Thomas R. Dye and Brett W. Hawkins, pp. 493–99. Columbus, Ohio: Charles E. Merrill, 1971. First published in *American Behavioral Scientist* 5 (May 1962).

Hawkins, Robert B., Jr. *Self-Government by District: Myth and Reality.* Stanford: Hoover Institution Press, 1976.

Hawley, Amos. *Human Ecology: A Theory of Community Structure.* New York: Ronald Press, 1950.

———. *Urban Society.* 2nd ed. New York: Wiley, 1981.

Heiman, Michael K. *The Quiet Evolution: Power, Planning and Profits in New York State.* New York: Praeger, 1989.

Hendriks Frank, and Theo A. J. Toonen. "The Rise and Fall of the Rijnmond Authority: An Experiment with Metro Government in the Netherlands." In *The Government of World Cities: The Future of the Metro Model*, edited by L. J. Sharpe, pp. 147–75. Chichester: John Wiley and Sons, 1995.

Henriques, Diana B. *The Machinery of Greed: Public Authority Abuse and What to Do About It.* Lexington, Mass.: Lexington Books, 1986.

Herbers, John. *The New Heartland.* New York: Times Books, 1986.

Hill, Dilys M. *Democratic Theory and Local Government.* London: George Allen & Unwin, 1974.

Hill, Melvin B., Jr. *State Laws Governing Local Government Structure and Administration.* Athens: Institute of Government, University of Georgia, 1978.

Hill, Richard Child. "Separate and Unequal: Government Inequality in the Metropolis." *American Political Science Review* 68 (December 1974): 1557–68.

Hirsch, Werner Z. *The Economics of State and Local Government.* New York: McGraw-Hill, 1970.

———. *Privatizing Government Services: An Economic Analysis of Contracting Out by Local Governments.* Los Angeles: Institute of Industrial Relations, University of California at Los Angeles, 1991.

Hirschman, Albert O. *Exit, Voice and Loyalty.* Cambridge: Harvard University Press, 1970.

Hoch, Charles. "City Limits: Municipal Boundary Formation and Class Segregation." In *Marxism and the Metropolis.* 2nd ed., edited by William K. Tabb and Larry Sawers, pp. 101–19. New York: Oxford University Press, 1984.

Hoffman. Charles. *Municipal Authorities in Pennsylvania*. Harrisburg: Pennsylvania Department of Community Affairs, 1988.

Honey, Rex D. "Conflicting Problems in the Political Organization of Space." *Annals of Regional Science* 10, no. 1 (1976): 45–60.

———. "Versatility Versus Continuity—The Dilemma of Jurisdictional Change." In *Pluralism and Political Geography*, edited by Nurit Kliot and Stanley Waterman, pp. 228–44. New York: St. Martin's Press, 1983.

Horan, Cynthia. "Beyond Governing Coalitions: Analyzing Urban Regimes in the 1990s." *Journal of Urban Affairs* 13, no. 2 (1991): 119–35.

Inman, Robert P. "The Fiscal Performance of Local Governments: An Interpretive Review." In *Current Issues in Urban Economics*, edited by Peter Mieszkowski and Mahlon Straszheim, pp. 270–321. Baltimore: Johns Hopkins University Press, 1979.

Institute for Local Self Government. *Special Districts or Special Dynasties? Democracy Denied*. Berkeley: Institute for Local Self Government, 1970.

Institute for Public Administration (IPA). *Special Districts and Public Authorities in Public Works Provision*. Draft Report. New York: IPA, 1987.

Isserman, Andrew M. "Interjurisdictional Spillovers, Political Fragmentation and the Level of Local Public Services: A Re-examination." *Urban Studies* 13 (1976): 1–12.

Jackson, Kenneth T. "Metropolitan Government Versus Suburban Autonomy." In *Cities in American History*, edited by Kenneth T. Jackson and Stanley Schultz, pp. 442–62. New York: Knopf, 1972.

———. *Crabgrass Frontier: The Suburbanization of the United States*. Oxford: Oxford University Press, 1985.

Jonas, Andrew E. G. "Urban Growth Coalitions and Urban Development Policy: Postwar Growth and the Politics of Annexation in Metropolitan Columbus." *Urban Geography* 12, no. 3 (1991): 192–225.

Jones, Victor. *Metropolitan Government*. Chicago: University of Chicago Press, 1942.

———. "Local Government Organization in Metropolitan Areas: Its Relation to Urban Redevelopment." In *The Future of Cities and Urban Redevelopment*, edited by Coleman Woodbury, pp. 481–608. Chicago: University of Chicago Press, 1953.

Judd, Dennis R. *The Politics of American Cities*. 3rd ed. Glenview, Ill.: Scott, Foresman, 1988.

Kaufman, Herbert. "Administrative Decentralization and Political Power." *Public Administration Review* 29 (January–February 1969): 3–15.

Keating, Ann Durkin. *Building Chicago: Suburban Developers and the Creation of a Divided Metropolis*. Columbus: Ohio State University Press, 1988.

Kenyon, Daphne A., and John Kincaid. "Introduction." In *Competition Among States and Local Governments: Efficiency and Equity in American Federalism*, edited by Daphne A. Kenyon and John Kincaid, pp. 1–33. Washington, D.C.: Urban Institute, 1991.

Kern, Richard. "Open Government?" *Alt* 5, no. 1 (February 1995): 1.

Kerstein, Robert. "Growth Politics in Tampa and Hillsborough County: Strains in the Privatistic Regimes." *Journal of Urban Affairs* 13, no. 1 (1991): 55–75.

King, David. *Fiscal Tiers: The Geography of Multi-Level Governments*. London: George Allen & Unwin, 1984.

Kingdon, John W. *Agendas, Alternatives, and Public Policies*. Glenview, Ill.: Scott, Foresman, 1987.

Koritansky, John C. "Decentralization and Civic Virtue in Tocqueville's 'New Science of Politics.'" *Publius* 5, no. 3 (1975): 63–81.

Kotler, Milton. *Neighborhood Government: The Local Foundations of Political Life*. Indianapolis: Bobbs-Merrill, 1969.

Krohm, Greg. "The Production Efficiency of Single Purpose versus General Purpose Government." In *Findings of the Organizational Structure of Local Government and Cost Effectiveness*. Sacramento: California Office of Planning and Research, 1973.

La Gory, Mark. "The Organization of Space and the Character of the Urban Experience." *Publius* 18, no. 4 (1988): 71–90.

Ladd, Helen, and John Yinger. *America's Ailing Cities*. Baltimore: Johns Hopkins University Press, 1989.

Lamb, Robert, and Stephen P. Rappaport. *Municipal Bonds*. New York: McGraw Hill, 1980.

Lee, Dwight R. "Special Interest Inefficiency: A Case For or Against Government Spending Limits?" *Social Science Quarterly* 70, no. 3 (1989): 765–71.

Leigland, James. "The Census Bureau's Role in Research on Special Districts: A Critique." *Western Political Quarterly* 43, no. 2 (1990): 367–80.

———. "In Defense of a Preoccupation with Numbers, A Response." *Western Political Quarterly* 43, no. 2 (1990): 385–86.

———. "External Controls on Public Authorities and Other Special Purpose Governments." In *Public Authorities and Public Policy*, edited by Jerry Mitchell, pp. 31–47. Westport, Conn.: Greenwood, 1992.

Leigland, James, and Robert Lamb. *WPP$$: Who is to Blame for the WPPSS Disaster?* Cambridge, Mass.: Ballinger, 1986.

Leutwiler, Nels R. "Playing Taps for Urban Growth Control: Restricting Public Utility Access to Manage Growth." *State and Local Government Review* 19, no. 1 (1987): 8–14.

Levine, Marvin J. *Privatization of Government: The Delivery of Public Goods and Services by Private Means*. Alexandria, Va.: International Personnel Management Association, 1990.

Libonati, Michael. "Reconstructing Local Government." *Urban Lawyer* 19, no. 3 (1987): 645–60.

Liebert, Roland J. "Municipal Functions, Structure, and Expenditures." *Social Science Quarterly* 54, no. 1 (1974): 765–83.

———. *Disintegration and Political Action*. New York: Academic Press, 1976.

Liebman, Lance. "Metropolitanism and Decentralization." In *Reform of Metropolitan Governments*, edited by Lowdon Wingo, pp. 43–56. Washington, D.C.: Resources for the Future, 1972.

Lindblom, Charles E. "The Science of 'Muddling Through.'" *Public Administration Review* 19, no. 1 (1959): 79–88.

———. "Still Muddling, Not Yet Through." *Public Administration Review* 39, no. 6 (1979): 517–26.

Lineberry, Robert L. "Reforming Metropolitan Governance: Requiem or Reality." *Georgetown Law Journal* 58, nos. 4–5 (1970): 675–717.

Lipset, Seymour Martin, and William Schneider. *The Confidence Gap: Business, Labor, and Government in the Public Mind*. Rev. ed. Baltimore: Johns Hopkins University Press, 1987.

Logan, John R., and Harvey L. Molotch. *Urban Fortunes: The Political Economy of Place*. Berkeley: University of California Press, 1987.

Long, Norton E. "Who Makes Decisions in Metropolitan Areas?" In *Metropolitan Politics: A Reader*, edited by Michael N. Danielson, pp. 100–109. Boston: Little, Brown, 1966. First published in *The Polity* (Chicago: Rand McNally, 1962), pp. 156–64.

Louv, Richard. *America II*. Los Angeles: Jeremy P. Tarcher, 1983.

Lowi, Theodore J. "Machine Politics—Old and New." *Public Interest* 9 (Fall 1967): 83–92.

Lyons, W. E. *The Politics of City-County Merger: The Lexington–Fayette County Experience*. Lexington: University Press of Kentucky, 1977.

Lyons, W. E., and David Lowery. "Governmental Fragmentation Versus Consolidation: Five Public Choice Myths About How to Create Informed, Involved, and Happy Citizens." *Public Administration Review* 49, no. 6 (1989): 533–43.

Lyons, W. E., David Lowery, and Ruth Hoogland DeHoog. *The Politics of Dissatisfaction: Citizens, Services, and Urban Institutions*. Armonk, N.Y.: M. E. Sharpe, 1992.

Maass, Arthur, ed. *Area and Power: A Theory of Local Government*. Glencoe, Ill.: Free Press, 1959.

McKenzie, Evan. *Privatopia: Homeowner Associations and the Rise of Residential Private Government*. New Haven: Yale University Press, 1994.

McLean, Joseph E. "Use and Abuse of Authorities." *National Municipal Review* 42, no. 9 (1953): 438–44.

MacManus, Susan A. "Special District Governments: A Note on Their Use as Property Tax Relief Mechanisms in the 1970s." *Journal of Politics* 43, no. 12 (1981): 1207–14.

———. "State Government: The Overseer of Municipal Finance." In *The Municipal Money Chase*, edited by Alberta M. Sbragia, pp. 145–84. Boulder, Colo.: Westview, 1983.

Macrae, Norman. "A Future History of Privatisation, 1992–2022." *Economist*, 21 December 1991–3 January 1992.

Manson, Robert. "*Ball* in Play: The Effect of *Ball v. James* on Special District Voting Scheme Decisions." *Columbia Journal of Law and Social Problems* 21, no. 1 (1987): 87–136.

Marando, Vincent L., and Mavis Mann Reeves. "States and Metropolitan Structural Reorganization." In *Subnational Politics in the 1980s: Organization, Reorganization and Economic Development*, edited by Louis A. Picard and Raphael Zariski, pp. 73–88. New York: Praeger, 1987.

———. "State Responsiveness and Local Government Reorganization." *Social Science Quarterly* 69, no. 4 (1988): 996–1004.

Margolis, Julius. "Fiscal Issues in the Reform of Metropolitan Governance." In

*Reform as Reorganization,* edited by Lowdon Wingo, pp. 41–70. Washington, D.C.: Resources for the Future, 1974.

Markusen, Ann R. "Class and Urban Social Expenditure: A Marxist Theory of Metropolitan Government." In *Marxism and the Metropolis,* edited by William K. Tabb and Larry Sawers, pp. 90–111. New York: Oxford University Press, 1978.

Martin, Roscoe C., and Douglas Price. "The Metropolis and Its Problems Reexamined." In *Metropolitan Politics: A Reader,* edited by Michael N. Danielson, pp. 135–42. Boston: Little, Brown, 1966. First published in *The Metropolis and Its Problems* (Syracuse, N.Y.: Maxwell School of Citizenship and Public Affairs, Syracuse University, 1959), pp. 11–18.

Marx, Karl. *Capital.* 3 vols. New York: International Publishers Edition, 1967.

Maxey, Chester C. "The Political Integration of Metropolitan Communities." *National Municipal Review* 11, no. 8 (1922): 229–52.

Meyerson, Martin, and Edward C. Banfield. *Politics, Planning, and the Public Interest.* Glencoe, Ill.: Free Press, 1955.

Miller, David Young. "The Impact of Political Culture on Patterns of State and Local Government Expenditures." *Publius* 21 (Spring 1991): 83–100.

Miller, Gary J. *Cities by Contract: The Politics of Municipal Incorporation.* Cambridge: MIT Press, 1981.

Miller, Gary J., and Terry M. Moe. "Bureaucrats, Legislators and the Size of Government." *American Political Science Review* 77 (1983): 297–322.

Minge, David. "Special Districts and the Level of Public Expenditures." *Journal of Urban Law* 53 (1976): 701–18.

Mitchell, Jerry. "The Policy Activities of Public Authorities." *Policy Studies Journal* 18, no. 4 (1990): 928–42.

———. "Policy Functions and Issues for Public Authorities." In *Public Authorities and Public Policy,* edited by Jerry Mitchell, pp. 1–13. Westport, Conn.: Greenwood, 1992.

Mitchell, John Thornton. "The Uses of Special Districts in Financing and Facilitating Urban Growth." *Urban Lawyer* 5, no. 2 (1973): 185–227.

Monkkonen, Eric H. *America Becomes Urban: The Development of U.S. Cities and Towns, 1780–1980.* Berkeley: University of California Press, 1988.

Morrill, Richard L. "State and Local Government Commissions and Governance of the Metropolis." In *Decentralization, Local Governments and Markets,* edited by Robert J. Bennett, pp. 297–308. Oxford: Clarendon, 1990.

Mueller, Dennis C. *Public Choice II.* Cambridge: Cambridge University Press, 1989.

Mueller, Dennis C., and Peter Murrell. "Interest Groups and the Size of Government." *Public Choice* 48 (1986): 125–45.

Mullen, Gerald E. "The Use of Special Assessment Districts and Independent Special Districts as Aids in Financing Private Land Development." *California Law Review* 53, no. 1 (1965): 364–85.

Mullins, Daniel R., and Mark S. Rosentraub. "Fiscal Pressure? The Impact of Elder Recruitment on Local Expenditures." *Urban Affairs Quarterly* 28, no. 2 (1992): 337–54.

Muniak, Dennis C. "Federal Divestiture, Regional Growth, and the Political Economy of Public Authority Creation: The Emergence of the Metropolitan Washington Airports Authority." *Policy Studies Journal* 18, no. 4 (1990): 943–60.

Musgrave, Richard A. *The Theory of Public Finance: A Study in Public Economy.* New York: McGraw Hill, 1959.

Musgrave, Richard A., and Peggy B. Musgrave. *Public Finance in Theory and Practice.* 5th ed. New York: McGraw Hill, 1989.

National Municipal League. Committee on Metropolitan Government. *The Government of Metropolitan Areas in the United States.* Prepared by Paul Studenski with the assistance of the Committee on Metropolitan Government. New York: National Municipal League, 1930.

Neiman, Max. "From Plato's Philosopher King to Bish's Tough Purchasing Agent: The Premature Public Choice Paradigm." *Journal of the American Institute of Planners* 41 (1975): 55–73.

Nelson, Michael A. "Searching for Leviathan: Comment and Extension." *American Economic Review* 77, no. 1 (1987): 198–204.

———. "Decentralization of the Subnational Public Sector: An Empirical Analysis of the Determinants of Local Government Structure in Metropolitan Areas in the U.S." *Southern Economic Journal* 57, no. 2 (1990): 443–57.

New Jersey Department of Community Affairs. *Interlocal Services: Working Together.* Trenton: New Jersey Department of Community Affairs, 1991.

New York Office of the State Comptroller. *Special Report on Municipal Affairs.* Albany: New York Office of the State Comptroller, 1991.

Newton, Kenneth. "American Urban Politics: Social Class, Political Structure and Public Goods." *Urban Affairs Quarterly* 11, no. 2 (1975): 241–64.

Nice, David C. "An Intergovernmental Perspective on Urban Fragmentation." *Social Science Quarterly* 64, no. 1 (1983): 111–18.

Nicholas, James C. "The Costs of Growth: A Public vs. Private Sector Conflict or a Public/Private Responsibility." In *Understanding Growth Management: Critical Issues and a Research Agenda,* edited by David J. Brower, David R. Godschalk, and Douglas R. Porter, pp. 43–58. Washington, D.C.: Urban Land Institute, 1989.

Niskanen, William A., Jr. *Bureaucracy and Representative Government.* Chicago: Aldine-Atherton, 1971.

———. "Bureaucrats and Politicians." *Journal of Law and Economics* 18 (1975): 617–43.

———. "A Reflection on Bureaucracy and Representative Government. In *The Budget-Maximizing Bureaucrat,* edited by André Blais and Stéphane Dion, pp. 13–32. Pittsburgh: University of Pittsburgh Press, 1991.

Norton, R. D. *City Life-Cycles and American Urban Policy.* New York: Academic Press, 1979.

Oakerson, Ronald J. "Size, Function, and Structure: Jurisdictional Size Effects on Public Sector Performance." *Proceedings of the National Rural Studies Committee,* pp. 84–93. Corvallis: Western Rural Development Center, Oregon State University, 1992.

Oakerson, Ronald J., and Roger B. Parks. "Citizen Voice and Public Entrepreneurship: The Organization Dynamic of a Complex Metropolitan County." *Publius* 18, no. 4 (1988): 91–112.

Oates, Wallace E. "An Economist's Perspective on Fiscal Federalism." In *The Political Economy of Fiscal Federalism*, edited by Wallace E. Oates, pp. 3–20. Lexington, Mass.: Lexington Books, 1977.

———. "Searching for Leviathan: A Reply and Some Further Reflections." *American Economic Review* 79, no. 3 (1989): 578–83.

———. "Decentralization of the Public Sector: An Overview." In *Decentralization, Local Governments and Markets*, edited by Robert J. Bennett, pp. 43–58. Oxford: Clarendon, 1990.

O'Connor, James. *The Fiscal Crisis of the State*. New York: St. Martin's Press, 1973.

Olin, Spencer. "Intraclass Conflict and the Politics of a Fragmented Region." In *Postsuburban California: The Transformation of Orange County Since World War II*, edited by Rob Kling, Spencer Olin, and Mark Poster, pp. 223–53. Berkeley: University of California Press, 1991.

Osborne, David, and Ted Gaebler. *Reinventing Government: How the Entrepreneurial Spirit is Transforming the Public Sector*. Chicago: Addison-Wesley, 1992.

Ostrom, Elinor. "Metropolitan Reform: Propositions Derived from Two Traditions." *Social Science Quarterly* 53, no. 3 (1972): 474–93.

——— ed. *The Delivery of Urban Services: Outcomes of Change*. Urban Affairs Annual Reviews, vol. 10. Beverly Hills: Sage, 1976.

Ostrom, Vincent. *The Meaning of American Federalism*. San Francisco: Institute for Contemporary Studies, 1991.

Ostrom, Vincent, Charles M. Tiebout, and Robert Warren. "The Organization of Government in Metropolitan Areas: A Theoretical Inquiry." *American Political Science Review* 55 (1961): 831–42.

Ostrom, Vincent, Robert Bish, and Elinor Ostrom. *Local Government in the United States*. San Francisco: ICS Press, 1988.

Paddison, Ronan. *The Fragmented State: The Political Geography of Power*. New York: St. Martin's Press, 1983.

Palumbo, George. "City Government Expenditures and City Government Reality: A Comment on Sjoquist." *National Tax Journal* 36, no. 2 (1983): 249–51.

Pane, Michael A. *Functional Fragmentation and the Traditional Forms of Municipal Government in New Jersey*. Trenton: New Jersey County and Municipal Government Study Commission, 1985.

Park, Robert E. "Human Ecology." *American Journal of Sociology* 42, no. 2 (1936): 1–15.

———. *Human Communities: The City and Human Ecology*. New York: Free Press, 1952.

Park, Robert E., Ernest W. Burgess, and Robert D. McKenzie, eds. *The City*. Chicago: University of Chicago Press, 1925.

Parks, Roger B. "Metropolitan Structure and Systemic Performance." In *Policy Implementation in Federal and Unitary Systems*, edited by Kenneth Hanf and Theo A. J. Toonen, pp. 161–91. Dordrecht, The Netherlands: Martinus Nijhoff, 1985.

Parks, Roger B., and Ronald J. Oakerson. "Metropolitan Organization and Governance: A Local Public Economy Approach." *Urban Affairs Quarterly* 25, no. 1 (1989): 18–29.

Peiser, Richard B. "The Economics of Municipal Utility Districts for Land Development." *Land Economics* 59, no. 1 (1983): 43–57.

Perin, Constance. *Everything in its Place: Social Order and Land Use in America.* Princeton, N.J.: Princeton University Press, 1977.

Perrenod, Virginia Marion. *Special Districts, Special Purposes: Fringe Governments and Urban Problems in the Houston Area.* College Station: Texas A & M University Press, 1984.

Peterson, Paul E. *City Limits.* Chicago: University of Chicago Press, 1981.

Piven, Frances Fox, and Roger Friedland. "Public Choice and Private Power: A Theory of Fiscal Crisis." In *Public Service Provision and Urban Development,* edited by Andrew Kirby, Paul Knox, and Steven Pinch. New York: St. Martin's Press, 1984.

Porter, Douglas R., Ben C. Lin, and Richard B. Peiser. *Special Districts: A Useful Technique for Financing Infrastructure.* Washington, D.C.: Urban Land Institute, 1987.

Press, Charles. "State Government in Urban Areas: Petty Tyrants, Meddlers, or Something Else?" *Urban Interest* 2 (Fall 1980): 12–21.

Price, Eli. K. *The History of the Consolidation of the City of Philadelphia.* Philadelphia: J. B. Lippincott, 1873.

Rainey, Hal G. *Understanding and Managing Public Organizations.* San Francisco: Jossey-Bass, 1991.

Reed, Thomas H. *Municipal Government in the United States.* New York: Century Co., 1926.

———. "Dual Government for Metropolitan Regions." *National Municipal Review* 16, no. 2 (1927): 118–34.

———. "The Government of Metropolitan Areas." *Public Management* 12, no. 3 (1930): 75–78.

———. "Progress in Metropolitan Integration." *Public Administration Review* 9 (1949): 1–10.

Rich, Richard C. "The Political Economy of Urban Service Distribution." In *The Politics of Urban Public Services,* edited by Richard C. Rich. Lexington, Mass.: D.C. Heath, 1982.

Robson, William A. *The Government and Misgovernment of London.* London: George Allen & Unwin, 1939.

Rogers, Bruce D., and C. McCurdy Lipsey. "Metropolitan Reform: Citizen Evaluations of Performances in Nashville-Davidson County, Tennessee." *Publius* 4, no. 4 (1974): 19–34.

Rusk, David. *Cities Without Suburbs.* Washington, D.C.: Woodrow Wilson Center Press, 1993.

———. *Baltimore Unbound: A Strategy for Regional Renewal.* Baltimore: Abell Foundation, 1996.

Sacks, Seymour. " 'The Census Bureau's Role in Research on Special Districts: A Critique': A Necessary Rejoinder." *Western Political Quarterly* 43, no. 2 (1990): 381–83.

Samuelson, Paul A. "The Pure Theory of Public Expenditures." *Review of Economics and Statistics* (November 1954): 386–89.

Sanders, Heywood T. "Building the Convention City: Politics, Finance, and Public Investment in Urban America." *Journal of Urban Affairs* 14, no. 2 (1992): 135–59.

Savas, E. S. *The Organization and Efficiency of Solid Waste Collection.* Lexington, Mass.: Lexington Books, 1977.

———. *Privatization: The Key to Better Government.* Chatham, N.J.: Chatham House, 1987.

Sbragia, Alberta M., ed. *Municipal Money Chase.* Boulder, Colo.: Westview, 1983.

Schiesl, Martin J. *The Politics of Efficiency.* Berkeley: University of California Press, 1977.

Schmandt, Henry J. *Metropolitan Reform in St. Louis: A Case Study.* New York: Holt, Rinehart and Winston, 1961.

Schneider, Eugene J. *The Challenge of Local Partnerships.* Trenton, N.J.: Governor's Task Force on Local Partnerships, 1992.

Schneider, Mark. "Fragmentation and the Growth of Local Government." *Public Choice* 48 (1986): 255–63.

———. *The Competitive City: The Political Economy of Suburbia.* Pittsburgh: University of Pittsburgh Press, 1989.

Schneider, Mark, and John R. Logan. "Suburban Racial Segregation and Black Access to Local Public Resources." *Social Science Quarterly* 63 (December 1982): 762–70.

Scott, Stanley, and John Corzine. "Special Districts in the San Francisco Bay Area." In *Metropolitan Politics: A Reader*, edited by Michael N. Danielson, pp. 246–60. Boston: Little, Brown, 1966.

Seidman, Harold. *Politics, Position and Power: The Dynamics of Federal Organization.* 2nd ed. New York: Oxford University Press, 1970.

Shannon, John. "Federalism's 'Invisible Regulator'—Interjurisdictional Competition." In *Competition Among States and Local Governments: Efficiency and Equity in American Federalism*, edited by Daphne A. Kenyon and John Kincaid, pp. 117–25. Washington, D.C.: Urban Institute, 1991.

Sharp, Elaine B. *Urban Politics and Administration.* White Plains, N.Y.: Longman, 1990.

Sharpe, L. J. "The Abolition of the Greater London Council: Is There a Case for Resurrection?" In *The Government of World Cities: The Future of the Metro Model*, edited by L. J. Sharpe, pp. 111–30. Chichester: John Wiley and Sons, 1995.

———. "The Future of Metropolitan Government." In *The Government of World Cities: The Future of the Metro Model*, edited by L. J. Sharpe, pp. 11–32. Chichester: John Wiley and Sons, 1995.

Shefter, Martin. *Political Crisis/Fiscal Crisis: The Collapse and Revival of New York City.* New York: Basic Books, 1985.

Sjoquist, David L. "The Effect of the Number of Local Governments on Central City Expenditures." *National Tax Journal* 35, no. 1 (1982): 79–87.

Smith, Michael Peter. *The City and Social Theory.* New York: St. Martin's Press, 1979.

Smith, Robert G. *Public Authorities, Special Districts and Local Government*. Washington, D.C.: National Association of Counties Research Foundation, 1964.
———. *Ad Hoc Governments*. Beverly Hills: Sage, 1974.
———. "Reorganization of Regional Transportation Authorities to Maintain Urban/Suburban Constituency Balance." *Public Administration Review* 47, no. 2 (1987): 171–79.
———. "The Changing Role of Funding in Authority Policy Implementation." In *Public Authorities and Public Policy*, edited by Jerry Mitchell, pp. 84–95. Westport, Conn.: Greenwood, 1992.
Soja, Edward D. "The Political Organization of Space in Metropolitan Areas." In *The Manipulated City: Perspectives on Spatial Structure and Social Issues in Urban America*, edited by Stephen Gale and Eric G. Moore. Chicago: Maaroufa, 1975.
Sokolow, Alvin D., Priscilla Hanford, Joan Hogan, and Linda Martin. *Choices for the Unincorporated Community: A Guide to Local Government Alternatives in California*. Davis: Institute of Governmental Affairs, University of California at Davis, 1981.
Squires, Gregory D., ed. *Unequal Partnerships: The Political Economy of Urban Redevelopment in Postwar America*. New Brunswick, N.J.: Rutgers University Press, 1989.
Starr, Paul. "The Limits of Privatization." In *Prospects for Privatization*, edited by Steve H. Hanke. New York: Academy of Political Science, 1987.
———. "The New Life of the Liberal State: Privatization and the Restructuring of State-Society Relations." In *The Political Economy of Public Sector Reform and Privatization*, edited by Ezra N. Suleiman and John Waterbury, pp. 22–54. Boulder, Colo.: Westview, 1990.
Stein, Robert M. "Federally Supported Substate Regional Governments: The Maintenance of Governmental Structure." *Urban Interest* 2 (Spring 1980): 74–81.
———. "Tiebout's Sorting Hypothesis." *Urban Affairs Quarterly* 23, no. 2 (September 1987): 140–60.
———. *Urban Alternatives: Public and Private Markets in the Provision of Local Services*. Pittsburgh: University of Pittsburgh Press, 1990.
Stephens, G. Ross. "State Centralization and the Erosion of Local Autonomy." *Journal of Politics* 36 (February 1974): 44–76.
Stetzer, Donald Foster. *Special Districts in Cook County: Toward a Geography of Local Government*. Chicago: Department of Geography, University of Chicago, 1975.
Stever, James A. *Diversity and Order in State and Local Politics*. Columbia: University of South Carolina Press, 1980.
Stewart, John D. *The Responsive Local Authority*. London: Charles Knight, 1974.
Stone, Clarence N. "Systemic Power in Community Decision Making." *American Political Science Review* 74 (1980): 978–90.
———. "Elite Distemper Versus Problems of Democracy." In *Power Elites and Organizations*, edited by G. William Domhoff and Thomas R. Dye, pp. 239–65. Newbury Park, Calif.: Sage, 1987.

Stone, Clarence N., and Heywood T. Sanders, eds. *The Politics of Urban Development*. Lawrence: University Press of Kansas, 1987.

Studenski, Paul. See National Municipal League.

Suleiman, Ezra N., and John Waterbury, eds. *The Political Economy of Public Sector Reform and Privatization*. Boulder, Colo.: Westview, 1990.

Suttles, Gerald D. *The Social Construction of Communities*. Chicago: University of Chicago Press, 1972.

Teaford, Jon C. *City and Suburb: The Political Fragmentation of Metropolitan America, 1850–1970*. Baltimore: Johns Hopkins University Press, 1979.

———. *The Unheralded Triumph: City Government in America, 1870–1900*, Baltimore: Johns Hopkins University Press, 1984.

———. *The Twentieth Century American City*. 2nd ed. Baltimore: Johns Hopkins University Press, 1993.

Templer, Otis W. "Adjusting to Groundwater Depletion: The Case of Texas and Lessons for the Future of the Southwest." In *Water in the Southwest*, edited by Zachary A. Smith, pp. 247–68. Albuquerque: University of New Mexico Press, 1989.

Texas Advisory Commission on Intergovernmental Relations. "Special District Governments in Texas." *Intergovernmental Report* 5, no. 3. Austin: Texas ACIR, 1977.

Tiebout, Charles M. "A Pure Theory of Local Expenditures." *Journal of Political Economy* 64 (1956): 416–24.

Tocqueville, Alexis de. *Democracy in America*. Modern College Library Edition. New York: Random House, 1981.

Tullock, Gordon. "Federalism: Problems of Scale." *Public Choice* 6 (Spring 1989): 19–29.

U.S. Bureau of the Census. *Governments in the United States in 1952*. State and Local Government Special Studies, no. 31. Washington, D.C.: U.S. Government Printing Office, 1953.

———. *Local Government in Metropolitan Areas*. State and Local Government Special Studies, no. 36. Washington, D.C.: U.S. Government Printing Office, 1954.

———. *1962 Census of Governments*. Vol. 1, no. 1, *Government Organization*. Washington, D.C.: U.S. Government Printing Office, 1963.

———. *1962 Census of Governments*. Vol. 5, *Local Government in Metropolitan Areas*. Washington, D.C.: U.S. Government Printing Office, 1964.

———. *1970 Census of Population*. Vol. 1, pt. 1, sec. 1, *General Population Characteristics*. Washington, D.C.: U.S. Government Printing Office, 1972.

———. *1972 Census of Governments*. Vol. 1, no. 1, *Government Organization*. Washington, D.C.: U.S. Government Printing Office, 1973.

———. *1982 State and Metropolitan Area Data Book*. Washington, D.C.: U.S. Government Printing Office, 1982.

———. *1980 Census of Population and Housing*. Vol. 1, chap. C, *General Social and Economic Characteristics*. Washington, D.C.: U.S. Government Printing Office, 1983.

———. *1982 Census of Governments*. Vol. 1, no. 1, *Government Organization*. Washington, D.C.: U.S. Government Printing Office, 1983.

———. *1983 City and County Data Book*. Washington, D.C.: U.S. Government Printing Office, 1983.

———. *County Business Patterns, 1982*. Various state issues. Washington, D.C.: U.S. Government Printing Office, 1984.

———. *1982 Census of Governments*. Vol. 6, no. 4, *Historical Statistics on Government Finances and Employment*. Washington, D.C.: U.S. Government Printing Office, 1985.

———. *1986 State and Metropolitan Area Data Book*. Washington, D.C.: U.S. Government Printing Office, 1986.

———. *1987 Census of Governments*. Vol. 1, no. 1, *Government Organization*. Washington, D.C.: U.S. Government Printing Office, 1988.

———. *1988 City and County Data Book*. Washington, D.C.: U.S. Government Printing Office, 1988.

———. *1987 Census of Governments, Directory of Governments File*. Washington, D.C.: U.S. Government Printing Office, 1989.

———. *1987 Census of Governments*. Vol. 4, no. 5, *Compendium of Government Finances*. Washington, D.C.: U.S. Government Printing Office, 1990.

———. *1992 Census of Governments*. Vol. 1, no. 1, *Governmental Organization*. Washington, D.C.: U.S. Government Printing Office, 1994.

———. *Government Finances: 1991–92*. Washington, D.C.: U.S. Government Printing Office, 1996.

———. *Census of Population and Housing*. Various editions, 1910–1980. Washington, D.C.: U.S. Government Printing Office.

Viteritti, Joseph P. "Bureaucratic Environments, Efficiency, and Equity in Urban Service Delivery Systems." In *The Politics of Urban Public Services*, edited by Richard C. Rich, pp. 53–68. Lexington, Mass.: D. C. Heath, 1982.

Vogel, Ronald K. *Urban Political Economy, Broward County, Florida*. Gainesville: University Press of Florida, 1992.

Vogel, Ronald K., and Bert E. Swanson. "The Growth Machine Versus the Antigrowth Coalition." *Urban Affairs Quarterly* 25, no. 1 (1989): 63–85.

Wagner, Richard E., and Warren E. Weber. "Competition, Monopoly, and the Organization of Government in Metropolitan Areas." *Journal of Law and Economics* 18 (December 1975): 661–84.

Walker, Richard A., and Michael K. Heiman. "Quiet Revolution for Whom?" *Annals of the Association of American Geographers* 71, no. 1 (1981): 67–83.

Walsh, Annmarie Hauck. *The Public's Business: The Politics and Practices of Government Corporations*. Cambridge: MIT Press, 1978.

———. "Public Authorities and the Shape of Decision Making." In *Urban Politics New York Style*, edited by Jewel Bellush and Dick Netzer, pp. 188–219. Armonk N.Y.: M. E. Sharpe, 1990.

Walsh, Annmarie Hauck, and James Leigland. "The Only Planning Game in Town." *Empire State Report* 9, no. 5 (1983): 6–12.

Warf, Barney. "The Port Authority of New York–New Jersey." *Professional Geographer* 40, no. 3 (1988): 288–97.

Warren, Charles R. *The States and Urban Strategies: A Comparative Analysis*. Washington, D.C.: U.S. Department of Housing and Urban Development, 1980.

Warren, Robert. "A Municipal Services Market Model of Metropolitan Organization." *Journal of the American Institute of Planners* 30, no. 3 (1964): 193–204.

Weiher, Gregory R. *The Fractured Metropolis: Political Fragmentation and Metropolitan Segregation.* Albany: State University of New York Press, 1991.

Weisbrod, Burton A. *The Nonprofit Economy.* Cambridge, Mass.: Harvard University Press, 1988.

Weiss, Mark A., and J. W. Watts. "Community Builders and Community Associations: The Role of Real Estate Developers in Private Residential Governance." In *Residential Community Associations: Private Governments in the Intergovernmental System?* edited by Advisory Commission on Intergovernmental Relations, pp. 95–104. Washington, D.C.: U.S. Government Printing Office, 1989.

Wells, Donald T., and Richard Scheff. "Performance Issues for Public Authorities in Georgia." In *Public Authorities and Public Policy,* edited by Jerry Mitchell, pp. 167–76. Westport, Conn.: Greenwood, 1992.

Willbern, York. "Unigov: Local Reorganization in Indianapolis." In *Regional Governance: Promise and Performance,* edited by Advisory Commission on Intergovernmental Relations, pp. 59–64. Washington, D.C.: ACIR, 1973.

Williams, Oliver P., *Metropolitan Political Analysis: A Social Access Approach.* New York: Free Press, 1971.

Williams, Oliver P., Harold Herman, Charles S. Liebman, and Thomas H. Dye. *Suburban Differences and Metropolitan Policies: A Philadelphia Story.* Philadelphia: University of Pennsylvania Press, 1965.

Williams, Oliver P., and Kent Eklund. "Segregation in a Fragmented Context: 1950–1970." In *Urbanization and Conflict in Market Societies,* edited by Kevin R. Cox, pp. 213–28. Chicago: Maaroufa, 1978.

Wingo, Lowdon. "Introduction: Logic and Ideology in Metropolitan Reform." In *Reform of Metropolitan Governments,* edited by Lowdon Wingo, pp. 1–6. Washington, D.C.: Resources for the Future, 1972.

Wood, Robert C. *Suburbia: Its People and Their Politics.* Boston: Houghton Mifflin, 1958.

———. "A Division of Powers." In *Area and Power: A Theory of Local Government,* edited by Arthur J. Maass, pp. 53–69. Glencoe, Ill.: Free Press, 1959.

———. *Metropolis Against Itself.* New York: Committee for Economic Development, 1959.

———. *1400 Governments: The Political Economy of the New York Metropolitan Region.* Cambridge: Harvard University Press, 1961.

Yates, Douglas T., Jr. *Neighborhood Democracy: The Politics and Impacts of Decentralization.* Lexington, Mass.: D.C. Heath, 1973.

Ylvisaker, Paul. "Why Mayors Oppose Metropolitan Government," In *Metropolitan Politics: A Reader,* edited by Michael N. Danielson, pp. 180–88. Boston: Little, Brown, 1966. First published in "Diversity and the Public Interest: Two Cases in Metropolitan Decision-Making," *Journal of the American Institute of Planners* 27, no. 2 (1961): 109–13.

Zaleski, Alexander V. "A New Authority for Massachusetts: Best Solution for a Difficult Task?" *National Civic Review* 74, no. 11 (1985): 531–37.

Zax, Jeffrey S. "The Effects of Jurisdiction Types and Numbers on Local Public Finance." In *Fiscal Federalism: Quantitative Studies,* edited by Harvey S. Rosen, pp. 79–103. Chicago: University of Chicago Press, 1988.

——. "Is There a Leviathan in Your Neighborhood?" *American Economic Review* 79, no. 3 (1989): 560–67.

Zeigler, Donald J., and Stanley D. Brunn. "Geopolitical Fragmentation and the Pattern of Growth and Need: Defining the Cleavage Between Sunbelt and Frostbelt Metropolises." In *The American Metropolitan System: Present and Future,* edited by Stanley D. Brunn and James O. Wheeler, pp. 77–92. New York: V. H. Winston and Sons, 1980.

Ziman, John. *Knowing Everything About Nothing.* Cambridge: Cambridge University Press, 1987.

Zimmerman, Joseph F. "Metropolitan Reform in the U.S.: An Overview." *Public Administration Review* 30, no. 5 (1970): 531–43.

# Index

New Orleans, La., 121–22
New York, 15–16, 82, 96, 111, 115n.
    8, 140, 144n. 7. *See also* Port
    Authority of New York and
    New Jersey
New York City, 1–2, 3, 115n. 8;
    Metropolitan Transit Authority
    (MTA), 116n. 16; World Trade
    Center, 117n. 22
Niagara Falls, N.Y., 122
Nice, David C., 68–69, 85n. 12
nonprofit (agencies or sector), 9, 92,
    93, 94
nontaxing districts, 7, 8, 12, 14, 105,
    107, 114; distribution of, 123–24,
    127, 132–33, 134, 135; formation
    of, 18, 19; and privatization,
    227. *See also* privatizing districts;
    public authorities
North Carolina, 79; North Carolina
    Municipal Power Agency, 186n.
    14
North Dakota, 146n. 22
Novato, Calif., 11

Oakland, Calif., 122. *See also* San-
    Francisco-Oakland, Calif.
Ohio, 80
Oklahoma, 83
Olin, Spencer, 49
Omaha, Nebr., 122; Omaha Public
    Power District, 186n. 14
Orange County, Calif., 49
Oregon, 74, 87n. 32
Owensboro, Ky., 122, 186–87n. 16

Park, Robert E., 59n. 53
parking (districts or function), 13,
    152, 153, 154, 155, 163, 200
parks and recreation (districts or
    function), 2, 8, 19, 34, 44, 52;
    and capital spending, 167;
    distribution of, 13, 139, 140; and

district multiplicity, 170, 171–72;
    and district reliance, 152, 153,
    154, 155, 161, 163, 174, 179,
    187n. 25; and metropolitan area
    age, 216n. 33; and resource
    allocation bias, 193, 196–97,
    198–99, 210–11, 213; and
    spending shares, 209; and state
    location, 141; and upward
    spending bias, 163, 164, 168,
    170, 171–72, 173, 174, 175, 178,
    180–81
particularizing districts, 105, 106,
    109–110, 219, 225, 226. *See also*
    subcounty districts
particularizing-collectivizing
    districts, 105, 109
particularizing-privatizing districts,
    105, 109–10
Peiser, Richard B., 76, 77, 143
Pennsylvania, 18, 77, 83, 135, 140,
    144n. 7
Peoria, Ill., 153
per capita spending: and district
    multiplicity, 169–72; index of,
    177–78, 188n. 31; measurement
    of, 150, 152, 185n. 11;
    nondistrict determinants of, 172;
    and political fragmentation, 69,
    70; and special districts, 74–75,
    148, 150, 183, 186n. 15; and
    upward spending bias, 155,
    163–65, 166–76, 179–84
Perrenod, Virginia Marion, 77, 78
Philadelphia, Pa., 3, 122, 129: Board
    of Prison Inspectors (1790),
    15–16
Phoenix, Ariz., 186n. 14; Salt River
    Project Agricultural
    Improvement and Power
    District, 186n. 14
Pittsburgh, Pa., 70, 113, 122
police protection (districts or
    function), 16, 70, 96, 106, 115n.
    8, 191, 200